Africa and the
International Economy

Africa
and the
International
Economy
1800–1960

An introduction to the modern economic
history of Africa south of the Sahara

J. Forbes Munro

J. M. Dent & Sons Ltd, London
Rowman and Littlefield, Totowa, N. J.

© J. Forbes Munro, 1976
All rights reserved
Made in Great Britain
at the
Aldine Press · Letchworth · Herts
for
J. M. Dent & Sons Ltd
Aldine House · Albemarle Street · London
First published 1976
First published in the United States, 1976
by Rowman and Littlefield, Totowa, New Jersey

This book is set in 10 on 12 point Times New Roman 327

U.K. Hardback ISBN: 0 460 10088 2
U.K. Paperback ISBN: 0 460 11088 8
U.S. Hardback: 0 87471 893 7
U.S. Paperback: 0 87471 894 5

Contents

List of Maps and Figures

List of Tables

Preface

This book is intended as a short introduction to a very large subject. It attempts to provide students in universities and polytechnics with an outline overview of the major trends and processes in the modern economic history of Africa south of the Sahara and hopes to offer a foundation from which further study may be undertaken. It has been written in the knowledge that the recent growth of scholarly interest in Africa's economic past has produced several important works on particular economies or regions but it seeks to complement this literature through a broader, more comparative perspective. The book takes as its central theme the integration of Africa into, and the subsequent structural shaping of African economies by, the modern international economy. To adopt such a framework is not to deny the possibility of alternative approaches, perhaps stressing more strongly the internal dynamics in African societies and the many elements of continuity in African history, but it reflects my view that exogenous influences arising from participation in the global system of production and exchange were the strongest determinants of economic change in nineteenth- and twentieth-century Africa.

My aims in writing this volume have been both ambitious and modest—ambitious in the sense that the literature upon which one might draw is so extensive, and yet the gaps in historical research are so many, that any brief general review of Subsaharan Africa's modern economic history must be regarded as a somewhat premature venture; modest in the sense that I have attempted little more than an account of broad trends and patterns. I have deliberately refrained from trying to apply or test any or all of the various theories of 'development' or 'underdevelopment' currently in vogue, since this would require entry into a *methodenstreit* which could all too easily overwhelm the empirical basis of my presentation. My account terminates

7

at 1960, a date taken to represent the end of colonialism in, and the opening of a new era in the political economy of, the greater part of Africa. Failure to carry the story through to the present day stems partly from a reluctance to lose the perspective of distance from events which is the historian's principal asset—but in the main from a belief that the last fifteen years deserve a separate volume. No short assessment of economic change between 1960 and 1975 could do justice to the range of economic strategies followed by post-colonial governments or deal adequately with the issue of 'neo-colonialism', which demands close consideration of theories of 'imperialism' and 'dependency' as well as critiques of such theories. This book, therefore, presents an historical background to, rather than a direct commentary upon, contemporary African economic problems.

The chapters which follow are not intended to be exhaustive, but rather pick out the important elements of change in particular periods. In this focus, and regrettably, certain aspects of the total picture—such as banking and currency developments, urbanization or land tenure—have been ignored or touched upon lightly. I have employed place and territorial names current during the colonial era and trust that this does not lead to any confusion. Since this does not claim to be a work of original research, notes have been kept to a minimum.

I wish to express my appreciation to all who assisted in the course of my work. The University of Glasgow generously granted a term's leave of absence for completion of the book, and the Centre of African Studies at the University of Edinburgh equally generously afforded me its hospitality and the use of its facilities during that term. To my colleagues in Glasgow, and to Nancy Porter, Orla Henry and Dorothy Milne who typed the manuscript, I also owe a debt of gratitude. Finally, and by no means for the sake of convention, I wish to thank my wife.

Introduction

Exchange transactions between the peoples of Subsaharan Africa and other parts of the world have a history which can be traced for centuries, indeed millennia, but Africa south of the Sahara was one of the last major regions to be fully integrated into the operations of the international economy. This apparent paradox can be explained by the fact that the international economy in question has a particular form—the modern global system for the exchange of goods and services which was created by the industrial capitalist countries of the West and the growth of which has been a relatively recent development in human history.

As late as A.D. 1500 world trade operated through several distinct, if overlapping, networks whereby each of the great clusters of urban-commercial culture—around the shores of the Mediterannean, in the Middle East, in North India and in China—traded with the various communities on their periphery and with each other. The commodities exchanged were seldom items of mass consumption, basic necessities of life for the average man, because the rudimentary state of the world's transport technology added great expense to the costs of moving goods over long distances. The standard items of inter-continental commerce were rather luxury and exotic products with a high value-to-bulk ratio—the precious metals and gemstones, fine textiles and pottery, spices and dyestuffs and rare furs and skins which were in demand among the wealthier minorities enjoying power and privilege in their respective societies. International trade therefore normally involved only a tiny fraction of a society's total output and was engaged in by a relative handful of specialists among its merchants, craftsmen and farmers. In a world where subsistence agriculture employed the energies of most of mankind,

9

exchange activities were largely local or regional in character.

Subsaharan Africa had a place in this early pattern of inter-continental commerce. By way of shipping routes across the Indian Ocean and Red Sea and overland trails across the Sahara desert, all of the world's major centres of market activity had links with African economies (although China's direct contacts were short-lived), and regional clusters of commercial centres had emerged in Africa to serve as entrepôts for external trade. Such towns as Jenne, Timbuktu and Gao in the savanna-steppe zones of West Africa and Sofala, Kilwa and Malindi along the East African coast tapped regional market networks for export commodities, of which gold was the most important but by no means the only item, and redistributed imports which were largely manufactured goods originating in the various concentrations of craft skill in the pre-modern world. Africa was no Dark Continent, totally isolated from external influences in the manner of the Americas or Australasia. For a number of societies south of the Sahara, interaction with Eurasian cultures and oppor-tunities for international exchange were already important elements in their economic, social, political and cultural history. Nevertheless, Subsaharan Africa, when seen in world perspective, may be said to have been an area of relative isolation. While the desert and oceans which surrounded it were never a total barrier to communications, they did place some limits on contacts with other continents, and the sheer scale of the African land mass, which restricted intra-African intercourse, tended to dissipate external influences. Only in the areas immediately south of the Sahara and along the Indian Ocean littorals can pre-modern international trade be said to have impinged strongly on the pattern of economic and political change. Most African communities had either only weak, second-hand connexions with intercontinental commerce or none at all, and remained largely unaffected by its operations.

From approximately A.D. 1500, however, Western Europe began the great transformation of world trade. The twin processes of aggres-sive expansion overseas and rapid economic development at home dramatically altered the role of Western European economies from that of periphery of the Mediterranean commercial complex to that of centre of a global system of trade, production and finance. Capita-lism and empire-building, in a relationship whose nature and signifi-cance are still hotly debated by historians, created the modern international economy with its large-scale trade in basic commodities, national and regional specialization in production, multilateral payments system, multinational companies and mass migration.

This international economy was no fixed and static entity but underwent continuous organic evolution, constantly responding to the changing conditions in and needs of its central core. Broadly speaking, four phases can be distinguished in its development. The first was the era of mercantile capitalism in which the shift of Europe's economic centre of gravity from the Mediterranean to the north-west, the rise of new commercial middle classes there, and the use of state power to achieve national economic strength went hand in hand with the systematic exploitation of overseas regions susceptible to European technology. This phase was primarily Atlantic-based, the mines, plantations, forests and fisheries of the Americas yielding valuable new resources for Western Europe's economic development, but European sea-power also brought societies along Asia's maritime littorals within the operations of the new international system.

Around 1780 there opened the phase of early industrial capitalism, when the economies of Western Europe, led by Great Britain, began to undergo the basic transformation from rural agrarianism to urban industrialism. Industrialization created new demands on overseas economies, for the scale and pace of change were too great to be satisfied by Western Europe's own internal resources alone. Raw materials for its factories and construction industries, markets for its products, food for its workers, and employment for those whom rapid demographic growth and a turn to larger-scale agriculture were forcing from the countryside, Europe obtained in growing measure from lands beyond its confines. At the same time, Western Europe achieved new levels of technological capacity, above all in the application of steam-power to production and distribution, which made possible extensive changes in both the commodity and spatial characteristics of intercontinental exchange. Trade in expensive luxury or semi-luxury goods, which had still largely dominated the earlier phase of mercantile capitalism, gave way to trade in cheaper machine-made goods and primary products in bulk. At the same time many new regions were pulled or pushed into the ambit of the international economy—as areas of European settlement, like Australia and Canada, as conquered territories, like India, or as

11

regions where naval and military power were used to remove obstacles to Western trade and investment, as in the Middle East and East Asia.

The third phase, commencing perhaps in the decade of the 1870s, was an era of maturing industrial capitalism in an enlarged but unstable international economy. The spread of industrialization, with Germany and America overtaking Britain and France as seats of technological and institutional innovation, and nations of non-Western culture, chiefly Russia and Japan, emerging as industrial economies, changed the international economy from an essentially single-centred system into a multi-centred one. The competitive forces which arose from this situation underlay the late nineteenth-century scramble for new colonies in regions of the world which had hitherto been only marginally involved in the activities of the international economy, and also made a substantial contribution to the outbreak of the First World War. The latter's distortion of international trade and monetary arrangements in turn coincided with another charac-teristic of the multicentred system—the tendency for capitalism's cyclical pattern of progress to become a global rather than a purely national phenomenon—to bring two disturbed decades for the international economy between 1919 and 1939. In the later stages of this phase, when the confident expansion of capitalism and colonial-ism gave way to crisis and doubt, the countervailing ideologies of socialism and nationalism made greater headway among the peoples of the centre and periphery.

The Second World War ushered in the fourth phase, that of the contemporary international economy. The central capitalist econo-mies, leadership of which now passed to the United States, regained their vigour, experiencing rapid and sustained growth. Greater governmental activity in economic planning and management at the national level was accompanied by increased co-operation between governments to provide the international economy with new institu-tional arrangements, and world trade expanded more rapidly than at any time since the late nineteenth century. A rival or alternative network of international trade and economic co-operation, that of the socialist or centrally planned economies, also emerged and the dismantling of Western colonial empires brought new hopes of rapid development for many of the world's poorer, primary-producing economies. Few of the latter disengaged from the operations of the Western-centred system to which colonialism had attached them, but a mood of frustration over the international economy's apparent inability to satisfy their aspirations became increasingly pronounced. The nature of relationships between rich and poor countries of the world therefore remains one of the key issues of international debate in the 1970s.

AFRICA AND THE INTERNATIONAL ECONOMY

Each of these phases in the international economy had its significance for economic change in Subsaharan Africa and made its mark on the evolution of African societies. Each involved Africa in changing patterns of centre-periphery relationships.

During the era of mercantile capitalism the older trading complexes of the West African savanna and the East African coast, which in world terms may be regarded as peripheries of Mediterranean and Middle Eastern centres of exchange dynamism, experienced destructive attempts by external forces to seize monopolistic control of their operations, and in the longer run were by-passed by the shift of commercial activity to the Atlantic and the mutation of Indian Ocean commerce by European sea-power. They lost their vitality and entered a period of apparent stagnation. By contrast, African communities along the western seaboard, previously remote from the influences of world trade, were drawn into the Atlantic sector of the nascent international economy—as suppliers of labour for the European plantation and mining enterprises in the Americas. Through the mechanism of the Atlantic slave trade, Western Africa joined the European-centred economy as a periphery to the American periphery.[1]

The phase of early industrial capitalism also had a differential impact on regions of Africa south of the Sahara. The gradual abandonment of European slave trading to, and slave-based production in, the Americas rendered the nineteenth century a period of adaptation for Western Africa. As the slave trade gave way to what Europeans called 'legitimate commerce', and Western Africa turned to supplying primary products directly to markets in Europe, the earlier relationship of periphery to periphery began to change towards that of periphery to the centre. European industrialization, meanwhile, created new peripheral or satellite economies around Africa's northern and eastern extremities. Algeria, Egypt, India and the scattered islands

13

of the Indian Ocean became areas of specialized primary production within the enlarged international economy, and their commercial links with Subsaharan Africa revived. Regions immediately south of the Sahara and large parts of eastern and central Africa now joined the intercontinental system in the same kind of relationship as Western Africa in the previous phase—as peripheries to peripheries. Finally, a satellite economy of a distinctive character, and one which was more closely connected to the international economy than any other in Subsaharan Africa, emerged in the far south, around the Cape of Good Hope, in what was the only major area of European settlement south of the Sahara.

The phase of maturing industrial capitalism completed the African transition from relatively isolated autonomy to full integration into, and dependence upon, the international economy. The partition of Africa among European colonial powers in the late nineteenth century initiated or reinforced processes by which the productive capacities of regions south of the Sahara were harnessed to the needs and demands of the Western industrial economies. With the creation of new political and administrative units, colonial investment in transport and other infrastructural projects, and the penetration of foreign business men, new economic structures were superimposed upon the existing ones. Such structures, the commanding heights of which were firmly under alien control, varied in their characteristics from region to region and colony to colony, but all operated to generate export-led economic growth. Subsaharan Africa experienced an unprecedented expansion in its external commerce. The emergent African nation states inherited these colonial economic structures, somewhat altered by half a century of internal evolution and inter-action with the international economy, when decolonization took place in the late 1950s and early 1960s.

Some measure of the changes which occurred in colonial Africa can be obtained from Table 1. This shows that in 1880 Africa as a whole, although clearly engaged in international commerce, had the smallest share of recorded world trade of any continent, but by 1960 its share was more than twice as great as that of Oceania and was not too far behind that of Latin America and the Caribbean. Between 1880 and 1960 the African share of world trade grew by 189 per cent, almost twice as much as that of North America. While the source for column 1 provides no data for Africa minus the North African

14

economies, it would appear that Subsaharan Africa's share of recorded world trade in 1880 was somewhere between 0·8 per cent and 1·2 per cent. In 1960 it was 3·9 per cent, a change in the region of 200–300 per cent. The trade of Subsaharan Africa, it seems, not only kept pace with the growth of world trade over a period of very great expansion in the latter's value, but so far exceeded it as to raise substantially Subsaharan Africa's share of the total.[2]

Such simple calculations, however, give no more than a general impression of the magnitude of economic change in Africa. They are silent about the character of change, its timing, and the means by which it was effected. They reveal nothing of the controversies over

TABLE 1   *Regional Distribution of World Trade, 1876–1960*

	Trade as % of Total World Trade 1876–80	1960	% Change 1876–1960
World	100	100	—
Europe	66·9	51·4	−23·1
N. America	9·5	18·4	+93·6
C. & S. America	5·4	7·6	+40·7
Asia	12·9	14·3	+10·8
Africa	1·9	5·5	+189·4
Oceania	3·4	2·4	−29·4

SOURCES: A. G. Kenwood and A. L. Lougheed, *The Growth of the International Economy, 1820–1960* (1971), p. 93; *U.N. Yearbook of International Trade Statistics* (1966).

strategies of economic 'development', the conflicts between different interest groups, the clash between indigenous and alien values, the manipulation of prevailing systems of production and distribution, the instabilities caused by fluctuating primary product prices or the growth of social inequalities which were just as much a part of Subsaharan Africa's modern economic history as the emergence of export staples and the spread of the market economy. Nor do they show the great variety of regional and local experience. These and other matters form the contents of the chapters which follow, chapters which do not attempt to examine in detail the long history of African interaction with the international economy from the first Portuguese voyages along the West African coast to the present day

One

The economics of Africa in 1800

For the historian, as for the playwright, a major problem is how to raise the curtain, introduce the characters, and set the scene for the action and dialogue which follow—and no account of Subsaharan Africa's modern economic history can avoid this difficulty. The year 1800 is to a large extent an arbitrary point of departure, selected for convenience in the absence of any date which clearly represents a watershed in the pattern of economic change in Subsaharan Africa as a whole. The African economies which would interact with the international economy in the nineteenth and twentieth centuries had already been shaped by a number of powerful influences, including the early phase of Europe's overseas expansion, and elements of stasis and change at work in 1800 had long-term as well as short-term significance for economic development. This chapter, therefore, outlines the principal economic characteristics of Africa in 1800 and the historical forces behind them as a starting point for a discussion of the nineteenth and twentieth centuries. No single chapter, however, can present a comprehensive treatment of Africa's early economic history for, quite apart from the difficulties of compressing lengthy chronology and differential patterns of local-regional experience into a brief framework, analysis is seriously limited by the nature of the source material available. Only a few broad, salient features can be discussed.

LAND AND POPULATION
Africa south of the Sahara has always been a land of great variety, as much in its economic systems and structures as in its cultures and politics. This diversity of means by which men obtained their livelihoods and provided for the material well-being of their families arose from the interplay of a number of factors, one of the most

17

important and influential of which was the environment they sought to use and control.

The succeeding chapters will use for descriptive purposes a division of Subsaharan Africa into four main regions. While the exact boundaries between the regions are difficult to delimit (those on Map 1 are drawn to follow present-day political boundaries), each is nevertheless fairly well defined in terms of its principal physical features. Southern Africa is an area of high plateau, surrounded by a narrow

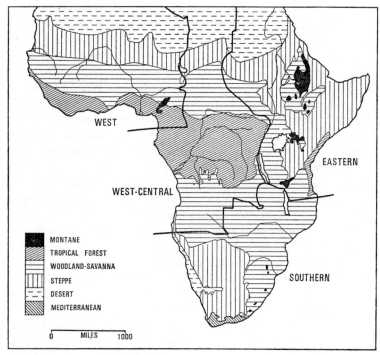

Map 1. Regions and Ecological Zones

coastal belt and sloping gradually from the mountainous terrain on its south-eastern flank towards the plains around the vast basin of the Congo river system. The latter is the heart of the second region, West-Central Africa. West Africa, the major river system of which is the Niger-Benue, is also an area of relatively low-lying plain but has a few isolated blocs of high land. Eastern Africa is the most diverse of

18

the four regions in its physical characteristics—folding into mountain ranges and plateaux and the faulting of the Rift Valley, with its associated lakes, present great intra-regional contrasts in land and ecology.

Climatic and vegetation belts, cutting across the somewhat artificial regional boundaries, add to the diversity of environmental conditions and create a number of distinctive sub-regions. In the western half of the subcontinent a pattern of some regularity prevails. Immediately north and south of the equator lies a zone of dense tropical forest and high levels of annual rainfall, comprising much of the Congo basin and the coastal strip of West Africa. North and south of the forest are the woodland-savanna belts, where drier conditions exist, rainfall has a more strongly pronounced seasonal distribution and the vegetation is a more open woodland interspersed with grassland. To the north and south again are zones of steppe country, semi-arid areas of open grassland with only occasional trees, which gradually give way to the arid conditions of the Sahara and Kalahari. In the eastern half of the subcontinent, however, the regularity is broken. Here the higher altitudes of the East African highlands and the Southern African high plateau, and the influence of Indian Ocean rather than Atlantic wind systems, create circumstances in which steppe and woodland-savanna belts extend much further to the south than in western Africa, moist tropical forest is confined to a few narrow coastal stretches, and isolated blocs of cool, moist zones with montane vegetation occur at high altitudes.

Forms of land use have been closely related to prevailing environmental conditions throughout African history. In the steppe lands and desert fringes transhumant pastoralism has been the dominant type of land use, employed by peoples for whom cattle are the principal assets but whose herds also include goats, sheep and donkeys. The woodland-savanna zone and its steppe fringes are the location of a mixed arable-pastoral way of life. Field production is mainly of cereals—millets, sorghums and maize—and legumes, but cotton and peanuts are also important crops. The care of livestock has a significant part in the operations of the domestic economy, perhaps more especially in the highland and high plateau areas of Eastern and Southern Africa where the absence or low prevalence of tsetse fly renders cattle-keeping less hazardous than in the woodland-savanna zone of West Africa. The farming practices of the forest zones are

19

distinguished from those of the woodland-savanna by a much greater reliance on root crops (manioc and yams) and bananas, and by the lack of large domestic animals.

A further element in Subsaharan Africa's regional and sub-regional differentiation is population density. Unfortunately, population—its numbers, growth and distribution—is one of the great unknown factors in African history. Measurement of any near-reliability becomes generally possible only in the late colonial period and discussions of pre-colonial conditions necessarily involve large elements of guesswork. In the absence of censuses, ecclesiastical records and tax returns which provide the historical demographer with his basic data, estimates of the population in recent centuries are commonly achieved by working backwards from the known facts of the present day, using assumptions which may or may not be accurate. Some indications of the difficulties which arise in such an exercise can be obtained from Table 2. Variant A postulates a decrease in population

TABLE 2   *Estimated Total Population South of the Sahara* (millions)

	1750	1800	1850	1900	1950	1960
Variant A	135	124	124	124	180	207
Variant B	54	61	69	89	160	207

SOURCE: J. D. Durand, 'The Modern Expansion of World Population', *Proceedings of the American Philosophical Society*, 111 (1967), p. 138.

between 1750 and 1800 as a result of the forcible migration and high mortality of the Atlantic slave trade, followed by a century of static population between 1800 and 1900 and sixty years of growth after 1900. Variant B supposes that, in spite of the slave trade, the population of Subsaharan Africa grew at the modest rate of 0·25 per cent per annum during 1750–1850 and more rapidly thereafter. Both sets of assumptions are tenable in the vast lacunae of African historical demography, but they give rise to startling differences in estimates of total population at any point in time. The divergence is greatest for the year 1750, when the inhabitants of Subsaharan Africa might have numbered anything between 54,000,000 and 135,000,000.

The distribution of population through time is also difficult to establish with any precision. Linguistic, archaeological and other evidence has enabled the historian of pre-colonial Africa to trace patterns of growth and movement—but only in broad terms. The northern savanna and steppe, from Senegal in the west to Ethiopia in the east, were the locations of the first major development of food-cropping techniques south of the Sahara, and the population of these areas appears to have undergone a long, slow growth from 2000 B.C. to the recent past. The West African forest, initially settled by migrants from the north-western savanna, in some places perhaps as early as 800 B.C., seems to have experienced its greatest expansion in population with the arrival of new crops suited to forest agriculture—the South-East Asian complex of bananas, plantains and new varieties of yams around A.D. 1000, and the American complex, including manioc and maize, from around A.D. 1500. Most of the rest of Subsaharan Africa has been populated in the last two thousand years by the expansion of the Bantu-speaking peoples, farming and iron-working migrants from the Niger-Benue confluence who crossed the Congo forest to the southern savanna. From there they dispersed into most of West-Central and Southern Africa, and into Eastern Africa where they met a southward expansion of pastoralists from the north-eastern steppe around A.D. 1300. While the Bantu speakers probably incorporated existing hunting-gathering and early neolithic peoples into their new social formations, their numbers may also have grown more rapidly in consequence of the absence of the anopheles mosquito and tsetse fly, carriers of malaria and sleeping sickness, from the highland and high plateau areas of Eastern and Southern Africa.

Map 2 shows the present-day distribution of African population. Rural distribution in 1800 was probably not too different in its general characteristics, the most populous areas being the West African forest and savanna, the Ethiopian highlands and the highland-plateau country around Lakes Victoria and Nyasa. West-Central Africa and Southern Africa had fewer concentrations of population density than other regions, their inhabitants being more thinly scattered across both forest and savanna.

Only a tiny proportion of the population lived in towns in 1800. While Eastern, Southern and West-Central Africa had a number of small towns with up to 10,000 inhabitants, mainly along the coasts, the Ethiopian capital of Gondar, with 60–70,000 people, was the only population centre of any size. West Africa, in line with its ancient state-building traditions and its greater density of market networks, was more urbanized—Kano, Katsina, Segu, Timbuktu, Benin,

21

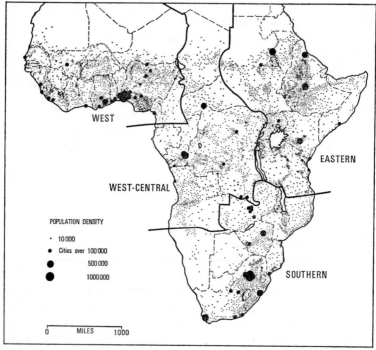

Map 2. Population Density, 1960

Kumasi, Ife and Old Oyo all had more than 10,000 inhabitants. Nevertheless, West Africa, too, was a region in which the overwhelming mass of the people lived in hamlets, villages or small towns.

Striking variations in growth and density make generalization about Africa's population hazardous. Nevertheless, two features of long-term significance for the subcontinent's economic history should be noted. The first is that in all probability demographic growth proceeded at a slow pace before the twentieth century. It was certainly slower than the rate of growth by which the population of Western Europe more than doubled between 1750 and 1900, and it was possibly more modest than the rates achieved by some pre-industrial societies in Asia. Famine-producing droughts were prevalent in the marginal agricultural areas of the steppe-savanna borders, and have been recorded by Arabic literary sources from the Niger Bend and oral traditions from the eastern fringes of the Kenya highlands. Such

22

epidemic diseases as cholera, smallpox and plague were not unknown, and in the lower-lying tropical areas malaria, yellow fever and try-panosomiasis were endemic, causing high infant mortality rates. Finally, African populations experienced the drain of slave exports.

Slow demographic growth combined with the vast expanse of exploitable land to produce population densities which were low by world standards. If the figures of 54,000,000 and 135,000,000 in Table 2 represent the lower and upper limits of Subsaharan Africa's population in 1750, they would indicate a population density of between six and fifteen people to the square mile. At that time penin-sular Europe (i.e. excluding Russia) *had* a density of 60 to 70 people to the square mile. Even allowing for the existence of sub-regions and localities with higher than average densities, it seems clear that Africa's early economic history cannot be expected to have paralleled too closely the pattern in such great centres of world population density as Western Europe, North India or China. If parallels exist, they are more likely to be found in the history of a territory like Russia where, as in Africa, land was abundant, population was thin on the ground, and fresh frontiers for agrarian colonization were continually opened up.

PRODUCTION AND EXCHANGE
While the relationship between population and economic activity is a complex one, and the historian must beware of too simple and deter-ministic a view of their interaction, some important features of pre-colonial African economies can be explained largely in terms of slow rates of population growth and low levels of population density. They include a high incidence of extensive land-use coupled with loosely defined proprietorship in land. Where population density is slight and there is no great variation in soil fertility, the cultivator is able to use land on a very temporary basis, abandoning both the land and his rights to it when its natural fertility is exhausted. As population grows, densities increase, and competition for land mounts, land must be used more intensively, which in turn may require innovation in agricultural technique, and the proprietary rights of individual or family assume greater importance. The movement of African agri-cultural systems along the spectrum from temporary to permanent land use, primarily if not solely in response to population growth, has undoubtedly been one of the central features of economic change in

both pre-colonial and colonial Africa. This movement, however, has gone largely unrecorded, except for a few communities under colonial rule, and the regional and sub-regional pattern which existed in 1800 cannot be easily established. It is unlikely to have been too different from that of the present day, in which the less densely populated areas of West-Central, Eastern and Southern Africa are associated with methods of shifting cultivation, whereby the land is cropped for a few years and then abandoned in favour of a fresh site, while the moderately populated areas, including most of West Africa and the interlacustrine area of East Africa, follow practices of rotational bush fallow in which field sites remain constant but are used in a system of recurrent cultivation. A few African communities—notably the Hausa around Kano, the Ibo of the Lower Niger and the Kikuyu of the Kenya highlands—practise intensive and permanent cultivation in which crops rather than fields are rotated. This, it would appear, has been a mainly twentieth-century development in densely populated and commercially oriented agricultural communities which in 1800 used techniques of rotational bush fallow.

Agriculture tended to be concentrated on the most naturally fertile areas, where satisfactory yields could be obtained by low productivity techniques. Implements were simple, the most important being the iron hoe. Clearance of timber and grass by burning provided the arable with small amounts of fertilizer but, even in woodland-savanna zones where cultivators kept livestock, the systematic application of animal manure to fields was not practised. The existence of large areas of waste, moreover, permitted a high incidence of foraging activities within the daily routine or seasonal cycle, and lessened dependence on field and pasture for the provision of food, clothing and shelter. In recent centuries specialist hunting-gathering societies, once fairly common in Subsaharan Africa, have been confined to such isolated corners as the deeper recesses of the Congo forest and the sands of the Kalahari by encroaching farmers and pastoralists. But the latter also drew heavily on the foraging potential of the land around their settlements—to collect the fruit, nuts and juices of local plants, to hunt wild animals for their skins and meat, to cut timber for fuel and construction, and to fish the rivers, lakes and seas. A distinction, admittedly one which is occasionally blurred, can be drawn between farm and non-farm sources of income or consumption goods in African domestic economies.

Slow rates of population growth and low-to-moderate densities also produced a tendency towards egalitarian distribution of land. While the supply of land to meet the demands of a growing population was never totally free from the social constraints of kin and polity, and from the natural constraints of soil infertility, aridity or inundation, the capacity of the household unit to clear new land from the waste and bring it under cultivation was the principal determinant of land allocation. Pioneering colonization by cultivator and herder was a basic feature of African agrarian societies—but, with a few possible local exceptions, colonization seldom outgrew the supply of land exploitable by the existing technology. Features of a restricted land supply, such as landlordism, tenancy, rentals and land sales, were either absent or more weakly developed than in the more densely populated regions of Eurasia, while landlessness through inability to obtain access to new land or near landlessness through fragmentation of holdings was virtually non-existent. African economies therefore lacked the large numbers of rural poor, obliged to hire their labour, which were to be found in many areas of pre-industrial Eurasia. The scarcity of labour and its consequent high price inhibited the emergence of agricultural systems employing non-family labour and was a major constraint on the development of commerce and manufacturing.

Pre-colonial African economies are often characterized as 'subsistence economies', comprising self-contained units of production and consumption. The description is not entirely inappropriate to the agriculturally based domestic or household economy. The goal of the average cultivator, governing his choice of production techniques, might be said to have been first and foremost to meet his family's needs for food, clothing and shelter. These he could supply by the application of household labour and capital (tools, seed and live-stock) to his land, any surpluses being incidental by-products of his subsistence aims. Such an analysis, however, would not be wholly accurate. Pure self-sufficiency was largely unattainable, if only because some necessary commodities could not always be obtained from the family fields and pastures or from their immediate environs. Minerals in particular tended to be concentrated in a few favoured localities, so that iron or salt were often procured solely or most easily through trade. Nor can it be demonstrated that auto-consumption was the sole or even the overriding goal of the agricultural producer, leading him to forgo any exchange possibilities which might arise and to exclude them from his calculations in farm management.

By 1800, in fact, the majority of Africans made some use of a market system to obtain part of their needs and to dispose of some of their output. Few areas lacked contact with a local or even a regional market centre, and West Africa in particular had market networks of some antiquity. The subsistence-orientation and market-orientation of production in pre-colonial Africa was therefore a matter of degree. Unfortunately, data which would permit comparative measurement of market activity are as scarce as data on population, and the historian is forced to rely on scattered, impressionistic and imprecise information.

The growth of the market in pre-1800 Africa, with its local and regional networks of market sites, trade routes, currency systems and merchants, was a lengthy and intricate process in which forces encouraging market development interacted with constraints against its growth to produce a wide variety of local conditions and circumstances.[1] One of the most important elements, it seems, was population density. Although the correlation between population density and levels of market activity is not absolute, the evidence suggests that areas with moderate to high densities were most favourable to the emergence and growth of local markets. The presence of larger numbers of people within easy walking distance of each other made possible the everyday personal contacts through which exchange might take place, and, conversely, sparse population inhibited such interchanges. Since large parts of Eastern Africa, and all of West-Central and Southern Africa were more lightly populated than West Africa, the latter tended to have a richer concentration of market sites and a wider use of the market system.

Population densities, however, are an insufficient guide to market behaviour because commercial transactions could, and did, take place in sparsely populated areas. Nature had an equally significant influence in that the variety of environmental conditions created opportunities for the exchange of commodities peculiarly suited to particular areas. The concentration of minerals in certain localities was part of this pattern, as were minor differences in soil fertility or rainfall distribution which gave rise to local scarcities and exchange. At a wider level, the differences in climate and vegetation between steppe, woodland-savanna and forest underlay regional commodity flows. Steppe pastoralists, for example, have traded their livestock for the grain and other arable products of the savanna throughout Africa's history.

The fact that animals transported themselves immensely facilitated dealings in livestock. Most other commodities lacked that advantage, and the cost of moving them over long distances dictated that some items could be more easily exchanged than others in regional trade. Transport facilities in pre-colonial Africa were inadequate for any large-scale transactions in farm produce. Small coastal craft and river canoes provided relatively cheap bulk carriage—the towns on the Niger Bend, for example, depended on river traffic for their food supplies. But patterns of supply and demand based on environmental variations rather than on urban-rural dichotomy could not easily be serviced by major waterways. The rivers Senegal, Congo and Zambezi, among others, flow for almost their entire length through terrain which is largely undifferentiated in its climatic and vegetational conditions. Since, for reasons that are not entirely clear, Subsaharan Africa lacked the horse- or ox-drawn cart which was an important means of overland transport in the pre-industrial economies of Eurasia, trade between forest and savanna or savanna and steppe depended in some areas on pack animals and everywhere mainly on expensive human porterage. The high costs of transport severely limited trade in staple foodstuffs and basic raw materials. This was largely confined to local-level transactions, more especially in areas where environmental differences were especially sharply defined or where political and commercial forces were sufficiently strong to create urban centres. The expense of porterage was more easily borne by what was, in the African context, luxury or semi-luxury goods with relatively high values—the manufactures of the specialist craftsman and the foraged products of extra-farm land.

Most African village communities had their own craftsmen—mainly blacksmiths, weavers and woodcarvers—who combined agricultural pursuits with the manufacture of items which others were unable or unwilling to supply for themselves within the domestic economy. While the bulk of craft goods were locally produced and distributed, some important regional centres of craft specialism had also emerged in consequence of a plentiful supply of raw materials or the accumulation through centuries of skills in some aspect of the craft, the best known being perhaps the city of Kano whose weavers

27

and dyers supplied a large part of the textile trade in the West African savanna and steppe. Outside West Africa, centres of craft excellence were less common because the regional distribution networks on which their existence depended were less highly developed.

In every region foraged or collected commodities figured prominently among the items in long-distance commerce. They included the skins and tusks of animals, valued for their decorative properties, and the dried fish produced by riverain communities. Unworked metals like iron, copper and gold, extracted by simple technological processes, may also be regarded as collected items, while the West African trade in kola nuts, gathered from the wild or the semi-wild of the forest and sold to Islamic communities in the savanna and steppe, was quantitatively the most important of widespread dealings in natural fruit and plant extracts valued for their medicinal or food-flavouring qualities.

Trade offered the African producer a highly differentiated 'vent for surpluses'. Agriculture, which employed by far the greatest part of Subsaharan Africa's labour and capital resources, could respond only to the relatively weak demands of local markets, made little direct contribution to regional or long-distance commerce, and drew from the market few of its necessary inputs apart from some iron. Regional commerce, by contrast, bore most directly on those who specialized, sometimes full time but more frequently part time, in extra-farm production—such as craftsmen, hunters, fishermen and miners—and the potential for innovation in response to changing market forces was almost certainly greater in these fields of activity. Similarly, long-distance trade, more volatile but more rewarding for the successful, held the greatest potential for the development of mercantile skills and capital and for the emergence of specialist merchant groups, and it was more closely intertwined with the ebb and flow of political affairs.

SOCIAL AND POLITICAL STRUCTURES

African systems of production and exchange were embedded in multifarious social and political formations, ranging from the band organization of hunting-gathering groups to large, complex state systems. Lineages, varying from small family units recognizing kinship through only two or three generations to large, sometimes territorially localized clans recognizing kinship through many generations, were the elemental socio-political organizations. The lineage provided security for its members, ensuring the individual's access to such resources as land, tools, seed and additional labour, and regulated the distribution of inherited wealth and the disposal of moveable goods. Cutting across the bounds of lineage loyalty were a number of organizations—village communities, religious institutions, secret societies, age-sets and men's clubs—which served to secure interlineage co-operation in matters of common concern, largely at a local or grass-roots level. Finally, dynastic authority over lineage and association was to be found in a number of areas, operating through political systems which ranged from very small states to large, sprawling kingdoms with hierarchic administrative arrangements.

The distribution of socio-political structures conformed to no clearly defined pattern of region, environment or population density. While West Africa might be said to have had the largest concentration of administratively sophisticated and militarily strong states, it also contained stateless groups like the Ibo and Tiv. In the Eastern African highlands and plateau there existed the ancient Christian kingdom of Ethiopia, the newer interlacustrine states ruled over by the descendants of pastoralist immigrants, and acephalous societies like the Kikuyu.

Each type of socio-political formation acted as a mechanism for the appropriation and redistribution of goods and services, giving rise to circulatory flows which were distinctly different from those of market exchange and to patterns of social differentiation which were not based on the market. Lineage heads and elders, exercising authority by virtue of seniority and age, enjoyed special claims on lineage output and received commodities and services from junior members. These they used partly for their own consumption and partly for redistributive purposes—to maintain lineage cohesion, to ensure its growth by obtaining wives from outside and to take care of its sick and weak members. The entrance fees and other charges of the various extra-lineage associations were expended not only on the upkeep of the institutions and their officials but also on ceremonies, feasts and charitable works.

The state, however, had the most powerful appropriation-redistribution mechanism. In every state the ruler and his corps of military-administrative personnel were necessarily involved in mobilizing revenues from below. By way of tribute, taxes and tolls on trade, foodstuffs, precious metals and other commodities flowed upwards to political and military élites, providing them with above average levels of consumption and resources to redistribute to retainers, clients and allies. But the burden of maintaining a state superstructure did not fall solely on those under its immediate authority, for the pre-colonial state was usually as much an instrument for conducting warfare outside its geo-political boundaries as maintaining social order within them. Successful external aggression ensured a redistribution of wealth from neighbouring societies by way of tribute and booty-raising campaigns. The powerful state surrounded by weaker peripheral polities from which it drew much of the resources for its upkeep can probably be said to have been typical of pre-colonial Africa.

To each set of arrangements, the market was both contradictory and complementary. The individual's ability to obtain new commodities and dispose of his own through commercial transactions was a threat to the non-market circulation of goods and services with which relationships of legitimacy and loyalty were intertwined. Lineage heads, priests and kings therefore had strong motives for attempting to control and regulate dealings between those under their authority and stranger merchants, controls which might include licensing traders, policing markets, setting prices or establishing monopolies over particular commodities. Conversely, the non-market systems presented opportunities for the trader. The figures who stood at their apex were potentially important suppliers of products bulked up through the appropriation mechanism and, as the wealthier elements in society, potentially important customers for the trader's goods. Their power could also ensure the merchant the peace and security his operations required. Consequently, lineages, religious organizations and states, the goals of which were far from purely commercial, were frequently participants in major exchange transactions.

A number of writers, mainly anthropologists, have laid great stress on the non-market elements in African life and suggest, explicitly or implicitly, that by obviating the need for the allocation of goods and services by a market system, and by cushioning the producer against market demand and prices, lineage, association and state restricted the growth of the market.[2] The truth, however, was usually more complicated than their models allow. Their arguments, indeed, might be reversed—for the market can be regarded as just as much a derivative of socio-political conditions as an independent variable imposing itself on and changing these conditions. That market expansion might result from the growth of inequalities in income and consumption generated by political innovation suggests the possibility that the relative weakness of the market in pre-colonial Africa merely reflects a relative absence of social stratification and inequality, and that African production, above all agricultural production, employed techniques of low-level productivity because the demands of élite groups did not press particularly heavily on output.

Such a thesis cannot be easily proved because of the lack of information and the complexity of socio-political conditions. Agrarian societies without state superstructures, many of which existed in the Africa of 1800, were fairly egalitarian and obviously did not experience the same pressure of demand from above as those who were subject to a state system and a ruling élite. Among the states, however, the ability of ruling groups to appropriate from below appears to have varied considerably, and there is some reason to believe that even the most efficient (or oppressive) failed to secure the same upward shift in income distribution achieved by élites in pre-industrial Eurasia. Comparative measurements of the share of output appropriated by fiscal arrangements cannot be made, but it is doubtful if any African state or aristocracy obtained the 15 to 20 per cent of total grain crop which the Chinese land tax produced in the fifteenth century or the 15 per cent of total income said to have been enjoyed by the political-military establishment in Moghul India. The castles, palaces, cathedrals, mosques and sundry public buildings which were the most visible manifestations of the consumption habits of Eurasian ruling classes, the patronage of the arts by the upper élites, and the concentrations of merchants, craftsmen and servants in urban centres around administrative capitals and military encampments, all had their equivalents in state-ruled areas of Africa—but on a greatly reduced and less lavish scale.

That conditions in the northern woodland-savanna and steppe—from Senegal to Ethiopia—most closely approximated those in Eurasian societies suggests that the key to differences in social equality and income distribution, and by extension in levels of market activity, was not so much the relative agricultural productivity of particular regions or localities but rather the relative efficiency of the means of social control at the disposal of ruling groups. In the African conditions of low to moderate population density, societal management through controls over land was relatively ineffective—too many avenues existed for flight to empty land or distant peripheral areas where central political authority was weak. Other sanctions, including religious ones, might be used, but the most effective would seem to have been the application of military power. Possession of superior military technology—horse-mounted cavalry borrowed from the example of North African societies with which they were in contact—gave the aristocracies of the northern woodland-savanna the means at least to counteract partially the egalitarian tendencies of abundant land and weakly defined political frontiers. Ruling groups in most of the rest of Africa, by contrast, lacked such a clearly differentiated military capacity until the introduction of firearms, and even then the clear superiority of firearms over other weapons and techniques of warfare was not immediately assured.

Where state and aristocratic power was strongest, the incidence of dependent labour tended to be greatest. As in other parts of the pre-industrial world where land was abundant and labour in short supply, such as eastern Europe in the fifteenth to seventeenth centuries, the rise of aristocratic privilege in Subsaharan Africa was associated with the growth of restrictions on individual liberties. A dependent or 'slave' labour force—drawn from such groups as debtors, criminals and war captives—relieved the élites from routine domestic and agricultural employment, being used mainly to provide household subsistence and seldom for exchange production. Depending on circumstances, bonded men might also be used as troops in war and for the carriage of goods. Although in Subsaharan Africa as a whole the 'free peasant' smallholding remained a more universal unit of agricultural production than the slave or serf estate, slavery and slave trading were present in a variety of degrees and forms before the growth of the European-controlled maritime slave trade. The latter, however, impacted on areas where, by and large, the incidence of slavery and slave trading was initially low.

MARITIME COMMERCE: THE SLAVE TRADE

To discuss Subsaharan Africa's external commerce of 1800 solely in terms of its links with European maritime enterprise is to adopt a somewhat traditional approach. It ignores the continuing trans-desert trade of the northern savanna-steppe lands which recent research suggests did not decline to total insignificance during the supposed 'dark ages' of the seventeenth and eighteenth centuries. It also overlooks the non-European seaborne trade between Asia and the small ports of the Red Sea and Indian Ocean littorals, the decline of which may have been exaggerated by earlier historians. But the vitality of each of these sectors of external commerce ultimately depended upon the progress of North African, Middle Eastern and Indian economies which seem to have reached a stagnant condition in the eighteenth century and which certainly lacked the dynamism of the West European economies.

To equate further Africa's international exchange with the European-operated slave trade does an injustice to the fact that Africa exported to the rest of the world a range of commodities other than human beings. Nevertheless, it remains broadly true that in the two centuries preceding 1800 an overseas demand for slave labour was the greatest single external influence on socio-economic conditions in Subsaharan Africa.

That Black Africa joined the emergent international economy more as an exporter of manpower than an exporter of commodities was in no sense pre-ordained, but it did reflect certain weaknesses of the African position in international commerce. Pre-colonial Africa did not lack mercantile skills—of which the Mande and Hausa trading diasporas in West Africa were prime examples—and until at least the last half of the nineteenth century almost all overland, intra-African trade remained in African hands and under African control. Nevertheless, the virtual absence of an indigenous maritime technology and capacity for constructing ocean-going ships severely restricted African initiatives in inter-continental commerce. When, from the late fifteenth century, European traders came to coastal markets south of the Sahara to buy and sell, African merchants—with the partial exception of the Arab-Swahili communities in East Africa— were in no position to challenge the European monopoly of maritime transport. Africans could now trade with Europe and the Americas, and via European shipping with Asia—but only on European terms.

They could respond to external demand and adjust their mechanisms of supply, but they were unable to take independent action to alter the character of that demand.

Western Europe's maritime connexions with other continents set limits on an African response. In the sixteenth century, before the full emergence of the slave trade, Africans were able to pay for their imports of European manufactured goods by sales of various 'exotic' non-farm products—gold, gum, ivory, timber, beeswax and wild peppers—bulked up through local and regional markets. Such direct trade between Africa and Europe continued to operate throughout the seventeenth and eighteenth centuries—but with Africa building up large deficits. The African deficit in trade with Britain, for example, averaged £78,000 per annum at the beginning and £833,000 at the end of the eighteenth century. This was in marked contrast to the experience of Asian societies which, with their exports of cotton and silk textiles, spices and tea, enjoyed positive balances of trade with pre-industrial Europe and obtained bullion and specie imports. The difference arose from the fact that technique and productivity in Asian agriculture and manufacturing were roughly on a par with, and in some respects more advanced than, those of pre-industrial Europe, and Asian societies were better placed than African to benefit from the growth of European demand for new or cheaper products. Asia was therefore, in a general way, a competitor with Africa for the European market—and so too were the Americans. It is conceivable that, in the absence of European colonization in the Americas, Subsaharan Africa's maritime littorals might have become important regions of agricultural and mineral export production, either through indigenous innovation or some form of joint European-African enterprise. Such possibilities as existed at the beginning of the sixteenth century, however, faded away as European mercantile capitalism found the Americans better suited to the production of such crops as sugar, tobacco, coffee, cocoa and cotton—because of abundant supplies of land, a lower prevalence of tropical diseases and easier access to Europe for windborne shipping—and gained control of major new sources of precious metals there. Africa's export potential was further narrowed.

The choice facing Subsaharan societies open to European maritime commerce came very close to one between abjuring the increase in imports made possible by sea transport or paying for such imports with the one item, manpower, for which there was any substantial external demand. The interests of military-administrative élites, who were the principal consumers of imports, and whose warfare and tribute-raising campaigns were easily adapted to the enslavement of weaker subjects and neighbours, tipped the scales and ensured that slave-exporting would be the principal African contribution to the early growth of the international economy. The export of slaves to Europe's colonial peripheries covered the African deficit in trade with Europe.

The centre of demand lay in the Americas, where some 8,500,000 Africans landed between 1450 and 1810, 6,000,000 of whom made the crossing in the years 1700–1810. If, as seems likely, mortality rates in the Atlantic passage were around 15 per cent, total slave exports from Africa's coasts probably amounted to 9,750,000 by 1810. The Atlantic slave trade was therefore the greatest intercontinental migration in the pre-industrial world, being surpassed in scale only by emigration from Europe in the nineteenth century.

West and West-Central Africa bore the brunt of the transatlantic demand. Table 3 presents a rough guide to the regional distribution of slave exports to the Americas in the eighteenth century, revealing that at the beginning of the century the West African coast, from Senegal to the Cameroons, was the most important single source of supply but that from 1730 onwards the share of other regions grew rapidly. Most of the increase came from West-Central Africa, from an expansion in the exports from Portuguese-ruled ports in Angola and even more from the growth of British and French trading along the coast from the Cameroons to the mouth of the River Congo. But in the later decades of the century, the slave-trading 'frontier', which had come to the various sections of the Atlantic coast at different points in time, began to penetrate the Indian Ocean, seeking new supplies from the Portuguese enclaves on the Mozambique coast and the Arab-Swahili ports in East Africa. There it overlapped with a newer, and still relatively small-scale, slave trade to meet the labour needs of sugar plantations in the French islands of Reunion and Mauritius.

West Africa's total maritime trade (exports and imports together) has been estimated as being worth a little over £4,000,000 in 1800,[3] which would suggest, assuming the same regional ratio in total trade as in slave exports, that the Atlantic-oriented commerce of West-Central and Southern Africa was worth £4,750,000 in the same year.

35

TABLE 3   *The Atlantic Slave Trade: Exports by Region, 1701–1800* (Totals of British, French and Portuguese Slave Exports)

	1701–20	*1721–40*	*1741–60*	*1761–80*	*1781–1800*
WEST AFRICA					
(000's)	497·9	594·2	619·1	654·1	648·7
% of total	77·6	67·6	61·0	63·2	45·9
WEST-CENTRAL & SOUTHERN AFRICA					
(000's)	144·0	278·5	379·3	379·3	758·9
% of total	22·4	31·7	37·4	36·7	53·7
OTHER & UNKNOWN					
(000's)	—	6·3	16·2	0·8	6·5
% of total	—	0·7	1·6	0·1	0·4
TOTAL (000's)	641·9	879·0	1,014·6	1,034·2	1,414·1

SOURCE: P. D. Curtin, *The Atlantic Slave Trade* (1969), p. 211.

In world terms the combined total of nearly £9,000,000 was not large—it was the equivalent of only 11 per cent of Britain's foreign trade and less than 2 per cent of the only known estimate of world trade in 1800—but it was nevertheless a significant sum for regions which three centuries earlier had engaged in no maritime trade at all.

The slave-trading networks which developed within Africa were in the main extensions of existing systems of long-distance trade in which dealings in slaves gradually became more important than, but seldom if ever displaced, transactions in various non-farm commodities. A certain superficial regularity prevailed in that three basic functions—exporting, 'producing' and intermediary or middleman activities—can be assigned to the traders and/or rulers of particular African societies. The critical nodal points between external demand and internal supply were the entrepôt ports, which along certain sections of the coast came under European rule—French posts in Senegal, British and Dutch castle-towns on the Gold Coast and Portuguese towns in Angola and Mozambique—but along others remained under African authority. In these coastal towns and harbours, slaves and other commodities were gathered together and stored for dispatch by sea and export-import prices were established between European shippers and African brokers. By the late eighteenth century, whatever the earlier situation, the main sources of slave supply lay in the interior, where warfare associated with the rise of new states such as Futa Jallon, Ashanti, Dahomey and the Yoruba empire of Oyo in West Africa—and the collapse and decline of others—of which the Kingdom of Kongo in West-Central Africa is the best known and possibly most tragic example—produced large numbers of captives who might be sold as slaves. Finally, between the entrepôts and the major slave-producing localities areas of middle-man operations were usually to be found—inhabited by intermediate peoples like the Fante of the Gold Coast, the Ovimbundu of Angola or the Yao of Northern Mozambique, the political authorities of which controlled the trade routes, and the merchant groups of which handled the commodities to and from the ports.

This tripartite division of commercial-political relationships, however, was by no means uniform. Some coastal exporters by-passed intermediary markets and dealt directly with slave-producing areas, and Dahomey, perhaps the eighteenth-century slave-trading centre *par excellence*, encapsulated all three functions within the framework of a single political system. Nor were militarily strong and expansive states the only slave 'producers'—virtually every society linked to maritime commerce yielded up some slaves for export, and among the stateless Ibo of the Lower Niger, a religious institution, the Aro-Chuku oracle, controlled a powerful mechanism for bulking up and re-selling slaves from local markets.

Did the maritime slave trade promote or retard the pre-1800 economic development of Subsaharan Africa? This, the most funda-mental question about Africa's early involvement in the international economy, is susceptible to no easy or satisfactory answer. It has greater relevance for West and West-Central Africa than for Southern and Eastern Africa, which became involved in pre-1800 external slave trading only partially and belatedly, and the debate which has arisen over the role of the Atlantic slave trade in the early economic history of the former regions cannot be resolved within these pages.[4] To argue either case convincingly would require the construction of a hypothetical or counter-factual model of the progress of African economies in the absence of the slave trade, and the data needed for such a task—on demography, the volume and value of internal trade, the incidence of 'domestic slavery', the amount of indigenous commercial capital, and so on—are unavailable to the historian. On the one hand it may be argued that maritime commerce enlarged the sphere of market operations within Africa, calling forth new entrepreneurial endeavour, creating stronger concentrations of commercial skill and capital, and promoting new consumer desires. On the other it may be pointed out that trade by itself is not development and that the demographic effects of slave exporting and its related warfare—a probable reduction of population in eighteenth-century West and West-Central Africa—must have had a deleterious impact on levels of output.

Certainly, any idea that the maritime slave trade acted as an engine of economic development must be seriously questioned, for its characteristics were such as to make little apparent improvement in the productive capacities of African economies. Opportunities for external exchange and access to firearms strengthened the power and wealth of rulers, warriors and traders, but the new consumption demands which arose from this increased social stratification would seem to have been satisfied more by the rise of imports and a greater use of household slavery by élites than by any expansion of African exchange production. Imports were mainly finished goods, which required little or no further processing by African craftsmen, while military and commercial innovation, rather than agricultural or manufacturing, provided the principal exports. There was little significant diffusion of technology from the rest of the world into Africa via maritime commerce—apart from the introduction of American crops and the training of a few African artisans in some European-ruled coastal entrepôts. All in all, the slave trade appears to have done little to promote higher levels of output in African economies.

Maritime contact with Europe and the Americas would seem to have strengthened, and in certain areas may have initiated, trends which were already well established in Subsaharan Africa—the growing application of slave labour to household subsistence and the expansion of exchange transactions in high-value non-farm products—and conversely did little to erode the compartmentalization between agricultural production on the one hand and long-distance trade on the other which arose from the prevailing conditions of vast expanses of land, low to moderate population densities, shortage of wage labour and above all the lack of cheap bulk transport. The few Europeans who in Southern Africa left the immediate environs of the coastal ports to live in the interior were scarcely more successful in overcoming such conditions, so that the Dutch Boer communities of the Eastern Cape and the Portuguese *prazeros* of the Lower Zambesi, with their slave-worked estates to provide subsistence and their trading in ivory, skins, hides and (on the Zambesi) slaves, may be said to have conformed to, rather than to have broken through, the limitations on economic development which existed in pre-1800 Africa. These limitations the early international economy did not, and perhaps could not, remove.

Two

New directions in the international economy, 1800 – 1870

The matrix of the modern world, for Subsaharan Africa as much as anywhere else, was Britain's Industrial Revolution. The deep-seated structural transformation of the British economy had global implications and repercussions which would ultimately penetrate to every human society. It pioneered the rapid industrialization through which, by continuous technological advance and organizational adaptation, cumulative economic growth became possible. The first in a series of shifts from rural-agrarian to urban-industrial national economies, it initiated the division of the world into wealthy industrial and poor agrarian societies. It also spawned new networks of international exchange—of goods and services, men and machines, ideas and institutions—which transformed methods and relationships of production on a scale and at a pace which were historically unprecedented. Between 1820 and 1880, the value of world trade in current prices rose from £341,000,000 to £3,033,000,000, the annual rate of growth, adjusted for price changes, being 5·03 per cent. Behind this enormous expansion of international exchange lay innovations in manufacturing technique, mainly in textiles and metallurgy, which gave Western industrialists a competitive edge over small-scale handicraft producers in the rest of the world, changes in transport technology—the railway, river steam-boat and ocean-going steamship—which broke through the natural barriers of distance, and the combination of military-naval power, diplomatic pressure and free trade ideology which eroded political restrictions on trade. From a handful of industrializing economies, among which Britain enjoyed a near hegemony as the pioneering industrial nation and the 'workshop of the world', came a rising tide of manufactured consumer and capital goods to be exchanged for the raw materials and foodstuffs of the less developed economies. There

40

also came an outflow of capital to finance trade, shipping, railway and harbour construction, mining and agricultural production, and an outpouring of European migrants—11,500,000 between 1820 and 1880—who sought new opportunities overseas. Around the British, and to a lesser extent the French, economy, concentric circles of international interdependence developed.

Most histories of the international economy in the first three-quarters of the nineteenth century pay scant attention to Subsaharan Africa. Alongside the great themes of the diffusion of industrialization in Europe and America, the growth of European settlement economies in the world's temperate regions, and the 'imperialism of free trade' in Asia, North Africa and Latin America, the economic history of Subsaharan Africa seems to be regarded as uninteresting or unimportant. There is, indeed, a strong hiatus in much of the prevailing literature. Subsaharan Africa is assigned a clear international role in the eighteenth century—as a supplier of slaves to the Americas, thereby making a substantial contribution to the preconditions for an industrial revolution in Europe—and again in the late nineteenth century as an object of the 'new imperialism' of the industrial nations. About the intervening periods, however, little is usually said, giving rise to the impression that little of consequence occurred in Africa's relationship with the international economy between 1800 and 1870.

That impression is both inaccurate and misleading. International commerce may not have been as strong a force for economic change in Subsaharan Africa as in, say, South Asia, but its influence was by no means absent, and in a variety of direct and indirect ways it made demands on, and challenged the adaptability of, African economies. The period 1800–1870 was, in fact, one of transition in African economic history, in which older connexions with the international economy were cast off and new ones evolved, in which an increasing penetration of European commercial and political power laid foundations for later territorial acquisitions, and in which the emergence of new systems of production and exchange and the rise of new interest groups created basic continuities between precolonial and colonial economic history. The events of these years, essential to any appreciation of the forces behind, and the forms of, African integration into the international economy in the late nineteenth century, can be most conveniently reviewed region by region.

41

WEST AFRICA: FROM THE SLAVE TRADE TO 'LEGITIMATE'
COMMERCE

The Act of Parliament of 1807 which prohibited British subjects from
dealing in slaves was not the first such move by a European state, but
withdrawal from the slave trade by the world's foremost commercial
nation, the shipping of which carried one-half of all the slaves crossing
the Atlantic, set a powerful precedent which the United States (1808),
Holland (1814) and France (1815) quickly followed. The reasons why
this group of Western nations should, at the beginning of the nineteenth century, turn their faces against a commerce which had played
an important part in their seventeenth- and eighteenth-century
economic development, lie deeply embedded in the social and intellectual history of each, in the demography and productive capacity
of their tropical and sub-tropical peripheries, and in the shared
experiences of the upheavals of the Revolutionary and Napoleonic
wars—and it would be a gross caricature to depict their retreat from
the slave trade as the triumph of industrial capitalism over the older
mercantile capitalism. Nevertheless, it remains an acceptable
generalization that the industrialization which each was experiencing
in a greater or lesser degree made possible the end of their slave-
trading activities—by creating social classes and political groups
which, lacking any strong vested interest in Atlantic slavery and
jockeying for power with older mercantile forces which did, allied
with those who opposed the dealings in human beings on theological
and humanitarian grounds.

Paradoxically, the industrialization which helped to undermine
commitment to the slave trade and to the institution of slavery in
metropolitan societies also tended to strengthen slavery and dealings
in slaves in some of the international economy's peripheries. The
rapidly growing demand for raw materials and foodstuffs in the
industrial economies encouraged agricultural expansion in the primary-producing economies, in a number of which labour was in
short supply. In the southern United States a high rate of natural
population growth among slaves and an internal slave trade rendered
the cotton-planting economy more or less independent of external
sources of labour, and in the British Caribbean the gradual shift of
sugar planting from the older settled islands to Trinidad and Guiana
was ultimately made possible by imported indentured Asian labour.
Two American centres of expanding plantation agriculture, however,

continued to look to Africa for slave labour—Spanish-ruled Cuba, where importing of slaves was only effectively suppressed from 1859, and Brazil, a Portuguese colony until 1822, the government of which took no strong measures to end slave importing until 1850. This continuing demand for slaves in the Americas, the profitability of meeting that demand, and the difficulty of securing international co-operation to halt slave-trading activities, both legal and illegal, all combined to bring a lingering rather than a sudden death to the Atlantic slave trade. The year 1807 marked merely the beginning of the end, for the compulsory transfer of Africans across the Atlantic went on virtually unabated for another forty or fifty years. Between 1807 and 1850, slaves were imported into the Americas at a rate which, although down on the peak period of the 1770s and 1780s, was still approximately equal to the rates for the first half of the eighteenth century, and only in the 1850s and 1860s did the Atlantic slave trade dwindle to insignificance. More than 2,000,000 slaves were exported from Africa's shores between 1810 and 1870, the destination of perhaps 60 per cent being Brazil and 30 per cent being Cuba.

Aggregate figures of slave exports, however, conceal important distinctions between regions of origin. Such information as is available suggests that, of the slaves crossing the Atlantic in the nineteenth century, perhaps only 17 per cent came from West Africa as opposed to 57 per cent from West-Central Africa and 26 per cent from Southern Africa (essentially from Mozambique). While these figures cannot claim absolute accuracy, they do indicate that the trend in slave-exporting away from West to West-Central and Southern Africa, already pronounced in the late eighteenth century, was accelerated by the end of British, French and Dutch slave-trading in West Africa, where the shipping of these three nations had predominated, and by the freedom from metropolitan or international control in seas south of the equator enjoyed by Portuguese and Brazilian dealers until the late 1840s. The decline of the Atlantic slave trade, therefore, came to West Africa as a whole earlier and somewhat more gradually than it did to the other regions of Sub-saharan Africa.

Within West Africa the timing of the change varied from place to place, depending upon the effectiveness of the European powers in blocking access to the Atlantic for slave exporters. In Senegambia,

Ivory Coast and the Gold Coast, where the British or French maintained a military presence or where the ports lay open to the warships of the Royal Navy, the slave trade had more or less died by the end of the 1820s. But along the Guinea-Sierra Leone coastline, heavily indented with creeks where illegal slave shippers could hide, slave-exporting carried on for another couple of decades. Similar conditions prevailed in the creeks of the Niger Delta and the lagoons of the Bight of Benin, and in the entrepôt ports of the latter the continuing slave trade was fostered by events in the interior. The disintegration of the northern Yoruba empire of Old Oyo, the incursions into its territory by the Fulani invaders from the savanna, and the outbreak of prolonged warfare between the southern Yoruba states enlarged the flow of war captives south to Lagos, Badagri, Porto Novo and Whydah. Whydah, the main port of the Kingdom of Dahomey, became a favourite haunt of Brazilian slave dealers, some of whom became royal functionaries, and Dahomey under King Ghezo went on exporting slaves in large numbers until the decline of Brazilian demand in the 1850s. The situation in Whydah, however, was somewhat atypical, it being virtually the only place where a large, militarily strong state controlling large sections of interior supply routes also had its own port, which enabled it to dictate conditions of trade to external merchants. This fact, coupled with British and French disagreement over intervention in Dahomean affairs, permitted Whydah to carry on with the slave trade after the rulers of most other West African coastal areas had been compelled or cajoled into its abandonment.

As exports of slaves declined, more rapidly in some areas than in others, a remarkable growth occurred in primary-product exports (the overall dimensions of which have still precisely to be quantified) and the old tri-continental exchange relationship, by which West Africa paid for its imports from Europe by exports to the Americas, began to change to a bilateral relationship between Europe and West Africa. The commodities with which West Africa now paid its way in international commerce had mostly been traded in small quantities in the eighteenth century, and in that respect their nineteenth-century export expansion was but an extension of a commerce which the slave trade had overshadowed. Such items as ivory and gum assumed a new importance in external exchange, but the most rapid growth came in exports of timber, of which the Sierra Leone forest was a major source of supply, and vegetable oils now in demand in Europe for the manufacture of soap and candles. Palm oil, extracted from the fruit of the oil palm which grew naturally in the West African forests, was exported from virtually every coast with a forest hinterland, but the principal source of supply was the Niger Delta where such small trading states as Old Calabar, Bonny, Brass and Warri tapped hinterland markets by canoe. Imports into Britain, by far the largest market, rose from 112 tons in 1807 to 31,457 tons in 1853. The coastal areas of Senegambia, with a savanna-steppe environment, offered an alternative source of vegetable oil in the form of groundnuts (peanuts), cultivated by peasant farmers and exported to France for processing. The groundnut trade began around 1840, and by 1854 Senegalese ports were exporting 5,500 tons per annum.

The growth of this 'legitimate' commerce was more than simply a response to the decline of the slave trade for, although the loss of income from slave-exporting encouraged West African merchants and rulers, more especially those of the entrepôt ports, to look for exports other than slaves, their search was powerfully assisted by the fact that the first half of the nineteenth century was a period, hitherto unprecedented, when barter terms of trade turned strongly in favour of primary producers in the international economy. The great increases in the productivity of British, and to a lesser extent French, industry reduced the price of manufactured goods in world markets more sharply than the price of primary commodities for which productivity increases were less marked. Britain's net barter terms of trade, expressed as an index in which 1880 = 100, fell from 176·5 in 1800 to 89·4 in 1855. What this meant for West Africa was that while prices of imported goods fell strongly (British textiles by around 75 per cent between 1817 and 1850), prices for primary products exported to Britain and France held firm, and in the case of palm oil, the largest export by volume and value, prices even rose. At Old Calabar, for example, palm oil sold for between £7 and £15 per ton in the early 1820s and around £25 per ton in 1855. By way of cheaper imports the external economy penetrated West Africa more thoroughly than before, the price of manufactured goods falling towards levels where they passed through regional networks of high-value exchange to local exchange networks, becoming available to the ordinary farmers and petty traders. The latter in turn responded to the changing international terms of trade by yielding up to the regional external networks the commodities now in greater demand overseas.

The coincidental timing of the closing of one type of overseas market and the emergence of another prevented any general or prolonged crisis in West African economies and polities, although the transition from the slave trade to 'legitimate' commerce was by no means equally painless for all. It proceeded most smoothly in a fairly narrow belt of territory from the coast inland, usually no more than 50 to a 100 miles in depth, where a combination of climate and transport factors favoured the new external commerce. Palm oil, as a product of the forest zone which lay close to the coast, had a comparative advantage in transport costs over equivalent low value-to-bulk products from the woodland-savanna, the only notable exception being found in the coastal hinterland of Senegambia. Apart from the groundnut commerce of Senegambia, therefore, the external trade of the woodland-savanna zone was, in the absence of slave exports, confined to small quantities of the more 'traditional' high value-to-bulk items—ivory, gold and gum. The problems of transition, it would appear, were most acute for slave-'producing' areas of the woodland-savanna like northern Dahomey and Ashanti. The rulers and merchants of some of these localities, however, found at least a partial answer in the redirection of trade away from the coast to the northern savanna-steppe.

Throughout the nineteenth century the economies of the northern savanna-steppe (with the exception of the western extremities near the Senegal river) remained remote from Atlantic commerce. Here the principal dynamic for change was not external commerce which, oriented across the Sahara to the Maghreb, was on a smaller scale than the Atlantic commerce of the south, but rather a series of political-theocratic movements which threw up new ruling groups and created new state systems in the late decades of the eighteenth and early decades of the nineteenth century. The economic implications of these 'Islamic revolutions' have yet to be explored, but it would appear that the political innovations initiated a new phase in the economic history of the savanna-steppe lands. An enlarged 'leisured' élite, its powers of social control strengthened by a combination of military and religious expertise, was supported by a population among which slaves were now a larger proportion and the freemen were subjected to stricter taxation in accordance with

46

Islamic law. The surplus-expropriating operations of the new ruling groups, by changing patterns of income distribution, gave a boost to both commerce and craft manufacturing, which the enlargement of scale of political units further assisted by providing security for commercial transactions over wider stretches of the savanna and steppe. Consequently, the northern localities constituted for at least some of the more southerly areas a growth pole which was independent of the international economy. The expansion of the kola nut and gold trades from Ashanti to the north is perhaps the best known example of the way in which the political and commercial élites of woodland-savanna areas found new outlets for commodities under their control and an alternative source of consumption goods.

How 'revolutionary' was the transition from the export of slaves to primary products in the economic history of the western and southern coastal/hinterland belt? Did it, as some historians argue, represent a clear break with the past, a phase in which the foundations of West Africa's 'modern' economic development were laid, or was it, as others insist, more a matter of continuity than change, the basic turning-point coming with the imposition of colonial rule in the last quarter of the nineteenth century?[1] To the extent that fundamental changes took place, these are perhaps more clearly found in production than exchange, for the structure of the externally oriented commercial system was only marginally transformed. In its upper levels European merchants and trading companies continued to conduct shipping and bulk import-export functions and to provide the credit which, transmitted downwards through the market hierarchy, financed West Africa's external trade. Some of the European merchants were ex-slavers, while others were new arrivals attracted to the coast by the commodity boom, but almost all came from ports —Liverpool, Bordeaux and Marseilles—which had West African connexions from the slave trade era. Similar continuities may be found in the personnel and methods of African brokerage operations in the entrepôts. In the landward networks, however, the situation was more complex and fluid. The bulking up, transportation and storage of commodities like palm oil and groundnuts, and the breaking down of imported goods into the quantities needed for the many small producers, required more manpower than the trade in slaves and the numbers of traders, porters and canoemen engaged in international exchange appears to have grown. The further implications of this development, however, are by no means clear. Since 'slaves' or household dependants were employed in 'middleman' operations in many areas, it is possible that the rise of commodity-exporting encouraged the continuation of slave-holding and slave-trading within West Africa. It is also possible, although historians strongly disagree in the matter, that the growing commercial activity and power of these groups generated conflict and new patterns of socio-political alliance in West African polities.

An argument for innovation of watershed dimensions is stronger in the case of production. Many exports—ivory, gold, gum and dyewoods—remained 'exotic' foraged items, produced by hunting, gathering and felling operations which were marginal to agriculture, but the growth of palm oil and groundnut exporting meant that at least some agricultural producers now had an overseas market for the commonplace, low value-to-bulk yields from their fields. This feature is clearly seen in the groundnut cultivation of Senegambia but is somewhat less easily perceived in the palm oil production of the forest zone. While the oil palm grew naturally in the forest, it could also be deliberately planted as a tree crop, and there is evidence of an emergence of oil palm-planting under the stimulus of external demand—by Krobo farmers in the eastern Gold Coast and military élites who used slaves to cultivate larger-scale oil palm-plantations in southern Dahomey and Yorubaland. While the ratio of 'planted' to 'gathered' palm oil in total exports cannot be calculated, the fact of its existence, when coupled with groundnut production, justifies the claim that for the first time in West Africa's economic history the international economy had an influence on the choice of crops and techniques employed in agriculture.

WEST-CENTRAL AFRICA: EXTENSIONS AND COLLAPSE OF THE SLAVE TRADE

If the beginnings of a distinctly different relationship with the international economy can be detected in West Africa, the same cannot be said of West-Central Africa, where an expansion of the Atlantic slave trade in the first half of the nineteenth century contrasts with its gradual demise in West Africa. Portugal's tardy prohibition of the slave trade in 1836 went unenforced in its African coastal settlements, while Portuguese shipping was safe from search by the British navy south of the equator until 1842 (Brazilian ships until 1845). Even then the Royal Navy, lacking the bases it had in West Africa, was too weak to do more than marginally limit the trade before mid-century. The slave trade from the Portuguese ports of Luanda and Benguela on the Angolan coast flourished unchecked until approximately 1850 and along the coast from the mouth of the Congo to Cape Lopez, Brazilian, Portuguese and Cuban slave-dealers moved in to replace departing British and French merchants. Between 1815 and 1850 West-Central Africa probably exported over 1,000,000 slaves.

In West-Central Africa, therefore, the rapid decline of manufactured goods' prices in international exchange did not co-exist with a contracting market for slaves, as it did in most of West Africa where it had helped to foster the shift to 'legitimate' commerce. Rather, it impacted upon a situation where slave-exporting remained fully operative and its chief effect would seem to have been to propel an extension of that trade. A lack of basic quantitative data on the region's commerce unfortunately prevents any full exploration of the phenomenon. It is possible that West-Central Africa felt the force of falling prices of manufactured goods less keenly than West Africa —exports to Brazil were paid for partly in Brazilian rum and tobacco —but some reduction in the costs of imported textiles, metal goods and firearms almost certainly occurred. The implication of this development, although the argument can be no more than speculation, would seem to have been a further extension of slave-trading operations deep into the interior of the region, the lower costs of trade goods at the ports of entry offsetting the higher costs of transporting these items to new sources of slave supply. Thus, rather than using the falling price of manufactures to penetrate local market networks close to the coast, the merchants and brokers of West-Central Africa elected to push forward the tentacles of long-distance commerce and draw the ruling élites of the far interior into the slave trade.

By the first decade of the nineteenth century the operations of Atlantic-oriented commerce already extended more deeply into the interior than had been the case in West Africa, the principal reason for this difference between the relative sparseness of population in West-Central Africa which meant that traders had to range more widely to obtain an equivalent volume of exports. Three axes of coast-to-interior lines of communication carried the bulk of the export-import trade. The most northerly, through the forest zone of the Lower Congo area, began at various ports and harbours at the Congo mouth and on the Loango coast and converged by canoe-traffic and/or overland porterage on Stanleypool, where Teke traders took over the largely water-borne commerce with communities further up-river. A central route, overland through woodland-savanna country, from Luanda to the town of Kasanje, controlled by Imbangala middlemen, was paralleled further south by a caravan route from Benguela to the Ovimbundu-inhabited plateau and thence to the interior. By 1850 Ovimbundu trading caravans were operating as far east as the general area of modern Katanga and Zambia, approximately 1,000 miles from Benguela, and had entered the great Western Lunda kingdom, the coastal trade of which had hitherto been the preserve of the Imbangala. The latter, by way of partial compensation, opened up trade with the Kasai basin, well into the forest zone. Although less is known about the northern route up the Congo, it would appear that here, too, the sale of imported goods and the purchase of export items underwent considerable territorial extension in the first half of the nineteenth century. These developments may be seen as no more than the continuation of an already existing trend, but it is suggested that the changing terms of trade at the coast underlay the commercial viability of ventures so deep into the interior.

Although the Ovimbundu, Imbangala, Teke and other long-distance traders were also involved in serving internal, sub-regional patterns of supply and demand, the principal *raison d'être* of their commerce was the satisfaction of external demand for exotic, high-value-to-bulk foraged products—some ivory, a little gum, beeswax and malachite—and above all the lucrative export trade in slaves. The latter, however, slumped drastically in the early 1850s, partly as a result of Royal Navy intervention but mainly as a consequence of the closing of Brazil to slave imports. Exporting of slaves lingered on in a minor way—there was a brief revival of the illegal Cuban trade in the late 1850s—but in general terms the early 1850s saw a collapse of West-Central Africa's transatlantic commerce which was more abrupt than the same process had been in West Africa. All along the coast a major trade depression set in, the magnitude of which can be indicated only by travellers' descriptions of stagnation and decay in the once-thriving ports of Benguela and Luanda (the latter's European population, for example, fell from 1,601 in 1845 to 830 in 1851).

Recovery was fairly quick along the northern coasts of the region. To the ports and harbours of the forest zone, more especially to those around the mouth of the Congo, the West African oil-trading frontier now came. While some British merchants from West Africa had a hand in the development, the leading part was taken by Dutch merchants for whom the Lower Congo represented a source of palm oil supply outside British control. By comparison with the West African palm oil trade, that of the Lower Congo has been little studied, but it would appear that here too the African brokers and traders found the shift from slave to palm-oil exporting relatively easy. There is little evidence, however, of an emergence of oil-palm planting, and it seems that the production of palm oil in the Lower Congo hinterland retained its essentially foraging characteristics. In coastal Angola, on the other hand, the effects of the abolition of the slave trade were longer-lasting. Lying in a woodland-savanna zone, it had no palm oil to offer and, apart from a short-lived burst of cotton planting during the American civil war, found few outlets for its agricultural produce. Coastal Angola's failure to develop an agricultural export may be contrasted with the success of Senegambia, the difference perhaps being explained, among other things, by relative distances from European markets. For most of the 1850s and 1860s, therefore, the commerce of Angolan ports rested on exports of foraged products from the interior, and although quantities of the latter, especially ivory, grew substantially, they were insufficient to compensate for the loss of earnings from slave-exporting.

For the long-distance caravan trade of the interior the end of the overseas slave trade meant the replacement of slaves by ivory as the standard item of commerce. Dealings in slaves did not fully disappear since an internal demand remained among élite groups, both at the coast and in certain interior societies, for additions to their household labour force; nor was the growth of the ivory trade entirely novel— the origins of its expansion in the woodland-savanna zone may be dated to the Portuguese crown's revocation of its ivory-exporting monopoly in 1836. Nevertheless, a shift into ivory purchasing was the principal response of Ovimbundu, Imbangala and Teke middlemen to the demise of slave exporting. Ivory production, however, differed from slave 'production' in at least one important respect— the latter rested essentially on military and political skills, and the former on hunting skills. The shift of external demand from the

51

productive power of the established state to that of the mobile band of hunters, whom rulers could not easily control and whose travels over long distances in search of elephant herds generated an ability to challenge the caravan trade of established operators, at least partially explains the political instability and disturbances which came to the interior in the 1860s and 1870s.

The transition from the slave trade to 'legitimate' commerce proceeded less smoothly in West-Central Africa than it did in West Africa. The territorial extensions of the slave trade in the first half of the nineteenth century, its relatively abrupt termination in the third quarter, and the inability of the region's trade networks to find an alternative bulk export (at a time when terms of trade in the world's markets were beginning to swing away from primary producers in favour of industrial producers), all combined to make 'crises of adaptation' a more pronounced feature of West-Central African history. The West African breakthrough into the cultivation of crops for the external market had no parallels (the Lower Congo's palm oil trade notwithstanding) in a West-Central Africa where production processes relevant to overseas trade remained those of hunting-gathering. The Atlantic slave trade may have ended, but the economies of West-Central Africa continued to tread old pathways in their connexions with the international economy.

EASTERN AFRICA: THE ASIAN PERIPHERY

A further variant in Subsaharan Africa's overseas trade is to be found in Eastern Africa which, throughout the period from 1800 to 1870, was less closely linked to, and less directly influenced by, the changing structure of the international economy centred on industrial Europe than either West or West-Central Africa. Its external commerce, rather, was locked into a more ancient network of international exchange—the series of overlapping and interconnecting maritime and overland routes which carried the foreign trade of North-East Africa and South-West Asia, linking Egypt and Syria, the Arabian peninsula, north-western India and the maritime littorals of Eastern Africa in a complex web of shipping and exchange transactions. External supply and demand conditions which impacted on Eastern Africa, therefore, had their most immediate origins in the economies of the eastern Mediterranean, and around the Red Sea and Persian Gulf, and the principal intermediaries in external commerce were Arab and Indian rather than West European merchants and shippers. Nevertheless, Eastern Africa was by no means totally immune from the influence of the European-centred international economy. On the one hand, some of the economies of North-East Africa and South-West Asia, including Egypt, Syria and India were being integrated into the modern international economy as centres of primary commodity production and industrial goods distribution, a development which appears to have generated a new vitality in the commerce of the Red Sea, the Persian Gulf and the northern Indian Ocean. On the other hand, the growing volume and value of commodity transactions in this Afro-Asian interchange gradually attracted European and American merchants to Eastern Africa's coastal ports, laying the foundations of direct trade between the region and the world's major industrial economies. In Eastern Africa, therefore, older patterns of external exchange intertwined with the newer commercial forces emanating from the West in a complicated set of inter-relationships which historians have yet fully to unravel.

The nineteenth-century growth of Eastern Africa's external commerce was most rapid and spectacular along the Swahili coast, from Kilwa in the south to Lamu in the north. The economic history of the Horn, Ethiopia and the eastern Sudan (which from 1820 came under a Turco-Egyptian regime) has been too little studied to permit any rounded assessment of developments there, but it is doubtful if the interlocking maritime and caravan trade of the region's northern areas approached either the scale or the dynamic thrust of the exchange activities conducted in and through the numerous small ports and harbours on the mainland and islands south of the Horn. In the first half of the nineteenth century the external trade of the Swahili coast and islands expanded at a pace which can only be generally indicated by a 500 per cent increase in customs revenues between 1804 and 1859. Much of the history of this commercial revival has been written in the heroic mould, focusing on the role of Seyyid Said of Muscat-Oman whose sovereignty extended to the Swahili coast and who eventually shifted his capital to the island of Zanzibar, which became the principal entrepôt of the entire sub-region. Said's activities—the example of his own trading and agricultural ventures, his encouragement of the settlement of Omani merchants and aristocratic estate holders, his welcome for Indian traders and bankers, his

53

reforms of currency and customs administration, his commercial treaties with America and major European trading nations—were undoubtedly an influential factor, but probably less so than deeper economic and commercial trends which, in the absence of appropriate information and data, cannot be so easily perceived. By 1859, the Swahili coast's external trade via Zanzibar was worth £930,030 (excluding slaves), a figure which seems to represent something of a peak since total trade values declined slightly in the 1860s.

In many respects developments followed an already familiar path, overseas trade being based to a very considerable extent upon exports of foraged products and slaves. Some of the foraged items—gum copal and cowrie shells—were gathered in the Swahili-inhabited coastal belt and offshore islands, but the most valuable commodity, ivory, was a product of the interior. So too were the slaves whose trans-shipment, mainly to ports in Arabia, at an average annual rate of some 15,000 in the period 1810–60 probably added an additional £88,000 per annum to export earnings. The interaction of coast and hinterland had strong parallels with the pattern of events in West-Central Africa, the Arab and Indian brokers passing on to African middlemen—the Kamba of the Mombasa hinterland, the Nyamwezi who dominated the long-distance trade route between Bagamoyo and Lake Tanganyika, and the Yao between Kilwa and Lake Malawi— the cheap industrial goods which enabled them to extend their particular combination of trading, hunting and raiding deep into the interior. By the 1850s, Nyamwezi hunter-traders from the east were operating in the same general area of Katanga as Ovimbundu from the west. The Eastern African and West-Central African patterns, however, diverged in at least two ways. First, the brokers of the coast did not remain content to leave up-country operations in the hands of established middlemen dealers in ivory and slaves; from the late 1830s they supplied capital and credit to promote the entry of entrepreneurs of coastal origin, which led to the creation of an Arab-Swahili trading-post empire in the interior challenging rather than displacing the longer-established middlemen. Second, the Swahili coast's Indian Ocean slave-exporting, based on Arabian rather than Brazilian demand, lasted longer than West-Central Africa's trans-Atlantic slave trade. An 1845 treaty between Said and Britain, agreeing to the end of slave-shipping to Arabia remained virtually unenforced and in the intervening years between 1845 and 1870 the volume of slave exports almost certainly rose. In the Swahili coast and its related hinterland the commercial crisis of slave-trade abolition would immediately precede the political crisis of the challenge of European colonialism.

Furthermore, despite the high incidence of foraged products and slaves in its exports, the Swahili coast and islands also became a centre of specialized agricultural production. Some members of its land-owning Arab aristocracy, more especially the Omani who had followed Seyyid Said to East Africa, gradually converted their estates from a household subsistence to a commercial footing, using slaves from the interior to enlarge the production of certain crops suited to local conditions. Cloves, grown on Zanzibar and Pemba islands and exported to both Asian and European markets, were the first success-ful cashc rop but mainland estates were drawn into externally oriented production in a minor way through sales of copra and sesame seed, oil-yielding materials for which France was the principal market. The scale of these operations was limited—in 1859 agricul-tural exports were worth less than half the total value of ivory, cowrie and gum copal exports—but nevertheless the emergence of a plan-tation system supplying overseas demand represented a break with the past and a precursor of future trends on a par with the palm oil plantations of West Africa.

SOUTHERN AFRICA: THE SETTLERS' FRONTIER

Foreign ownership and management of export-oriented units of production, as represented by the Arab slave plantations of the Swahili coast, was an even more pronounced feature of Southern Africa, in large parts of which European-African interaction rested on a fundamentally different basis than the arrangements in West and West-Central Africa. Sir Keith Hancock's well-known paradigms of the West African 'traders' frontier' and the South African 'settlers' frontier'[2] sum up the essential distinction between the regions where the relationship between European and African enterprise was almost exclusively mercantile, production and most intermediate exchange remaining in African hands, and Southern Africa where the evolving international economy spawned a socio-economic system in which European immigrant settlers carried out both exchange and produc-tion functions, competed with African economies for the resources necessary to production, and enjoyed most of the gains which accrued from international commerce. The early origins of this system predate the nineteenth century, taking place in the small Dutch colony at the Cape of Good Hope where a coastal belt of land with a Mediterranean-style climate and free from tropical diseases permitted the relatively easy transfer of people, crops and domestic animals from Europe and provided the setting for Subsaharan Africa's first substantive European agricultural settlement. Some of the most significant steps in the system's rise to eventual domination of the entire Southern African region, however, occurred in the six decades following the British seizure of Cape Colony in 1806.

Cape Colony's links with international trade in 1806 were slight and precarious, being almost totally dependent upon the passing shipping which used Cape Town for provisioning and the spare freight capacity of which made possible some small-scale exporting of agricultural produce, mainly to trading ports and military garrisons strung along the maritime routes between Europe and Asia. A European population of approximately 20,000, assisted by a labour force drawn from the Cape's dispossessed indigenous Hottentot population or imported as slaves from West Africa and South-East Asia, was supported by agrarian enterprises which were subsistence-oriented to a high degree—less so within a radius of 50 to 60 miles from Cape Town, where wheat and wine were produced for the maritime market, than in the more extensive but drier lands of the eastern Cape, where pastoralism predominated. Here a settlement frontier of cattleherding Trekboers had expanded eastwards at the expense of Hottentot and Bushmen until, in the general area of the Fish River, it met Bantu-speaking, mixed-farming communities with whom it existed in an uneasy relationship, alternating between trade and warfare. By way of horse and ox-cart transport, the eastern Cape farmers maintained tenuous links with Cape Town's maritime commerce, exchanging pastoral products and hunted items for imported firearms, textiles, metal goods and tools.

Possession of Cape Colony brought Britain the strategic advantage of control over the shipping lanes around Africa's southernmost tip, but little in the way of direct commercial gain. For Cape Colony, on the other hand, the shift from a relatively stagnant Dutch imperial-commercial system to a more dynamic, expansive British one had somewhat greater significance. One of its most immediate effects was a substantial increase in the shipping, mainly British, which called at the Cape, in turn generating a larger demand for the colony's provisions and a greater excess freight capacity for bulk exports. By 1835 the volume of maritime traffic at the Cape was 800 per cent greater than it had been in the 1790s, coastal shipping had developed to tap the eastern Cape countryside for its hides, skins, ivory and tallow, and the colony's exports were worth £435,280, only a little short of the value of West Africa's palm oil exports to Britain (£450,185 in 1834).

Despite its growing commercialization, the eastern Cape's land-extensive, low-productivity pastoralism did not match British colonial administrators' agrarian ideals. Governor Sir George Craddock's declaration of 1812 that 'to encourage grazing and an indolent easy life . . . is not the object of His Excellency, but progressive civilization, agricultural improvement and common defence'[3] set the general tenor of official policy, which favoured a more intensive use of land, preferably through arable farming with its higher output per acre and denser population settlement. Pursuit of this goal, however, merely served to heighten dissatisfaction with British rule among the Trekboers of the eastern Cape. A state-assisted settlement of 5,000 British colonists in Albany district, partly as a buffer between Boer and Bantu and partly to demonstrate the benefits of wheat farming, a new system of land tenure to raise land values and limit the migratory tendencies of Boer pastoralism, and the government's reluctance to sanction or assist expansion across the Fish River, all conflicted with Boer expectations of cheap and quick access to fresh supplies of land. These land policies combined with the administration's intervention in labour relations—regulations of conditions for Hottentot workers and the abolition of slavery in 1834 —to produce the major Boer exodus known as the Great Trek.

The Great Trek of 1836 to 1846, during which some 10,000 Boers left Cape Colony to settle on the grasslands of the high veld to the north, might be interpreted as an act of economic as well as political defiance—a rejection of the market economy and external trade, and a major extension of subsistence-oriented pastoralism into interior lands which, remote from the markets and ports of the coast, could not sustain any significant commercial production. Certainly, the latter was the immediate economic consequence of the Trek, but it cannot be claimed as the goal of the migrants, whose settlement on the high veld was partly determined by the British occupation of the

Natal coast in 1842 to block any Boer access to the sea which was independent of British colonial authority. Commerce and communications became intertwined with strategic considerations in a way which would bedevil South African politics for several decades.

Viewed from a wider perspective than that of Anglo-Boer relations, however, the diaspora of the Great Trek assumes the character of just one more stream in a tide of social upheaval which overwhelmed much of Southern Africa in the first half of the nineteenth century. Just as it is possible to see the Trekboers as being driven by pressures from behind, so too might it be claimed that they were sucked forward into the interior by the existence of unoccupied land on the high veld and parts of Natal, land which had been depopulated in the course of the vast and complex clash of African societies which followed the rise of the Zulu state. The socio-economic dynamics of emergent Zulu militarism are barely understood. Suggestions that disequilibrium came to the small-scale African polities of the southeast as a result of the opening-up of overland and coastal trade with either Cape Colony or the Portuguese post at Delagoa Bay to the north are no more convincing than the explanation that population growth in the Bantu-speaking communities, hemmed in between the sea, the mountains and the Cape Colony's eastern frontier, created the tensions which sparked off the political upheavals. Alternatively, a growth in livestock numbers, generating conflict over water and pasture, may have been at the root of the problem.[4] Whatever its origins, devastating warfare spilled out from Southern Africa's southeast corner in the 1820s and 1830s, the military and political backwash of which reached almost every African society in the region. Depopulation through warfare and migration and the reconcentration of population into defensible areas like the Sotho mountains cleared large swaths of country on the high veld and in Natal, into which the European frontier of settlement pushed between the late 1830s and the early 1850s. As that frontier enveloped the principal areas of African occupation, hostilities between European and African communities developed, at the root of which lay competition for land. Out of this periodic warfare the broad outlines of a distribution of land between the respective communities began to emerge.

The penetration of the high veld by the Trekboers' cattle grazing and hunting economy and the establishment there of two independent republics, while carrying important implications for the future, contributed little to the immediate evolution of Southern Africa's links with the international economy. The key locus of international exchange remained the Cape Colony where a new phase of economic development, beginning in the mid-1840s, transformed the colony's economic role from that of a provisioning way-station for the commerce between Europe, Asia and Australasia, to that of a centre of production for the world market in its own right. Basic to this phase was the growth of an export staple, a single bulk commodity which could be exported in sufficient volume to encourage both specialization in its production and diversification of production and services around it. The staple was wool, for the mechanization of Britain's woollen industries, somewhat later than cotton manufacturing, and the consequent growth of over 800 per cent in Britain's raw wool imports between 1830 and 1870, created a mass market for a pastoral product eminently suitable to the Cape's natural conditions. As in Australia, and in conscious imitation of developments there, the introduction of high-yielding merino sheep laid the foundations for an export trade with a greater value and growth potential than the older trade in cattle hides, which it overtook in the 1840s. While British immigrants supplied much of the pioneering initiative, among them the Albany settlers who had found the district unsuited to wheat growing, the Boer pastoralists who remained in the Cape also took to commercial sheep-rearing. Wool-production spread into the new British colony of Natal and into the southern parts of the Orange Free State, on the high veld, but Cape Colony remained the largest producer and the centre of the wool trade. It became a source of raw wool for Britain second only to Australia, its exports rising from £5,900,000 in 1850, to £28,200,000 in 1860, and to £37,200,000 by 1870, at which date the Cape and the much smaller Natal exports together provided 12 per cent of Britain's raw wool imports, exceeding in value if not in volume Britain's palm-oil imports from the forest zones of West and West-Central Africa.

The Cape economy also paralleled the Australian settlement colonies in the manner, if not the scale, of its diversification around sheep rearing—the development of a few small-scale local manufacturing industries, government road construction programmes, the rise of county banking and the arrival of two London-based banks, the influx of a few thousand state-assisted British immigrants, and the growth of small market towns in the rural areas. But it differed from the Australian model in the fundamental respect that the labour for its agricultural and commercial enterprises was drawn less from European immigrants than from indigenous and imported non-European populations. Cape society was multiracial and multicultural, differences in skin pigmentation and culture being related to and reinforcing lines of social stratification based on economic function, and it was therefore closer in style and ethos to the societies of the tropical and sub-tropical Americas than to those of North America or Australasia. Its pattern of social relationships would be recreated, with numerous local variants, as the frontier of European settlement expanded northwards.

One such variant had already appeared in Natal which, between 1842 and 1870, was gradually converted from an ivory-exporting territory to an area of commercial agricultural production by a few thousand British immigrants. Natal's settlers, however, could not readily follow the Cape's path to development, because much of its sub-tropical coastal land was inappropriate to sheep rearing, which had a high land-to-labour ratio, and because it lacked the Cape's pool of relatively cheap labour, provided by the descendants of dispossessed Hottentots and freed slaves. The greater emphasis on labour-intensive arable production in Natal, particularly the sugar-planting which supplied the colony's second most valuable export, combined with the colonial administration's land allocation policies, which in opening up land for European farming left the colony's Bantu-speaking communities in possession of reserved areas, to produce acute problems of labour shortage for the European-owned agricultural enterprises. This was only partially solved by the importation of indentured Indian labour for the sugar plantations; some 6,000 arrived in the colony by 1870, adding a further element to its cultural diversity.

Although the growing economic and political ascendancy of British and Boer agrarian settlement is the dominant theme in Southern Africa's nineteenth-century economic history, substantial parts of the region, mainly in the north, remained untouched by the influences originating at the Cape. The region's north-east corner in particular was linked to world trade in a manner closer to that prevailing in West-Central or Eastern Africa. The scattered Portuguese ports and settlements along the Mozambique coast and up the Lower Zambezi, like those in Angola, had been drawn into the transatlantic slave-trading of the first half of the century, Portuguese and Brazilian merchants shipping perhaps as many as 6,000 slaves per annum to Brazil. The slaves were obtained partly by the predatory raids of Portuguese *prazeros* (estate holders) on weaker African neighbours along the Lower Zambezi, partly by purchase from African middle-men among whom the Yao slave and ivory dealers, operating in the relatively densely populated country around Lake Malawi, were especially prominent. The closure of Brazilian markets in 1850, however, did not bring the same abrupt termination of the slave trade as occurred in Angola. Mozambique's slave exports, although apparently reduced in numbers, were merely redirected by various subterfuges to outlets in the Indian Ocean, satisfying the disguised slavery of the 'contract labour' system of French sugar-planting islands and the Arab-Swahili slave markets of Eastern Africa. Mozambique and its hinterland, shifting the orientation of its external commerce from an Atlantic to an Indian ocean nexus, would be drawn into the ambit of the Anglo-Boer economies only after 1870.

With the exception of the Mozambique hinterland, the African agrarian economies in most of Southern Africa entered a relationship to rather than a connexion with the international economy in the years between 1800 and 1870. European settler-farmer intermediaries presented the latter less as an opportunity for the exchange of pro-ducts than as a demand for land on which European-managed production might be established; trading in ivory, livestock, hides and skins across frontiers was overshadowed by military conflict between the respective communities. One important qualification must be added to the generalization. As the violence of the settler-farming frontier passed, and once major expropriations of land had been accomplished at African expense, commercial production by African peasant farmers began to appear in the Eastern Cape and Natal. There, on land belonging to mission stations or rented from European farmers and land companies, enterprising African small-holders took to wool-farming for the export market and the sale of grain and meat to the domestic market. Such activities, despite uncertainty about their scale, indicate that, even in a period princi-pally characterized by conflict over land, avenues remained open for Africans to enter the market as independent producers. By 1870 the division of the land into areas of indigenous and areas of immigrant occupation had been largely completed in the Cape, Natal and the

Boer republics, but the relationship between the African and European economies was also beginning to change. Labour was becoming the resource which the European enterprises now needed from the African economies, a demand which would swell to an imperative when mining overtook agriculture as the mainstay of the immigrant-dominated economies.

In 1870 the external trade of Cape-Natal was worth £5,800,000, as compared with West Africa's maritime commerce of £6,200,000. While equivalent figures for West-Central and Eastern Africa cannot be calculated, they were almost certainly considerably less, perhaps around £2,500,000 each. Assuming Subsaharan Africa's total maritime trade to have been worth some £17,000,000 in 1870, this would mean a rate of increase from 1800 of only 0·7 per cent per annum in current prices as compared with a five per cent per annum increase in world trade in constant prices, and a fall from the equivalent of 11 per cent of Britain's foreign trade in 1800 to around three per cent in 1870. Such measurements, although subject to large margins of error, suggest that Subsaharan Africa's external commerce failed to keep pace with the enormous expansion in international exchange which followed Britain's industrial revolution. When one adds to this the absence of any significant investment from the world's metropolitan economies, an import structure heavily dominated by consumer goods and in which few producers' goods appear, and systems of internal transport which continued to rest on the porter, the canoe and (in Southern Africa) the bullock cart, it is easy to conclude that the main currents in the international economy of 1800 to 1870 by-passed Africa south of the Sahara.

But such a view misses the fact of a fundamental change in Africa's relationship with the international economy—the gradual shift from exporting labour to overseas centres of production towards exports of commodities produced in Subsaharan Africa by its own manpower. This transformation proceeded slowly because Western industrialization tended, at least initially, to strengthen Africa's propensity to export manpower—by fostering the growth of demand for slave labour in the tropical Americas, various Indian Ocean islands and possibly, although the linkages are less clear, in Arabia, as well as by supplying the mercantile systems meeting that demand with the cheaper manufactured goods which enabled them to expand their operations. In most of Subsaharan Africa the shift in terms of trade in favour of the world's primary producers encouraged rather than discouraged the slave trade, and the counterforce of political/ military action, undertaken mainly by Great Britain, consistently lagged behind these commercial pressures. Nevertheless, the slave-exporting which had been the basis of Africa's external exchange in 1800 had disappeared from all but Asian-oriented Eastern Africa by 1870.

A further important change occurred in the nature of the productive processes related to commodity-exporting. Around Africa's maritime littorals—in Senegambia, parts of the Gold Coast, the hinterland of Lagos, the islands of Zanzibar and Pemba, Natal and the Cape Colony—the reproductive principles of agriculture, including both cropping and animal husbandry, overtook the essentially destructive principles of hunting-gathering as the basis of exchange production for external markets. Although differing from each other in scale of enterprise, type of commodity, systems of labour, and degree of dependence on the market for inputs and sale of outputs, these scattered pockets of commercially oriented agriculture were the precursors of the later integration of African agrarian economies into the world market, influencing by their very existence the subsequent patterns of economic change in their areas and regions. They also, however, shared the characteristic of a location fairly close to the sea—for the high cost of internal transport remained the principal barrier to their emulation by farmers and herders in more distant localities. The advanced transport technology of the industrial revolution, which came to the West African and South African ports in the shape of the steamship in the 1850s and 1860s, had yet to penetrate the interior of the great land-mass of Subsaharan Africa. With the exception of steamship navigation on the Lower Niger, barely under way in 1870, that development would await the major extension of European political control in the last quarter of the nineteenth century.

Three

The economics of Partition, 1870-1896

The headlong rush of West European powers into Subsaharan Africa during the last three decades of the nineteenth century, in a scramble to convert the subcontinent's polities into appendages of European states, stands in marked contrast to the relative absence of colonial annexation in the course of the adjustments of African links with the international economy reviewed in the previous chapter. Outside the southern extremities which were the scene of settler-colonial expansion, the sovereignty of metropolitan Europe had been extended to only a few areas beyond the existing enclaves—to the small British- and French-ruled settlements of freed slaves in Sierra Leone and at Libreville in Gabon, to the little entrepôt kingdom of Lagos, and to a somewhat larger tract of land annexed to Senegal by an expansionary governor in the 1850s. Between 1870 and 1900 on the other hand, the whole of the subcontinent with the exception of Liberia and Ethiopia was partitioned into some twenty-three colonial possessions of six European powers in an outburst of unparalleled territorial acquisitiveness. A substantial part of Africa's historiography revolves around the events of these decades, in the shape of analyses of and arguments about the causes and consequences of European colonialism in Africa, and the debate about the origins of the Partition has been particularly lively, producing a voluminous literature but little in the way of general agreement.[1] This chapter, rather than reviewing the many strands in that debate, far less attempting any new synthesis which would provide an over-arching explanation of late nineteenth-century colonial expansion, will confine itself to an examination of the economic factors linking Europe and Africa in the period of the Partition. It focuses on the continuing evolution of African interaction with the international economy as a means of understanding not only the economic forces that promoted colonial annexation but also the subsequent structural development of colonial economies and policy decisions of colonial governments.

'GREAT DEPRESSION' EUROPE AND AFRICA

Historians are generally agreed that the last three decades of the nineteenth century, sometimes more precisely defined as the years 1873–96, constitute a distinctive phase in the development of the European heartland of the international economy, although they may differ about the nature and significance of its various components. For Lenin it was a transitionary phase in the evolution of capitalism, when the competitive industrial capitalism of pre-1870 Europe began to give way to the monopoly finance capitalism which would predominate after 1900. D. S. Landes sees it as a period of international climacteric between the productivity gains of the cluster of technological innovations of the Industrial Revolution and the second cluster (electrics, chemicals and automobiles) which brought a new cycle of industrial growth from the late 1890s. The period may also be seen as a transitionary phase in the centre-periphery relationships of the international economy—the movement from a single to a multi-centred system of global trade, finance and technological diffusion, as the nineteenth-century world economy which revolved around Britain's industrial leadership gave way to the twentieth-century world economy in which Germany, the United States, France and latterly Russia and Japan were also loci of advanced industrial production around which international specialization took place.

However one summarizes the developments of these decades, there can be little doubt that the industrial and industrializing economies of Europe were experiencing difficult, occasionally painful, adjustments in the wake of the expansionary boom of the 1850s and 1860s. Two interrelated, but at least partially contradictory, trends in the nineteenth-century world economy, advancing progressively but most rapidly in the 1850s and 1860s, brought pronounced economic instability to Western Europe after 1870. The rise of international exchange production of raw materials and foodstuffs, fostered by the movements in terms of trade in the first half of the century and long-distance transport innovations in the third quarter, so changed the conditions of supply, that, from 1870, declining prices of primary products, above all temperate zone agricultural commodities, threatened the incomes of Western Europe's still sizeable farming

65

communities. On the other hand, the growth of industrialization beyond Britain, mainly in the economies of Western Europe and America which had been among the first to take advantage of large-scale primary product-exporting to Britain, so enlarged manufacturing capacity as to drive down prices and generate intense competition for markets both within and beyond Europe. In Britain prices, interest rates and profits fell so sharply as to persuade contemporaries, whatever the doubts of later commentators, that they were afflicted by a 'Great Depression'; the growth rates of the French economy, its large agricultural sector hit by the phylloxera infestation of vineyards and the competition of cheap American and East European grain, declined to something under one-half of the rates experienced during Napoleon III's Second Empire; the economy of the newly united Germany, although making rapid structural changes, did not escape the sharp downturns in the trade cycle which also affected Britain and France in 1873–79, 1882–6 and 1890–96; around these three large and powerful national economies, the manufacturers, merchants and farmers of smaller or less-developed European countries struggled to maintain or improve their relative positions.

In this setting, the operations of European economic and political systems became progressively interdependent, in what can only be described as a turn to neo-mercantilist philosophies and policies. A retreat from the liberal free trade and *laissez-faire* policies, which had permitted the relatively free flow of commodities, labour, capital, technology and entrepreneurship between economic regions, into the tariff protection and subsidy of national autarky became the hallmark of post-1870 Europe. Behind the protectionist barriers erected by Austria (1875), Spain (1877), Italy (1878), Germany (1879), Switzerland (1884) and France (1881 and 1892), cartelization of domestic markets appeared as an attempt by producers to restrict competition and reduce market instability. British metropolitan politicians and businessmen, the mid-century apostles of free trade and the open economy, remained largely aloof from the neo-mercantilist ideas and influences spreading through continental Europe. The direction of their efforts, rather, turned outwards in a defensive posture—to ensure that, as barriers to British trade arose in Europe, they should not also be raised to the detriment of British trade with the peripheries of the international economy. In most of

Subsaharan Africa, where in 1880 Britain's trade was still three times the value of the combined trade of France, Germany, Holland, Portugal, the U.S.A. and India, these considerations underlay official British policy.

The connexions between economic instability and the trend towards state regulation of the market in Europe and the advance of colonial empire in Africa are by no means simple or direct, and it would be overly deterministic to argue that the former alone caused the latter. The scramble for colonies engaged the energies of too many individuals and interest groups with diverse motives for any such monocausal explanation. Nevertheless, the unsettled and changing political economy of Europe was one of the key elements in the transformation of political relationships between Europe and Africa. On the one hand it generated a climate of opinion strongly infused by a mistrust of foreign initiatives, which rendered metropolitan governments receptive to pleas for assistance from their businessmen—whether industrialists wishing to 'open up' new markets or overseas merchants facing foreign competition on the peripheries. In such parts of the world as China that assistance took forms other than outright colonial annexation, but Subsaharan Africa was particularly susceptible to a colonial 'solution' because in European concepts of international relations Africa had become something of a geo-political vacuum, its indigenous states regarded as archaic and barbaric and even the Sultan of Zanzibar dismissed as an 'Oriental Prince to whom are not accorded the usual rights prescribed by international law'.[2] On the other hand, the spread of neo-mercantilist ideas and practices in Europe had a parallel in the thinking of European businessmen in Africa, many of whom came to view the creation of colonial dependencies as a means by which the powers of the modern bureaucratic state might also be used to overcome their particular difficulties or advance their ambitions. State control and regulation of the market became a favoured device both to secure adjustments in existing commercial situations undergoing stress and to forge new links between Africa and the international economy.

This approach, in which events in Europe and Africa are seen to move in analogous, if not necessarily exactly similar, directions, offers a better insight into the economics of the Partition than the now much discredited explanation of surplus capital leading to investment and then to annexation, which is associated with the writings of J. A. Hobson and sometimes erroneously attributed to Lenin. It raises problems of economic change on the African peripheries of the international economy to at least a shared importance with the economic conditions of Europe in interpreting the new politics of control, for the stimuli to colonial expansion did not originate in the metropolitan economies alone. Subsaharan Africa of the 1870s was no subcontinent of totally closed, stagnant 'traditional' economies waiting to be 'opened up' by European rule. Several areas were already engaged in external commerce, and each of the coastal economies which figured prominently in the transformations of 1800–70 had a key role in the post-1870 advance of colonial authority—precisely because they lay open to international market forces which upset existing political relationships and called into question their control of the hinterland.

Such forces for change, however, were not necessarily the same in every region. Table 4 demonstrates that one important dimension to the economics of the Partition must be the downward movement in commodity prices which were a manifestation of Africa's connexions with 'Great Depression' Europe. The steady fall during the last three decades of the century of the prices for the two great export staples developed in the middle decades of the century—the palm oil and kernels of the West and West-Central African forests and the wool from Southern African grasslands—obviously had implications for the production and exchange activities, as well as the political economy, of these regions. But the same table also reveals that prices for ivory, for which West-Central and Eastern Africa were the principal producing regions, ran counter to the prevailing trend, as did those of another foraged item, the wild rubber which began to be exported from Africa in quantity during the last quarter of the nineteenth century. Given such a pattern, analysis of Africa's economic history in the period 1870–96 must proceed again on a regional basis.

WEST AFRICA: INSTABILITY AND DEFLATION IN EXTERNAL
COMMERCE

The economics of Partition in West Africa involved an intricate interaction between two phenomena—the short-term cyclical fluctuations of periodic slump interspersed with boom and the longer-term

secular trend of price deflation—which affected the industrial economies of Western Europe as well as the raw material exporting areas
of the West African coast. The origins of the scramble in the region
can be traced to the particular French response to the slump of
1873–9. To pull the French economy out of depression, politicians
and bureaucrats devised a programme of large-scale state expenditure
on railway, canal and road construction, and this Freycinet Plan, as
it was called, was extended to France's colonial possessions in Algeria
and Senegal. The moving spirits behind the scheme, it would appear,
had visions of using these colonies as a springboard for the creation
of an empire in North and West Africa which would perform the
role for the French economy which India was assuming for the
British economy—as a market for such capital goods as railway
materials and, through the provision of cheaper transport, for such
consumer goods as textiles. In the search for new markets for
hard-pressed sectors of French industry, great hopes were placed
on the largely illusory potential of the still relatively autonomous
economies of the West African savanna and steppe zones (the
Western Sudan). The scheme's more grandiose elements, especially
the proposed trans-Sahara railway to link Algeria and Senegal, did
not survive the French economy's recovery from recession in 1880–
1881, but nevertheless had a powerful influence on the scramble for
colonies in West Africa—by providing a set of ideas to which the
French state could refer in the course of subsequent slumps and by
initiating the construction of a railway line from Dakar to the Upper
Senegal which it was intended should eventually be extended to the
Upper Niger. The French army, called upon to provide security for
the eastern sections of the railway, clashed with the forces of
neighbouring African states and began a series of campaigns of
conquest which were justified partly on the grounds of local defence
requirements and partly on the grounds that they served wider goals
of 'opening up' savanna-steppe markets for France.

The French advance into the Western Sudan, which commenced
between 1879 and 1883, upset the status quo between European political interests in West Africa and unlocked the scramble for colonies.
During the next phase of the economic cycle, that of the depression
of 1882–6, Britain and Germany moved in defence of their 'interests'
by asserting their colonial authority over various sections of the
coastline, primarily in the important palm-oil exporting belt between

the Gold Coast and the Cameroons. British initiatives were possibly less immediately linked to the slump in Europe than were those of Bismarck who, facing elections at a time of socio-economic stress in Germany, was prepared to use the creation of a colonial empire in Africa and the Western Pacific in 1884 as a means of obtaining the political support of those elements of the German middle classes favouring colonies for reasons of commerce or national prestige. His motives, however, like those of British policy-makers, also included concern over conditions facing his country's merchants in West African trade.

In the course of the 1860s, 70s, and 80s, commerce along the West African coast had become fiercely competitive. This developed partly within the framework of a long-standing Anglo-French commercial rivalry—as French vegetable oil merchants, initially engaged in the export of peanuts, diversified into palm oil and kernel-purchasing, and began to penetrate the palm oil belt of Lower Guinea, including the Lower Niger which was hitherto a preserve of British merchants. But the arrival of increasing numbers of merchants from North German ports, in line with Germany's industrial growth, added a further dimension to European national-commercial rivalries. The character of West African entrepôt trade also underwent change, as the development of shipping lines with regular sailings between European and West African ports separated trading from shipowning and permitted the entry of men with more limited capital resources into import-export operations. The activities of the smaller capitalists, including in certain ports African businessmen from the older British coastal settlements of Sierra Leone and the Gold Coast, were further assisted by the gradual replacement of local African by European currencies in entrepôt transactions. This fluidity in commercial operations imparted itself to middleman operations between the entrepôts and interior markets by giving the African middlemen a wider range of customers, supplies of credit and sources of imported goods.

The competitive situation received a powerful twist from the downward spiral in commodity prices after 1870. Deflation in Western Europe affected the price of a range of products, but West Africa's major vegetable oil staples, both palm and groundnut, had especially adverse price trends as a consequence of the Suez Canal's opening of European markets to peasant producers of vegetable oils in Southern

Asia and a rising world production of mineral oils. The secular decline in prices, which brief recoveries in the trade cycle were unable to reverse, had repercussions for everyone connected with West Africa's maritime trade. Producers of most West African commodities experienced deteriorating terms of trade since the prices of imports fell more slowly than the prices for exports. African rulers and colonial administrators, facing static or declining revenues from taxes on trade, tended to favour enlargement of the area under their fiscal control and thereby contributed to local political conflict. Above all, the principal entrepôt merchants responded by trying to control deflationary trends through price-fixing cartels, but were unable to prevent ring-breaking by African middlemen, smaller import-export brokers and foreign rivals. They therefore began to call for political action up to and including colonial annexation, as a means of checking or suppressing commercial competition and, by reducing the political independence of African middlemen, forcing them to accept lower prices.

The character, intensity and influence of mercantile pressures for colonial expansion varied from locality to locality. They were most significant in the great palm oil belt between Dahomey and the Cameroons. In the Niger Delta the establishment of a British protectorate in 1887 was the prelude to colonial action against such middlemen-princes as Jaja of Opobo and Nana of Itsekiri, whose activities were a threat to the oligopolistic aspirations of the local British merchants. Further up the Niger, where the introduction of river steamboats had facilitated the penetration of British trading-houses into the palm-oil producing areas between the Delta and the Niger-Benue confluence, George Goldie amalgamated the competing British traders into a single commercial concern in 1879, and under-cut a rival French firm with such success as to force it to sell out to him. In 1886 Goldie persuaded the British government to grant a charter giving administrative powers to his company which, as the Royal Niger Company, laid the foundations of British rule in Northern Nigeria. Goldie sought political power to defend the monopoly which permitted his company to pass falling prices on to local African middlemen and producers without fear of competition. Although the various European states insisted at the Berlin Conference of 1884 that there should be free trade on the Niger, the Royal Niger Company's assumption of political authority enabled it, by judicious use of licensing and customs regulations, to keep out French and German merchants as well as African middlemen from the Delta.

While mercantile fears of foreign competition and customs posts, and desires to influence pricing arrangements in interior markets, made a significant contribution to the spread of colonial rule along the coast and into those areas of the immediate hinterland where vegetable oils were produced, the impact of deflationary forces on external commerce cannot be held responsible for European annexations everywhere in West Africa. In areas like the Gold Coast or Upper Guinea, where exporting of wild rubber developed in addition to the trade in vegetable oils, and merchants had the opportunity of dealing in a commodity with buoyant rather than depressed prices, the pressure on firms' profits and consequently their need to appeal for political action would appear to have been somewhat less. Moreover, the woodland-savanna zones north of the forest and east of the River Senegal, lying outside the palm and groundnut belts, were remote from and little involved in external commerce. To the extent that European territorial aggrandizement in such areas had economic antecedents, these would seem to rest in the unsettled political economy of Europe itself—where, especially from 1892 onwards, renewed industrial depression and heightened tariff barriers generated a French will to claim any domain which could be brought within the tariff system of the French empire, and a corresponding British and German determination to occupy areas to forestall the French where possible. In its final stages the European Partition of West Africa, and indeed of other regions, tended to lose contact with the very real problems on the periphery of the international economy and became a mere reflection of neuroses at its unstable centre.

WEST-CENTRAL AND EASTERN AFRICA: THE OPPORTUNISTS' SPHERE

In West-Central and Eastern Africa, too, the scramble for colonies was intertwined with commercial tensions arising in the periphery of an unstable international economy. In the former region, the British, Dutch, French and German merchants who traded along the coast from the Cameroons to Ambriz, the northern limits of Portuguese-ruled Angola, and up the Lower Congo to its waterfalls, and in the latter region the merchants operating from the entrepôt of Zanzibar, were all engaged in a competition for commodities rendered more fierce by the introduction of the steamship, the severity of the cycles of business activity and the deflationary forces of the late nineteenth century. Like their counterparts along the West African coast they were drawn into the international rivalries of their respective metropolitan government and into schemes to advance European authority over interior markets. Unfortunately, the commercial elements in the advance of colonial rule in these regions, more especially the role of established mercantile groups, have still fully to be explored by historians, and their relative importance in determining the pattern of events remains somewhat unclear.

Nevertheless, the economics of the Partition in West-Central and Eastern Africa differed from those in West Africa in certain important respects. The export trade of these regions, although smaller in scale, was more evenly balanced in its commodity structure, being less dominated by vegetable oils, which were undergoing severe price falls. While some of their exports—palm oil from the Lower Congo, cloves and copra from Zanzibar—had static or declining values, these regions also supplied external markets with large quantities of ivory and wild rubber, the prices for which rose through the last quarter of the century. Why ivory ran counter to the prevailing trend in world commodity prices remains something of a puzzle; the case of rubber is explained by a combination of rising demand resulting from new industrial uses and periodic attempts by dealers in Amazonian wild rubber to operate cartels. The rise in value of an existing export and the boost to the development of a new one, strengthening the hunting-gathering element in Africa's external exchange activities, had an impact in every region—but West-Central and Eastern Africa, with relatively abundant elephant herds, possibly a more extensive distribution of rubber-yielding trees and lianas, and certainly a lesser reliance on vegetable oil exports, benefited more than West Africa from differential price movements. Absence of quantitative data prevents any close examination of the terms of trade in these two regions, but in view of the price rises for ivory and rubber at a time of falling prices for imported manufactures, it may be suspected that terms of trade were more favourable than in most parts of West Africa.

A growth in exports of ivory and rubber gave the external commerce of West-Central and Eastern Africa a degree of expansionary vitality. From the ports of Benguela and Luanda came increasing quantities of the two foraged products—supplied by such interior hunter-traders as the Cokwe, whose penetration of woodland and forest from the south-west received continuing momentum from commercial conditions at the coast—and in the area of the Lower Congo, too, ivory and rubber originating in the Upper Congo basin began to assume greater significance in the profitability of European trading houses. In East Africa, the prominence of the two commodities, and more especially the emergence of wild rubber exporting from such ports as Kilwa, was partly a consequence of the abolition of the external slave trade. From 1873, the Sultan of Zanzibar, succumbing to British pressure, prohibited the shipping of slaves from the mainland and closed the slave markets in his territories. Termination of the slave trade, besides leaving the Sultan highly dependent on British political and military support, would seem to have had a differential economic impact—raising labour costs for plantation producers, particularly on the offshore islands, at a time when prices for their commodities were static or declining, but doing nothing to raise the costs of collecting ivory and rubber in and from the interior. For Indian capital and Arab-Swahili enterprise, the trade in foraged products began to have an even greater allure—and the Arab-Swahili penetration of markets and trade routes beyond the Great Lakes of the East African Rift went on apace.

By and large, therefore, deflationary pressures on trade and profits were less acute in West-Central and Eastern Africa and European merchants at the coast had less reason to be dissatisfied with commercial conditions. The forces seeking to change the status quo came less from the ranks of established mercantile groups, and more from among interloping figures who saw in the relative commercial vitality of these regions a potential for the creation of commercial empires. The leading figure among the new opportunists was Leopold II, King of the Belgians. Leopold's intervention in the affairs of these regions brought a unique dimension to the manœuvrings among European powers in Africa. In the context of Europe's political economy and policy-making, Leopold stood out as an aberrant, indeed anachronistic, figure, closer in style and philosophy to the dynastic empire-builders who guided Europe's earlier phase of mercantile capitalism than to the neo-mercantilist statesmen of late nineteenth century Europe. Like the monarchs of the seventeenth century, who identified the interests of their dynasty with those of the national economy, he was prepared to invest his family fortune in a colonial enterprise which would hopefully bring prestige and profit to both dynasty and nation, and to gather around him a motley alliance comprising his own courtiers and the 'buccaneering' adventurers of several nations. Foremost among the latter was William MacKinnon, the British shipping-line owner, whose steamships began regular sailings between Aden and Zanzibar in 1872 and who conceived a plan for a company to lease the Sultan of Zanzibar's mainland territories, thereby obtaining control over the points of access to interior trade. This scheme, although scotched by the British government in 1877, was the forerunner of an analogous plan devised by Leopold, and with which McKinnon co-operated, to obtain control of the commerce of the Congo basin. The Leopold-MacKinnon axis was the principal, if by no means the only, opportunistic force upsetting the political economy of West-Central and Eastern Africa.

The partition of West-Central Africa originated in a rivalry for the trade of the Congo river, more specifically for access to and domination over the interior distributive centre of Stanleypool, where the canoe-borne traffic of the Congo basin converged and interior commodities for export were concentrated in bulk prior to redistribution by overland routes to a number of coastal ports. As a strategic location from which the commerce of an extensive African trade network could be regulated and monopolized, Stanleypool was unrivalled in Subsaharan Africa. The competition for this prize, which came to a head during 1879–82, was between Leopold's agents and the French explorer, de Brazza, representing an ill-defined group of French colonial administrators and merchants who wished to see the redirection of Stanleypool's external trade towards French posts in Gabon. When, in 1882, the French government ratified de Brazza's treaties creating a French protectorate over the area between Gabon and the north bank of Stanleypool, Leopold came to enjoy the support and assistance of Dutch and British trading companies on the Lower Congo. The latter, fearing a French colony in the Congo basin and facing metropolitan governments unwilling to undertake pre-emptive annexations, saw in Leopold and his scheme for an independent Congo Free State a more acceptable and less dangerous claimant to political authority in the region—especially since Leopold promised free trade and navigation on the river. The British government, abandoning its support for Portuguese claims to the

Lower Congo area, followed its merchants' lead and provided diplomatic backing for the creation of Leopold's personal kingdom in the Congo after 1884.

Meanwhile in East Africa the intervention of another opportunistic promoter, Carl Peters of the German Society for Colonization, fortuitously backed by Bismarck as part of his electoral strategy, caused the British government to revise its attitudes to MacKinnon's ambitions. In the ensuing Anglo-German rivalry, it abandoned its support for the Sultan of Zanzibar's sovereignty on the East African coast and acquiesced in the division of the mainland into spheres of influence for Peters' German East Africa Company and MacKinnon's Imperial British East Africa Company.

That West-Central and Eastern Africa should have been the scene of several speculative, opportunistic ventures, which raised issues of 'national' interest and added yet further complications to the rivalry between European nation-states, owes as much to the commercial conditions in these regions as to the personalities of the main participants. The latter's wheeling-dealing activities must be seen against a background where product and price held out some prospect of profitability for new enterprises rather than one, as in most of West Africa, in which deflationary trends encouraged monopolistic combination to defend existing enterprises. Nevertheless, monopolistic tendencies were just as strongly embedded in the schemes of Leopold, MacKinnon or Peters as in those of Goldie on the Niger. Price trends were favourable, but the volume of trade in ivory and rubber in the 1870s and 1880s was not sufficiently great to guaranteee the commercial success of new concerns which did not engross a large share of that trade. The assumption of political-administrative powers, necessary to that goal, was rendered more expensive by the long-distance character of the trade in ivory and rubber—which required the extension of authority deep into the interior and so prevented the redirection of commodities from distant sources of supply to the coastal entrepôts of rival concerns. As it turned out, neither the German nor the British companies in East Africa attracted sufficient initial capital to turn potential into reality. Both were short-lived, their areas of activity being taken over by their respective metropolitan governments. Only Leopold, in his unique position as a dynastic mercantilist, operated on a scale and with sufficient ruthlessness to realize his ambitions.

SOUTHERN AFRICA: ORIGINS AND EXTENSIONS OF THE MINING
FRONTIER

In Southern Africa, yet a different set of economic circumstances lay behind the expansion of colonial rule. Factors common to the Partition in other regions were by no means absent. Bismarck's declaration of protectorate over the German ivory and ostrich feather trading post at Angra-Pequena in South-West Africa in 1884, and the British response in establishing a protectorate in Bechuanaland, partly to secure unrestricted access to interior trade for the merchants of Cape Colony, were but further variants of the politico-commercial rivalries played out in other African peripheries of the international economy. The agricultural communities of the areas of British and Afrikaner settlement were also affected by the deflationary tendencies of the period, for falling wool prices, together with recurrent drought, brought hardship to the pastoral farmers of the Cape, Natal and the Orange Free State. The dominant characteristic of Southern Africa's late nineteenth-century political economy, however, was neither rivalry over trade in foraged products nor difficulties created by falling prices for established export staples. It was rather the instability of rapid structural change in the immigrant-based economies of the south and the emergence of a new set of relationships between them and the international economy. The almost fortuitous discovery of extensive deposits of two valuable minerals, diamonds and gold, not only shielded these economies from any major slow-down in economic growth but, by introducing high-technology mining, so transformed their productive capacities as to render them the focal points of a new region-wide economic complex. Depressed rural incomes reinforced, but did not initiate, a drift from the land, mainly by agricultural labourers, which was one manifestation of a shift away from purely agricultural production which began in Southern Africa between 1870 and 1896.

The diamond strike in the northern extremities of Cape Colony in 1867 set in train a series of innovations, the immediate effects of which were largely confined to that colony. The rapid growth of the new mining town of Kimberley, the rise in the numbers of immigrants, the emergence of a need for railway construction to enable the mining centres to import equipment and supplies, more especially the heavy capital goods, and the enhanced state revenues which came from increased external trade were all features of a new direction in economic development which would be reproduced on a larger scale and over a wider area following the gold discoveries in the Transvaal in 1886.

Nevertheless, the introduction of diamond mining into the Cape economy of the 1870s and early 1880s had an important bearing on the subsequent pattern of Southern Africa's political economy. To the expansionary forces already inherent in Cape society—in the long-range activities of hunter-traders and the land-acquisitiveness of colonizing farmers—was added the powerful new dynamic of a mining frontier, in which prospector and magnate combined to seek out and exploit mineral deposits within and beyond the boundaries of the Cape. From the concentration of ownership of the diamond mines there emerged an autonomous colonial capitalism capable of both financing and securing state assistance for the forward movement of that frontier. Finally, the northerly location of the diamond workings brought a new south-north orientation to the Cape's communications and transport network and raised questions about whether or how far the productive potential of yet more northerly territories could be connected with the commercially and financially dominant Cape economy. Through the figure of Cecil Rhodes, with his visionary scheme for a Cape-to-Cairo railway linked with European colonization, his ultimate control of the Cape's diamond production and marketing, and his participation in Cape politics, first as an MP and from 1890 as Prime Minister, all of these forces found expression.

The speculative fever which overtook Southern Africa after the revelations in the Rand shifted the mining frontier further to the north. Rhodes and his diamond-mining associates moved quickly into the Transvaal to participate in the exploitation of the gold-bearing reef and share in the company and syndicate promotion which brought a massive inflow of capital from Europe. By 1895 over £41,000,000 had been invested in Transvaal gold mining, output had risen to £8,500,000, gold bullion accounted for 42 per cent of the exports from Natal and Cape Colony, and the new city of Johannesburg, with a population of over 100,000, had become the pivotal point of a new phase in the long-standing rivalries between Afrikaner and British colonists in Southern Africa.

The intrusion of technologically advanced, highly capitalized mining operations into the little-developed, near-subsistence, pastoral economy of the Transvaal raised questions about the political status of that Afrikaner republic and its relations with neighbouring polities. Around the gold mines there emerged a northern pole of economic growth surpassing the wool-exporting south in scale and value of production, a new economic region with linkages transcending existing political boundaries. The needs of the Rand for labour, foodstuffs, fuel and construction materials were drawn as much, if not more, from the Cape, Natal and the Orange Free State as from within the Transvaal. Above all, the Rand depended heavily upon the ports and transport systems of the two British colonies for its access to external markets and supplies, and investment by the governments of the Cape and Natal in railways to link Port Elizabeth, East London and Durban with the Rand followed closely on the heels of the expansion of mining. But if economic forces tended to work towards the integration of the Rand with a wider South African economy, these forces the Afrikaners of the Transvaal, and more especially their President, Kruger, were determined to check. The Transvaal government, strongly imbued with nationalist sentiment, favoured autarky over integration. It followed a strategy of using the gold mines as a 'leading sector' around which a more diversified, but still relatively independent, Transvaal economy might be developed by fostering within its boundaries related manufacturing and service industries. The maintenance of a separate tariff and the construction of a railway by-passing the ports of the British colonies, eventually achieved by a link-up with a Portuguese railway from Delagoa Bay, were central elements of the strategy. By raising costs to mine owners and mine workers, partly through administrative inefficiency, the Transvaal government's economic policy combined with its unwillingness to grant franchise rights to the *uitlanders* of the mining frontier to produce strong resentment on the Rand. Kruger's attempt to divert traffic away from the railway linking the Transvaal to Cape ports towards the railway to Delagoa Bay also brought conflict with the government of Cape Colony.

The contradiction between reliance on foreign capital and desires for 'national' autonomy in the policies of the Transvaal resulted in political crisis—in the shape of the ill-fated Jameson Raid of December 1895, which was intended to promote and assist rebellion on the Rand. Rhodes and Beit, the two leading representatives of Cape colonial capital, organized the raid for a variety of reasons, but the most compelling motive would appear to have been the fact that deep-level gold mining, in which both men, and the companies they headed, were heavily engaged, was proving costly and in 1895 was still unprofitable. The plotters attributed this to the policies of the Transvaal government, which should therefore be removed. The raid, although failing to achieve its goals, opened the way to the final solution of war, strengthening Kruger's resolve to resist any federation of South African states and destroying the unity of interest which previously had been growing between the Cape and the Orange Free State. For British metropolitan statesmen the Free State's transfer from a Cape to a Transvaal 'sphere of influence' seemed a portent of the future. 'The commercial attraction of the Transvaal', one wrote, 'will be so great that a Union of the South African States with it will be absolutely necessary for their prosperous existence. The only question . . . is whether that Union will be inside or outside the British Empire.'[3] The Boer War of 1899–1902, fought to answer that question, was a direct, if not necessarily inevitable, consequence of the shift from wool to gold as the principal export staple of European-settled South Africa.

The men of the force which raided the Transvaal in 1895 were Cape colonists who were also employees of Rhodes' third great venture, the British South Africa Company. Through this organization the Cape's mining interests, armed with memories of the gold trade from the Upper Zambezi to Sofala and hopes of a 'Second Rand' on the plateau country north of the Transvaal, penetrated the interior territories of Zambezia, in the hinterland of the Portuguese settlements in Mozambique. By contrast with the Beers and Consolidated Goldfields, actively engaged in mineral production, the British South Africa Company was an enterprise designed to stake a claim to future production. To forestall possible Transvaal or Portuguese occupation of the interior, and establish clear monopoly rights to any new mineral discoveries there, the enterprise required political power. This it obtained in the 1889 charter from the British government, which gave the Company administrative responsibility for a vast and ill-defined area of territory north of the Limpopo river. While the dramatic story of the diplomacy and warfare which created the new territories of Southern Rhodesia, Northern Rhodesia and Nyasaland lies beyond the scope of this chapter, it should be noted that the venture was the outgrowth of colonial rather than metropolitan aspirations and initiatives. The allure of mineral wealth for the

81

Cape's recently evolved and self-confident mining capitalism provided the impulse behind an outburst of territorial expansion which British governments were unable or unwilling to halt. Within one year of the granting of the charter agents for Rhodes were attempting to gain sovereignty over Katanga, where copper deposits were known to exist. Although the British South Africa Company failed to add Katanga to its possessions, its early presence in an area some 1,200 miles from Kimberley illustrates the powerful pull of potentially profitable mineral exploitation which drew the Cape mining frontier, and in its wake footloose elements of Cape colonial society, into the deep interior of Southern Africa. In the character of the European occupation of these areas lay the initial foundations of an economic system in which, as in the older, settled Anglo-Afrikaner territories, European-owned mining and agricultural enterprises would compete with African agrarian societies for the resources necessary to production for the international economy.

Gold, the commodity upon which the international economy's monetary system was based, the price of which was fixed at £3. 7s. 10½d. per ounce and which therefore rose in value against other commodities at this time, gave the economics of Partition in Southern Africa a distinctive cast. While the international economy as a whole, as well as its West African periphery, continued to experience a downward spiral of price deflation, the exploitation of the Rand initiated an inflationary trend in Southern Africa (one measure being the fact that prices for food and light in Cape Colony rose by 25 per cent between 1889 and 1897). This inflation carried with it a speculative investment in property and land, of which Rhodes's willingness to underwrite the occupation of Zambezia was but an extreme example. Rhodes's Zambezi venture—as a risk-taking operation in buoyant economic circumstances rather than a risk-shedding device in straitened conditions—had more in common with Leopold's Congo enterprise than with Goldie's undertaking on the Niger.

Gold also produced a dramatic change in Southern Africa's relative importance within the international economy. In 1870 the external commerce of West and Southern Africa was roughly equal in value. By 1897, West Africa's maritime trade had expanded by only some 40 per cent to £10,000,000, a rate of growth which, although exact measurement is impossible, was almost certainly surpassed by

West-Central and Eastern Africa. Southern Africa's trade, by contrast, rose by a staggering 800 per cent to some £52,200,000 and the region was responsible in 1897 for nearly three-quarters of the total external commerce of Africa south of the Sahara (see Appendices I–III). West Africa's dependence upon export staples experiencing a severe collapse of prices, and an apparent inability to diversify quickly into alternative export commodities, places that region in a group of peripheries of the international economy, including perhaps India, Chile and the Caribbean sugar-producing islands, which suffered most from price deflation in the 1880s and 1890s. The other regions of Subsaharan Africa fared somewhat better, and Southern Africa in particular had the advantage of becoming a major gold-producing area at a time when, according to at least some analysts, shortage of gold and a slow-down in the growth of the world's monetary stock was a significant factor behind the 'Great Depression' in the international economy. To the extent that such monetarist explanations of events are valid, the transition which took place in the Anglo-Afrikaner south in the 1880s—from depression caused by falling wool prices to boom caused by gold discoveries—may be seen as a precursor of the shift of the international economy from the 'Great Depression' phase of the late nineteenth century to the expansionary phase which preceded the First World War.

The considerable variety of conditions on the African peripheries of the international economy highlights the difficulties and dangers of reducing the late nineteenth century rush for colonies to any simple formula. Viewed from the perspective of the peripheries, the Partition comprised several different scrambles, each rooted in distinctive sets of regional economic circumstances, rather than a single, all-embracing competition among European powers for territorial sovereignty in Africa. On each periphery, integration with the international economy was an ongoing process, involving adjustments in methods and/or relationships of production and exchange and creating pressures for territorial annexation which, even in the absence of rivalry between the governments of European states, would almost certainly have led to some limited advance of colonialism.

But while the corrosive effects of market forces on politics at the periphery helped to trigger the Partition, the enormity and speedy satisfaction of the European appetite for African colonies ultimately rested upon the unstable political economy of Europe itself. In the 1870s and 1880s few European statesmen, with the possible exception of those of France, had much enthusiasm for the expense of acquiring and administering new colonies; conversely, however, the trend towards neo-mercantilist policies in Europe generated such tensions that few statesmen, once convinced that a division of Africa was underway, were able to refrain from staking claims and defending 'national interests', however minor or illusory. Such action was rendered easier and more palatable by the fact that merchants, mining magnates and speculative adventurers on the peripheries were prepared to share the burden of administration by raising capital for chartered and concessionary companies. This return to an old device for financing and legitimizing overseas operations, one which had been abandoned by European capitalism in the preceding liberal phase of the international economy, was but one more element in the neo-mercantilist tendencies asserting themselves in European thought and action, and underpinning the Partition of Africa.

The advance of colonialism into Africa was a product of a European uncertainty about the future shape of international relations, caused by the spread of industrialization and a consequent changing balance of power. It was also, somewhat paradoxically, a product of a European confidence in the technology of that industrialization—not just the military technology, the maxim gun of the jingoist refrain, which in the final analysis secured European authority over African agrarian societies, but also the transport technology which had increasingly drawn the world's regions into a single system of international exchange. To men who had seen the completion of transcontinental railway networks in Europe and America, and the beginning of further networks in India and Latin America, the railway seemed to hold the key to Africa's future development. Behind the French scheme for a Senegal-Niger railway, Leopold's plans to build a line from Matadi to Stanleypool, by-passing the Congo rapids, MacKinnon's hopes for a railway to Lake Victoria, and the Cape-to-Cairo visions of Cecil Rhodes, therefore, lay a belief in the availability of a solution to the high costs of internal transport which had hitherto restricted African sales of bulk commodities to a few coastal areas. This means to a fuller African integration into the international economy, it was assumed, could not be provided by indigenous African states, which seemed to lack the capital, technical expertise and scale of territorial authority. Colonialism, Europeans believed, was a necessary prerequisite for the reduction of Subsaharan Africa's economic autonomy.

Four

Colonial foundations, 1896–1914

No period in the economic history of Subsaharan Africa has a stronger claim to being a watershed than the approximately two decades from the mid-1890s to 1914, when the infrastructural foundations of most contemporary national economies were laid down by colonial governments and commerce between Africa and the rest of the world grew at an historically unprecedented rate. Between 1897 and 1913 the value of Subsaharan Africa's external trade more than doubled, from £71,000,000 to £188,000,000 (see Appendix I), thereby keeping pace with total world trade which grew from $1,274,000,000 in 1899 to $2,769,000,000 in 1913, in current prices. This increase in African trade, moreover, was not confined to any one region or sub-region, such as the British- and Afrikaner-settled territories which became the Union of South Africa in 1910, but was shared by all regions and almost all of the new European colonial possessions south of the Sahara. South Africa, it is true, retained its position of dominance in external commerce, still responsible in 1913 for more than half of all Subsaharan exports and imports by value, but the 'lead' it had established in the era of mineral discoveries was eroded between 1897 and 1913 as other territories, more especially in West Africa and to some extent Eastern Africa, raised their share of Subsaharan Africa's total external trade. Such evidence suggests that the period saw a fairly dramatic strengthening of Africa's connexions with the international economy, and possibly the final, conclusive transformation of its economies into peripheries of the industrial capitalist centre of world exchange. The forces behind, and forms of, this extraordinary and general upsurge of trade with the rest of the world require assessment, before any conclusion can be reached about the significance of this phase in the economic evolution of Subsaharan Africa.

86

THE INTERNATIONAL ECONOMY AND COLONIALISM

The later stages of the advance of European colonialism in Subsaharan Africa, the terminal point of which might be considered to be either the Fashoda crisis of 1898 or the Boer War of 1899–1902, coincided with the beginning of a recovery in the international economy from the faltering growth and uncertainties which had characterized the last three decades of the nineteenth century. From the bottom of the trade cycle in 1895, a vigorous upswing in production and investment carried the industrial economies at the centre of world trade into a period of boom conditions and rapid economic growth which lasted, with only short, intermittent checks, until the outbreak of the First World War. For the economies of Western Europe and America, as well as the international economy as a whole, the years from 1896 to 1914 constituted an era of rising output, prices, interest rates and profits, a late 'Golden Age' in global economic activity between the difficulties of the 'Great Depression' and the dislocations of world conflict. The causes of the recovery and expansion were multifarious—the boost to the world's money supply from the gold discoveries of the Rand, Western Australia and the Klondyke, the productivity gains of new technology in electrics, chemicals, steel-making and automobiles, the closing of the US land frontier and the consequent stimulus to temperate zone agriculture in, as well as the migration of labour and capital to, Canada, Australia and Argentina, and a shift in government expenditures in Western Europe towards welfare and armaments programmes. Whatever the true weight of each of these factors, they collectively generated an expansion in intercontinental exchange which transmitted itself to many corners of Subsaharan Africa.

The interplay between Africa and the rest of the world in these years cannot be reduced to any simple formula of cause and effect, initiative and response. Nevertheless, events taking place outside Africa, in wider world markets, were just as significant a determinant of economic and social change as developments within Subsaharan Africa itself. No discussion of, say, the economic consequences of the advent of colonial rule can be conducted without a recognition that renewed vitality in international trade and investment was likely to lead to some innovation in African economies already engaged in international exchange, and possibly in others as well, even in the absence of European colonial authority, and that measures under-

87

taken by colonial governments were ultimately made possible by expansionary conditions in world trade and production. One such externally derived force for change was a rise in demand for, and prices of, raw materials and foodstuffs. World prices for tropical agricultural products rose by 12·1 per cent between 1896 and 1913. This average figure, of course, conceals variation between commodities—from 1899 to 1913, prices for cotton rose by 91 per cent, hides by 75 per cent, palm oil 64 per cent, tobacco 38 per cent, rubber 11 per cent, sugar seven per cent and coffee a mere two per cent.[1] All were commodities produced by Africa's agrarian communities and were actual or potential exports to overseas markets. In a broad sense, therefore, Subsaharan Africa's export boom of 1896 to 1913 can be regarded as a response to favourable world market conditions.

What was the role of the recently inaugurated colonial administrations? One must be wary of the conclusions of an earlier generation of scholars for whom African economic history was 'largely a branch of administrative history',[2] whose analysis of economic change focused almost exclusively on colonial policies and practices, and who therefore tended to assign all innovation to the command powers of the colonial state. One should also appreciate that in certain localities—such as the coast and immediate hinterland of Senegal, the Gold Coast or Angola—colonial rule was already well established and was therefore less of a force for change than in newly annexed areas. Furthermore, in one extremely important case, that of the Afrikaner states of Southern Africa, formal external colonialism (in the sense of British metropolitan control) was extremely short-lived, disappearing in the negotiated arrangements by which the Union of South Africa became a self-governing Dominion in 1910 (although leaving behind an internal colonialism in the shape of rule by European colonists over indigenous African societies). When all of these qualifications are made, however, the advance of colonialism in the last quarter of the nineteenth century can still be said to have been a dominant force behind the growth of commodity-exporting which carried Africa through into the early twentieth century. Overseas demands on African economies were articulated as much—more here, less there—by way of administrative mechanisms as through the market—for colonialism rendered the greater part of Subsaharan Africa subservient to prevailing European views that the role of colonies should be to assist and complement the development of the metropolitan economies. Colonial administrations were therefore expected to suppress or at least limit forces which tended to perpetuate African autonomy from the international economy in general, and from interaction with the 'home' economy in particular, and conversely to advance such forces as tended to enlarge the external orientation of economic activity in Africa.

Colonialism was first and foremost a political phenomenon, usually involving a considerable enlargement of scale of state power, exercised by alien regimes, and a reduction, both relative and absolute, in the powers of indigenous polities and ruling groups. But this enlargement of political scale also had economic significance. Its achievement and maintenance created a need for increased taxation, since metropolitan politicians and taxpayers also demanded that colonies be, as far as possible, financially self-supporting. The need for revenues to pay for civil servants and soldiers as well as the supporting facilities deemed necessary for even a pale imitation of the modern bureaucratic state—above all, improved transport and communications—in turn generated a fiscal pressure on the subjects of the colonial state which, whether applied directly through hut and poll taxes or indirectly through taxes on imports, obliged them to raise the level of their monetary incomes by selling more on the market. Since administrators almost invariably considered the external rather than the internal market as the means by which taxable incomes could, and should, be generated, fiscal considerations reinforced the bias in their other policies towards increasing external trade. Where the gap between the colonial state's revenue needs and actual levels of trade-generated incomes was greatest, colonial governments tended to be most receptive to private business propositions and to promote or accept the penetration of foreign, predominantly European, capital, institutions and personnel into productive and distributive activities.

Enlargement of scale also resulted in some erosion of political barriers to the mobility of factors of production within the boundaries of the colonial state. Reduction of the power of the indigenous ruling groups to tax trade or demand tribute from travellers, the adoption of police powers by the colonial regime, and the introduction of colony-wide legislation, including commercial legislation, which superseded local laws and judicial processes, all served to create larger 'free trade' areas within which goods and men moved relatively

89

unhindered. The true significance of this development, however, cannot be easily gauged, for it is by no means clear how far, if at all, pre-colonial political arrangements acted as a serious or effective restraint on trade—certainly it was considerably less than that suggested by the greatly distorted and highly inaccurate European presentation of pre-colonial African societies as a collection of warring states and savage tribes between whom and with whom trade was impossible before colonial 'pacification'. The colonial powers, moreover, did not remove all institutional barriers to commercial intercourse—they merely replaced them with their own. Customs and excise duties, commercial codes, currency and labour legislation, administrative structures and transport systems, all tended to operate against inter-colony transactions while advancing both intra-colony exchange and commerce between the colony and its European metropolis.

TRANSPORT

Where colonial governments made the most obvious direct contribution to the further extension of intercontinental exchange, largely with a view to strengthening colony-metropolis relationships, was in the field of transport innovation, eroding the physical barriers of distance and terrain to intercourse between Europe and Africa. Maritime transport remained the preserve of private European capital, an increase in the number and tonnage of ships and the development of regular steamship sailings between various African and European ports being largely a function of the growth of commercial traffic. But in certain cases, where the volume of commercial traffic seemed insufficient to justify frequent maritime connexions, metropolitan and/or colonial governments offered inducements through subsidy—for example, the contracts for the carriage of mails given to British and German shipping lines in East Africa, and the monopoly of transporting government personnel and equipment given to the Compagnie des Chargeurs Réunis in 1912 in return for regular sailings to ports in French West and Equatorial Africa. The history of shipping in African waters during these decades is an intricate story of competition and amalgamation, rate wars and combination. The emergence of shipping conferences (or rings)—the South African conference of 1886, the agreements of which were subsequently extended to operations in Eastern Africa, and the West

African conference of 1895 which united the principal British, German and Belgian lines in West and West-Central Africa—set a trend towards oligopolistic control of African maritime trade, higher freight rates being justified by shipping line owners on the ground that they made regular, scheduled sailings feasible.

Shipping companies, and the export-import houses they served, benefited substantially from public investment in, and management of, transport developments designed to assist the flow of commodities from the interior to the sea. Colonial governments had access to funds from Europe, including loans from imperial treasuries and capital raised in metropolitan money markets on less than strictly commercial terms because the state stood as guarantor. Such funds made possible expenditures on major public works requiring the 'lumpy' investment that ordinary revenues could not provide. Some part of this capital went to improve harbour facilities at ports—occasionally the introduction of new facilities from scratch, as at Mombasa in Kenya or Beira in Mozambique, but more commonly smaller-scale improvements in existing harbours. But with the single notable exception of the French loan of 10,000,000 francs in 1903 to finance the construction at Dakar of the only truly deep-water harbour in West Africa, colonial transport strategies prior to the First World War gave less emphasis to port and harbour development than to the introduction of new methods of internal transport in the hinterlands of the ports.

The railway was the *deus ex machina* of colonial Africa, both a symbol of the advanced technology underpinning European political domination and the principal means by which bureaucrats, businessmen and politicians hoped to launch a dramatic transformation in Africa's productive capacity and its ability to consume the products of Western Europe. Every colony and every metropolitan society had its railway-building enthusiasts, perhaps none more strategically located than Joseph Chamberlain, British Secretary of State for the Colonies from 1893 to 1903, whose programme for 'developing the imperial estates' gave a powerful impetus to railway-building in British colonies. But France too had its heirs of Freycinet, while lively German and Belgian traditions of railway promotion and construction at home and abroad ensured an interest in railway development in their respective African spheres. The motives behind railway-building in colonial Africa were many and diverse—

91

metropolitan industrialists looking for new markets for their iron and steel, machinery and locomotives, Chambers of Commerce in European and African ports who sought an increase in African external trade, shipping companies wanting more freight, statesmen concerned with geo-strategic issues of 'effective control' in arenas of imperial rivalry, colonial administrations faced with the difficulties of supplying up-country administrative centres or moving troops quickly to scenes of 'disorder', and fringe speculators hoping to dump railway shares on a gullible public, all combined to set in motion the laying down of the twin tracks which probed the African interior.

The colonial state normally assumed direct financial and operational responsibility for the railways, but in certain cases private capital and companies were permitted a role—as in the arrangements beween the Gold Coast government and Ashanti Gold Fields Corporation which financed the latter stages of the line from Sekondi to Kumasi. Private risk capital appeared most readily where prospects of mineral traffic held out hopes of a quick return on investment, and private ventures were therefore most common in the Congo, the Rhodesias, Angola and Mozambique. Even in these areas, however, a distinction between public and private enterprise becomes somewhat artificial when arrangements are examined in detail. Thus Rhodesia Railways Ltd was able to raise capital for railway construction because its debentures were guaranteed by the British South Africa Company, which was itself vested with governmental powers. Because the colonial state was concerned with the politico-administrative and strategic benefits of railways, as much as with the commercial benefits, railways were frequently built in advance, although seldom without some hopes, of sufficient commercial traffic to cover operating costs or repay construction costs. Where this proved a particularly large burden on colonial budgets—for example, in the case of the Kenya-Uganda Railway in Eastern Africa—the need to create revenues for a newly built railway line became a pressing consideration on colonial economic policy-making.

Some of the principal characteristics of railway development in Africa are indicated in Map 3. By 1914, few territories lacked some section of line, but only the Union of South Africa had anything approaching a complete system of trunk and feeder routes. In South Africa, the period between the Boer War and the First World War

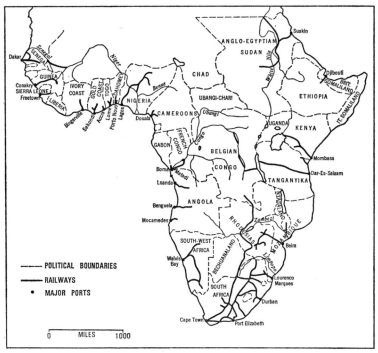

Map 3. Railways and Ports, 1914

was one in which priority was given to linking farming areas with the major lines constructed earlier between the ports and the mining centres. Elsewhere, railway-building was largely a matter of erecting the first spinal column of a modern transport system, routes and mileage being heavily determined by either the existence of mineral deposits, as in the case of the railways into the Rhodesias and Katanga, or the opportunity of linking the coast with navigable sections of river or lake. The Senegal-Niger Railway of French West Africa, the connections with the Lower Niger and the Upper Nile in the British-built railways of Nigeria and the Anglo-Egyptian Sudan, the Belgian concern with by-passing obstructions to navigation in the River Congo, and in East Africa the British and German railways from Mombasa to Lake Victoria and Dar Es Salaam to Lake Tanganyika, all illustrate the early colonial focus on rail-steamship arteries for purposes of control and commerce. On the

93

whole, railways were intended to serve the needs of a particular colony and there were few interterritorial connexions, one major exception being the lines built through Mozambique to the land-locked Rhodesias and Nyasaland.

Railway construction in Africa, as in almost all peripheries of the international economy, had virtually no direct backward linkages with African production. All manufactured components came from Europe and, outside Southern Africa, even fuel tended to be imported as bunker coal. Nevertheless, the arrival of the railway represented a considerable advance in transport facilities in Africa, its potential for relatively cheap and rapid transit of commodities and travellers contrasting sharply with the expensive and slow methods of internal transport hitherto available. Railway freight rates per ton/mile undercut head porterage by perhaps as much as 75 per cent and there began a shift from the latter to the former in the carriage of goods. The railway had greatest advantages over long distances and its impact was therefore felt most keenly beyond the coastal zones. It challenged long-distance caravan trades in foraged products, contributing to the commercial crisis which overtook established up-country trading enterprises in West-Central and Eastern Africa, and made possible for the first time the production and exporting of low-value-to-bulk commodities in areas where transport considerations had hitherto been a major, if not the only, limitation on such a development. By lowering the cost of freighting interior commodities to the ports and the carriage of imported capital and/or consumer goods which made production for world markets either possible or desirable, by facilitating the up-country penetration of merchants and traders from the coastal entrepôts, and by speeding up the exchange of commercial information, the implications of the railway and related steamship for African integration into the international economy might appear little less than revolutionary.

One must appreciate, however, the spatial limits to that 'revolution'. Except in South Africa, rail densities per square mile remained among the lowest in the world and extensive areas of the African land-mass were still remote from a railway station or steamer point. In the absence of feeder lines or roads, which colonial governments were either unwilling or more commonly unable to provide, the cost-reducing effects of railway innovation were confined to a fairly narrow belt of country on either side of the line, outside of which continuing reliance on porter or pack animal progressively raised costs to a point where any gain from the arrival of a railway disappeared. One major effect of railway construction, therefore, was the introduction of pronounced local inequalities, in which the inhabitants of some areas were less well placed than others to take advantage of the market opportunities opened up by transport changes. Consequently, in the routing of railways or the reallocation of land alongside railways, governments possessed powerful instruments to shape the structures of colonial economies.

If rising primary product prices, colonial rule and railways were universal (or near-universal) phenomena in Subsaharan Africa in 1896–1914, the social and environmental milieu in which they operated varied according to region. Across the continent, therefore, considerable differences could be found in the methods of production for world markets and in the structure of colonial economies. It is possible, at a first level of approximation, to distinguish between those colonial economies in which foreign or expatriate enterprise was restricted to commerce and finance, with production remaining in the hands of Africans, and those in which foreign enterprise, in the shape of mining companies, settler farmers and plantations, also became the dominant force in commodity production. But while such a categorization has some basis in fact—and represents the two paradigms of interaction with the international economy already developed in nineteenth-century West and Southern Africa—it is a generalization which cannot adequately describe, far less account for, the rich variety of economic conditions in early twentieth-century Africa.

WEST AFRICA: PEASANTS AND TRADERS

Between the mid-1890s and the outbreak of the First World War, West Africa's trade by value grew faster than any other region south of the Sahara—yet West Africa was the region in which there were fewest changes in basic economic arrangements. The foundations of its maritime commerce remained, as they had always been, African production of natural and farm commodities, essentially by small-scale methods, linked by competitive intermediate market systems to coastal export-import houses of varying size and influence. Change occurred, to be sure, but largely in the direction of modification and extension rather than any radical alteration in fundamental structures. In no other region of Subsaharan Africa do historical continuities appear so strong and the impact of colonialism on economic life seem so limited. That peasants and traders were the archetypal figures of the West African scene, and between them generated such a significant expansion in commerce, was a standing challenge to those contemporaries, both in metropolitan countries and in colonies in other regions, who argued that enlargement of external trade required the introduction of different agencies. The economic history of West Africa in this period, therefore, is of interest not only in its own right but also for its illumination of the debate about the appropriate forms of economic activity for dependent territories which was conducted, with varying degrees of passion, in colonial circles.

Why did the mines, joint-stock plantation companies, concession-ary companies with monopoly rights, and European settler-planters whose activities, singly or collectively, dominate the twentieth-century economic history of other regions, fail to penetrate West Africa to any great extent? The answer to this question lies partly in environ-mental considerations. By contrast with other regions, especially Southern Africa, West Africa is not particularly well endowed with mineral resources and the exploitation of such deposits as existed tended to be delayed by the need for expensive and time-consuming geological surveys. Prior to 1914, therefore, mining activities in West Africa were limited to the extraction of gold from the Tarkwa and Ashanti areas of the Gold Coast and tin from the Jos area of Nigeria. The environment also tended to discourage the European immigrant settler-farmer or plantation-estate proprietor. By the turn of the century, medical discoveries, especially in the control of malaria, removed much of the reality of West Africa's reputation as a 'White Man's Grave'. Nevertheless, the convention that tropical forest and woodlands were unsuited to permanent European habitation lingered on and combined with European tastes for cooler or less humid climates to steer the private planter or settler-farmer elsewhere. West Africa held few of the apparent climatic (and social) advantages which drew British and German settler-planters to the plateau or highland areas of Southern or Eastern Africa or French colonists to Algeria. A relative handful of French settlers attempted banana-planting in Guinea and coffee-growing in the Ivory Coast, but by 1914 the only sizeable concentration of settler-planters—and that not particularly large—was the German cocoa-planting estates on the slopes of Mt Cameroons.

Environment, however, cannot explain the relative absence of the concessionary trading and plantation companies which operated with salaried managers in roughly similar conditions in West-Central Africa. The exclusion of such institutions would appear to rest on the particular historical experience of Euro-African interaction in West Africa which, even before the full-scale advance of colonial authority in the late nineteenth century, had seen the establishment at the coast of fairly large European mercantile houses locked into, and profiting from, trade with African producers and consumers. With the difficulties of the period of depressed primary product prices giving way from the late 1890s to improved profitability, a slackening in rivalry between firms (partly a consequence of amalgamation into larger enterprises), and a diminution of trade hold-ups by African intermediaries, the leading import-export agencies (which were sometimes linked financially to important shipping concerns) appear to have regained confidence in existing commercial arrangements and become hostile to innovations which might disturb the status quo. The commercial revival, by contributing to administrative revenues, also relieved colonial administrations from the necesssity of having to consider alternative methods of production and exchange. Between trading companies and local administrations, therefore, an informal alliance, or tacit understanding, appears to have emerged against the introduction of two kinds of enterprise—on the one hand concessionary companies with monopoly trade rights in a particular area, which would not only disrupt 'free trade' in the interior but might be used as an excuse to relieve metropolitan governments from supplying funds for railway and other infrastructural projects, and on the other plantation companies with sufficient capital to operate on a very large scale and deal directly with major metropolitan purchasers of West African commodities, as competitors of the existing mercantile houses. Considerations of the former kind appear to be responsible for scotching suggestions that the concessionary system of French Equatorial Africa should be extended to French West Africa, and were at work among the forces resulting in the British decision to strip the Royal Niger Company of its monopoly reinforcing charter in 1900. Considerations of the latter type, rendered even more extreme by the fact that the initiative for large-scale plantations came from the biggest British purchaser of vegetable oils, openly seeking to break the 'stranglehold' of the mercantile houses, underlay the rejection of W. H. Lever's campaign, from 1906 until the early 1920s, to obtain land for palm-oil planting in British West Africa. In the absence of detailed studies of the relationship between commercial firms and colonial governments, such conclusions must remain tentative; nevertheless, the influence of long-established mercantile organizations seems crucial to any explanation of why the economic history of West Africa between 1896 and 1914 should take such a markedly different path from that of West-Central Africa, in the debates about the affairs of which European business interests in West Africa were closely concerned.

Some account should also be taken of general metropolitan satisfaction with the prevailing methods connecting West Africa to external markets. West Africa's remarkable export performance over this period was matched by rising imports of metropolitan manufactures, including for the first time capital goods in the form of railway and steamship materials, and for Britain at least, a sizeable balance of trade with its West African colonies made a useful contribution to overall balance of payments arrangements. The French, more openly neo-mercantilist, tried to achieve a similar result by extending the differential tariffs of Senegal, favouring imports from France, to their other West African possessions (except for Dahomey and the Ivory Coast which were covered by 'free trade' agreements with Britain).

At bottom, therefore, everything rested on the fact of a rapid growth in both volume and value of West African primary product-exporting from the mid-1890s onwards, a growth which owed as much to African initiatives as to the expatriate firms in articulating world demand and colonial governments in providing transport and currency facilities. The intermediate marketing system, its role in these years largely unstudied, was still firmly in the hands of African traders, although new entrants to middleman commerce appeared in the shape of the Lebanese who began to establish themselves in Senegal and from there spread into other parts of French and British West Africa. African initiatives in production took three basic, although by no means mutually exclusive, forms—an expansion of output of existing export commodities in areas in which they were already produced, the development of export production in new areas, and diversification into new export commodities.

The first form of activity predominated in peanut-growing coastal Senegal, and the palm oil and kernel-producing Niger Delta area of Nigeria, parts of Dahomey, the Ivory Coast and Sierra Leone. In coastal Senegal there was a trend towards concentration by cultivators on peanut production at the expense of foodcrops, which began to be imported from surrounding areas, but the means by which increased output of palm oil and kernels was achieved in areas of existing production is somewhat unclear. Whether, for example, the ratio of planted to gathered palm products rose in these years of buoyant prices has yet to be established. The second category is most dramatically represented by the emergence of peanut-exporting from inland localities of Senegal and from Northern Nigeria, both connected with the construction of railways into areas of savanna agriculture. A steady eastwards movement of peanut production accompanied the construction of the Senegal-Niger railway, but an additional factor in the adoption of the crop by Wolof and Serer peasants was the role of the Moslem Mouride brotherhood in diffusing knowledge about techniques and commercial returns among its growing number of adherents. The northern Nigerian 'breakthrough' came slightly later. The railway line built in the hopes of tapping Hausa cotton production for British industry reached Kano only in 1911, but its arrival triggered off a substantial jump in sales of peanuts, hitherto grown as a local foodcrop. Hausa traders, already active in long distance kola nut and livestock ventures, were quick to appreciate, and persuade cultivators of, the potential of a crop which gave a better return than cotton.

A development which fits neatly into neither category was the rubber boom which came to the West African forest and woodland-savanna zones in the wake of sharply rising rubber prices. Its antecedents lay in the growth of wild rubber tapping in several areas during the 1880s and early 1890s, but these early origins were insignificant by comparison with the outburst of activity which accompanied the doubling of rubber prices in European markets between 1895 and 1906, largely as a consequence of the growth of automobile manufacturing. In Western Nigeria, the Gold Coast, the Ivory Coast and Guinea, bands of rubber tappers, closely followed by dealers, scoured the countryside for the *funtumia* trees and various latex-yielding vines. The boom was relatively short-lived, peaking around 1907–8 and falling off thereafter as a result of the wholesale destruction of rubber-bearing plants by what are called slaughter-tapping methods and price-reducing competition from South-East Asian plantations, but it had a long-term as well as short-term significance. From its earnings there would appear to have come much of the capital, and from the experience of selling in bulk to coastal markets perhaps some of the incentive, behind the initial stages of the phenomenal shift into cocoa-growing by farmers in forest and woodland between the eastern Ivory Coast and western Nigeria.

Cocoa, an entirely novel crop for West African cultivators, arrived on the mainland from the plantation island of Fernando Po, its principal *points d'appui* being Agege near Lagos and Akwapim in the hinterland of Accra. From the latter area its cultivation spread so rapidly that by 1914 the Gold Coast, with exports worth over £2,000,000, was the world's largest producer, accounting for one-half of total world output. Cocoa-farming, requiring the planting of a tree crop incapable of producing returns over a single growing season, was a considerable risk for African peasants; on the other hand, it enjoyed no economies of scale, so that smallholders could compete favourably with plantation-production elsewhere in the world, it fitted fairly easily into forest and woodland agricultural techniques, and it needed little investment in new tools. Production initially concentrated in southern areas of the Gold Coast where a westward migration of Akwapim farmers, beginning in the late 1890s when local rubber supplies were apparently exhausted and palm oil prices were still low, carried cocoa-farming into uncultivated forest land. Extensions of cocoa-farming to the agricultural communities of Ashanti to the north and into the eastern Ivory Coast followed the decline of rubber-exporting from these areas, while in Yoruba-inhabited western Nigeria, where cocoa-growing had early origins, expansion of acreages also seems to have been delayed by the counter-attraction of rubber, and more latterly, palm oil prices, so that Nigeria's cocoa exports of £172,000 in 1914 were significantly lower than those of the Gold Coast.

The foregoing account, capable of presenting no more than a brief outline, does scant justice to the several fine studies which have been made of the African contribution to the growth of West Africa's external commerce.[3] Such studies are unanimous that African, rather than colonial or expatriate, enterprise was critical at the local level, with African traders seeking out new sources of supply of primary products and African cultivators reacting with considerable entrepreneurial skill. In altering old, or initiating new, methods of acquiring land for cultivation by sale or lease, in re-allocating the labour effort of the household unit and hiring casual labour (often from men of neighbouring communities anxious to get experience of new crops or techniques), and in mobilizing the savings and credit necessary to the introduction and/or expansion of cash cropping, the actions of African producers belied cosy conventional wisdoms about the peasant's lack of response to market incentives. Colonial governments, by contrast, made almost no direct contribution to agricultural change, the budgets of departments of agriculture being too tiny to make any appreciable impact and agricultural officers usually giving priority to crops—cotton in Nigeria or coffee in the Gold Coast—which commercial experience taught Africans to ignore in favour of others. Only in the provision of cheaper transport by the railway can colonial administrations be said to have taken vitally significant action—and even then, any idea that the introduction of a railway was everywhere a necessary prerequisite to enlargement of primary product-exporting is challenged by the fact that the most explosive and innovative case of agricultural change, the rise of cocoa-farming in the southern Gold Coast, did not rely on railway transport at all.

WEST-CENTRAL AFRICA: PREDATORY COLONIALISM AND
CONCESSIONARY COMPANIES

The West African pattern of economic relationships from 1896 to 1914 was one in which African enterprise in bringing under-used land, labour and capital into production combined with the commercial activities of a restrained, if by no means disinterested, European mercantile capitalism and the policies of a relatively paternalistic colonialism to produce a major expansion in external trade, the gains from which were shared with some measure of equity between the various participants. This stands in stark contrast to developments in West-Central Africa, the scene of the notorious 'Red Rubber' scandals, where the gains from trade accrued almost exclusively to the colonial governments and the European capital to which the administrations abrogated much of the task of wringing wealth from the region's forest and woodlands. For most of the inhabitants of West-Central Africa, the arrival of colonialism did not mean an opportunity to respond to, and benefit from, the rise in world prices for primary products, but rather subjection to a system of exploitation which produced, at best, little or no return for toil and at worst meant savage coercion by avaricious concerns. Admittedly, along stretches of the coast where trade with European mercantile houses had sprung up in the nineteenth century, relationships closer to those in West Africa continued to prevail—but the salient feature of the region's post-1896 economic history was the colonial governments' adoption of the concessionary system whereby enormous areas of land in interior localities were leased to private companies. The latter obtained monopoly rights of trade and, usually, *de facto* if not *de jure* administrative and police powers over their respective concessionary blocs which enabled them to extract surpluses from the African inhabitants at an extraordinary rate.

The concessionary system's centre of gravity lay in Leopold II's Congo Free State, where a regime meriting Hobbes's felicitous phrase, 'nasty, brutish and short', held sway. But it also spread extensively into the neighbouring territories of French Equatorial Africa (A.E.F.)—and even penetrated parts of the Cameroons, where the South and North-West Cameroons Companies, and northern Angola, where the Cabinda Company, conducted operations similar to those of the more numerous concessionary companies of the Free State and A.E.F. Domination of the Congo basin by concessionary companies arose in part from the relative backwardness of the region's external trade at the time of colonial annexation. The value of French Equatorial Africa's total external trade in 1897 was only ten per cent of that of French West Africa, while the Congo Free State's was equal to only 25 per cent of British West Africa's value— yet the colonial governments of West-Central Africa were expected to occupy, administer and provide modern infrastructure for roughly equivalent, although less densely populated, areas. To the pressing needs for administrative revenues, and the obvious attractions of concessionary companies sharing the burden, must be added the character of colonial governments in the Congo basin, which were brand-new, lacked the stabilizing anchor which previous rule over coastal enclaves brought to the personnel and policies of British or French West Africa, and attracted to their service the inexperienced, the inept and the fortune-hunting. They were not, in brief, colonial administrations likely to resist the allure of short-term gains held out by concessionary company promoters. Finally, established mercantile houses had less influence on policy-making in West-Central Africa, not simply because they were fewer in number but also because as mainly British and Dutch concerns, they had virtually no pull in Brussels or Paris. British mercantile houses took no part in the promotion of concessionary companies, which were mainly speculative ventures mobilizing the capital of small investors in Western Europe's stock exchanges, but the leading Dutch firm, N.A.H.V., joined the scramble for concessions in the French Congo.

Leopold's determination to transform his personal kingdom in the Congo into a paying proposition gave birth to the system. From 1892 a series of decrees turned the greater part of the Congo Free State into a private domain in which the exploitation of uncultivated land was reserved to the state. The private domain was further divided into three parts—that in which Free State officials monopolized trade in non-farm products on behalf of the State itself, that in which officials monopolized trade on behalf of the Crown (i.e. Leopold), and that which was leased to private companies in return for a proportion of their shares and a tax on their operations. Seven companies in all obtained grants amounting to thousands of square miles, the largest and most profitable being the Antwerp Company and the Anglo-Belgian India Rubber Company—on the boards of directors of which members of the Belgian aristocracy figured prominently. The phenomenal dividends which these companies paid in the late 1890s, and the active trading in their stocks, in turn encouraged company promoters' hopes of penetrating French Equatorial Africa. There the removal of A.E.F.'s founder-governor, Brazza, from his post, the direct intervention of Guillain, the Minister for Colonies, and the creation in 1898–9 of a public domain (equivalent to the Free State's private domain) cleared the way for the concessionary system. In the ensuing scramble for land forty companies, mostly smaller and with less capital than those in the Free State, obtained concessions in Gabon, the French Congo and riverain areas of Ubangi-Chari, where the largest concern, the Sultanates Company, had its sphere. In terms of the proportion of total land occupied by concessionaires French Equatorial Africa can perhaps be said to have been even more strongly subjected to concessionary exploitation than Leopold's

Congo—but the distinction becomes less significant in view of the fact that the Free State was itself a private venture and that the failure rate was higher among companies in the French colonies.

The concessionary companies, and indeed the Free State in its economic role, were neither classic plantation enterprises investing capital in the cultivation and processing of crops, nor trading organizations competing with others for the farm products of an African peasantry and using the price mechanism to encourage expansion of output. They were, rather, the most predatory form of European capitalist enterprise operating in Subsaharan Africa— institutions which with little initial investment or plough-back of profits monopolized the foraged products of forest and woodland and coerced the labour of African villagers into hunting and gathering operations. Timber, ivory and above all wild rubber, the rising prices of which fostered speculation in company shares, flowed from the Congo basin at an unprecedented rate. The Free State's rubber exports by value rose from 2,800,000 to 43,700,000 Belgian francs between 1895 and 1905, while those of A.E.F. grew from 2,600,000 to 8,600,000 French francs in the years 1896–1906. This export performance, the high profits accruing to most, although not all companies, and the revenue returns to colonial administrations, however, rested upon severe compulsion and repression. The introduction in both the Free State and A.E.F. of taxes in kind to be paid to the state or the concessionary companies, in a form which left state or company officials to decide how much ivory or rubber represented adequate payment, laid Africans open to virtually unlimited demands on their labour. Behind the fiscal demands stood naked aggression, ranging from bullying by troops or company guards to the seizure of hostages and 'punitive' expeditions against tax-defaulting villages.

The system evolved in the Congo basin in the wake of colonial annexation was unjust, inhumane and almost certainly inherently unstable. Its methods would probably have proved counter- productive in the longer term, if not from rebellion or flight by African populations (the former more common in A.E.F. than the Free State) then at least from the depletion of elephant herds and rubber plants. Two external factors, however, hastened its demise. The first was the awakening of metropolitan concern and assertion of metropolitan control following disclosures of atrocities by, among others, the Casement report of 1903 and the International Commission of 1905 on events in the Free State, and the Brazza Commission of 1905 on the system in A.E.F. E. D. Morel's Congo Reform Association, an essentially humanitarian movement which also received backing from British mercantile houses chafing at restrictions on their trade, added further publicity. In 1908, Belgium, pressed by Britain and America, annexed the Congo Free State, ended Leopold's personal rule, and commenced a series of reforms which, by changing tax regulations, stripping companies of their quasi-administrative powers and cutting back the area of concessions, terminated many of the former abuses. From 1909 to 1912, the French government followed a similar line in A.E.F., amalgamating the forty companies into eleven new ones with reduced powers of control.

Although concessionary companies retained title to large areas of land, a second external factor began to impose change on the character of their operations. The secular decline of rubber prices, initially the result of the American financial crisis of 1907 which pricked the bubble of the rubber boom, but from 1910 onwards caused by the arrival of large quantities of South-East Asian plantation rubber on world markets, presented the companies with a different commercial situation from that which had previously made the plunder of forests and woodland profitable. They began to turn in new directions. Some, like the Antwerp and ABIR companies, which merged in 1911, turned into plantation enterprises; others took to general trading, buying a wide range of products from and selling to the African inhabitants of their spheres; yet others, through mismanagement or inability to compete with 'free trade' competitors on the fringes of their concessions, went into liquidation. The system of naked exploitation which characterized the Congo basin in the early years of colonial rule, therefore, had a lingering death, its last vestiges still to be found, and powerfully denounced by André Gide, in Ubangi-Chari in the early 1920s.

The more obvious consequences of the predatory phase in West-Central Africa's colonial economic history are its rape of the countryside, its destruction of human life, its disruption of social systems and its wholesale expropriation of surpluses from the region. Less obvious, perhaps, is its stifling of the human spirit, its frustration of the individual and collective initiatives which West Africans evinced in their relations with the international economy. Any possibility that the farmers and traders of West-Central Africa would have responded like those of West Africa to changes in world commodity prices was blocked by colonial-concessionary regimes determined that opportunities for external trade should be exploited to their advantage and under their direction. The African role was circumscribed, independence of action denied by the pressure of alien demands. The system therefore reinforced popular European stereotypes about African economic behaviour and, despite recognition of its horrors, left its legacy in official policies more favourably disposed to large-scale, European-managed concerns than to small-scale African enterprise. When Lever, his plantation schemes baulked in West Africa, turned to the Belgian Congo and signed an agreement with its administration in 1911, he became an heir of West-Central Africa's concessionary traditions.

SOUTHERN AFRICA: MINING AND SETTLER ECONOMIES

In Southern Africa, too, concessionary companies were instruments of European economic and political penetration of the interior. In Portuguese Mozambique, German South-West Africa, the Katanga province of the Congo, and above all in Southern and Northern Rhodesia, which were under the authority of the largest and most persistent British chartered company in Africa, the ruling power's grants of land to joint-stock companies of varying size, capital-raising potential and interlocking connexions were the principal means by which economic change was imposed on local societies. By contrast with the concessionary regimes of the Congo basin, however, the companies of Southern Africa had little interest in the foraging of natural animal and vegetable products. Nor were they normally capitalized to purchase the harvest of African-owned fields and pastures. Rather, their expectations focused elsewhere, first and foremost on rights to mineral prospecting and extraction in selected areas and secondarily on title to land on which European colonists might be settled. The companies were the cutting-edge of a process by which metropolitan and colonial capital combined to extend into new locations the mining-settlement duality of the older Anglo-Afrikaner territories. Whether the initiatives originated from within the latter or from Europe, the South African 'model' provided the inspiration and reference-point for the economic transformation of the rest of the region. By its very size, moreover, the performance and characteristics of the South African economy impacted directly upon the structural evolution of the newer colonial territories in the region, by way of a variety of commercial, financial, transport and cultural linkages, so that the economic history of Southern Africa in this period is a matter not merely of economic innovation under colonial rule but also of the growth of regional interdependence in a unique degree.

Mining and the export sector were practically synonymous in Southern Africa. Minerals accounted for over 76 per cent of the region's exports in 1913—and a substantial proportion of the rest comprised agricultural produce, principally foodstuffs, which surrounding territories sold to the mining-based urban markets of South Africa. Only in the region's southern and eastern flanks did sales of agricultural commodities to overseas markets have any significance. Such exports came mainly from established centres of production in the Cape and Natal, but during the years 1896–1914 the latter's settler-planting traditions also infiltrated new areas to the north-east. Anglo-Natalian capital found a niche in the subsidiary plantation enterprises of the Mozambique Company, which administered central Mozambique for Portugal, but the true 'New Natal' was the Shire Highlands of Nyasaland, where the British administration's policy of reserving 'vacant' land for the Crown assisted the settlement of a few hundred coffee- and tea-estate proprietors amidst a cotton-exporting African peasantry. By and large, however, commercial farming in Southern Africa rested upon 'internal' regional, sub-regional and local markets, the principal dynamic in the growth of which was the expansion of mining and its related service and manufacturing activities.

Mining operations, their location dictated by geology, lay along a roughly south-north axis through the central high plateau. The most important centres of production were, of course, the diamond-fields around Kimberley and the gold-bearing reefs of the Rand. The latter's output, although temporarily checked by the Boer War, almost quadrupled by weight between 1897 and 1913, when it was worth £37,000,000 and represented 40 per cent of total world production. Successful development of deep-level mining techniques, substantial investment in ore-crushing and processing plant and the discovery of new reefs all contributed to this growth of the Transvaal's gold-mining industry. North of the Transvaal, in Southern Rhodesia, gold mining by British and Anglo-South African companies commenced in the wake of the Chartered Company's occupation. Hopes for the discovery of a Second Rand gradually evaporated as it became clear that the deposits on which the ancient gold trade of the Upper Zambezi had rested were smaller and more scattered than the great concentrations of ore which existed in the Transvaal—and the British South Africa Company was progressively forced to reduce its terms for leasing mineral rights to companies. Nevertheless, mining was the mainstay of Southern Rhodesia's early colonial economy and accounted for 93 per cent of its exports in 1913. Prospecting in Northern Rhodesia uncovered few commercially viable bodies of minerals, apart from lead at Broken Hill and a handful of copper oxide deposits worked in a desultory fashion. In the context of pre-First World War copper markets only the highest grade oxides could bear the cost of transport from the African interior, and such ores were far less prevalent in Northern Rhodesia than across the border in Katanga, where the Southern African mining frontier established its furthest output. A British prospecting company, Tanganyika Concessions penetrating Katanga from Northern Rhodesia, reactivated Belgian interest in this province of the Congo and initiated the negotiations which led to the formation of the Union Minière du Haut-Katanga in 1906. By 1913 Union Minière, in which the principal share-holder was the large Belgian trust, the Société Générale de Belgique, was producing over 7,000 tons of smelted copper per annum, although it had yet to make a profit. British capital also played a subsidiary part in the exploitation of diamond deposits in South-West Africa which, from 1907 onwards, gave that struggling German colony its only export commodity of any value.

The domination of mining in external exchange relationships gave the pattern of economic transformation in Southern Africa a distinctive cast. It attracted to that region the greater part of the foreign capital invested in Subsaharan Africa. Frankel's estimates suggest that some £400,000,000 or 62·5 per cent of capital inflow between 1870 and 1913 went to South Africa and the Rhodesias,[4] and if one added to this the sums invested in Katanga, South-West Africa and Mozambique, the region's share of total capital imports would probably be closer to 70 per cent. Most of that capital went directly into extractive enterprises and the railway lines which mining operations required, but such investment had powerful secondary effects, in the shape of demands for inputs and ancillary services, which produced change at every level of material life. Energy requirements led to the development of coal-mining in the Transvaal and Natal, and at Wankie in Southern Rhodesia which supplied mines and railways as far north as Katanga. Construction, engineering and haulage enterprises also sprang up in the shadow of the bigger mining concerns. The incomes generated by the mines, railways and related activities, in turn created demands for a wide range of consumer goods and services which supported businesses ranging from carpenters' shops to breweries and flour mills. Large-scale, capitalist mining, in short, produced in Southern Africa a concentration of urban-industrial activity which supported a greater proportion of population outside agriculture than any other region. By 1913 this process had proceeded furthest in South Africa, where it originated, but in neighbouring territories embryonic urban-mining growth poles had also emerged.

The growth of domestic markets for foodstuffs meant increased opportunities for commercial agricultural production—but these opportunities largely accrued to European mixed-farming settlers. Outside South Africa, the principal new locus of immigrant mixed-farming was Southern Rhodesia where, from approximately 1904 onwards, the British South Africa Company deliberately encouraged and assisted the settlement of several thousand, mainly British or Anglo-South African, farmers who produced maize and livestock for local and South African markets. A small offshoot of this settler society emerged alongside the railway in Northern Rhodesia to supply the Katanga mines. German colonists in South-West Africa, fewer in number than the Rhodesian settlers, sold their pastoral products mainly to South Africa. The success of these farmers, and their South African counterparts, in virtually monopolizing regional and local markets for foodstuffs was not based, to any clearly demonstrable extent, on command of superior methods or scale of production— for in the initial stages of mining development, African smallholders, employing family labour but turning from subsistence- to market-oriented agriculture, frequently competed successfully with European, labour-hiring farmers in the sale of grains and meat to mining and urban centres. From the late 1890s, however, this competition became progressively unequal as administrative policies of resource allocation throughout the region gave preferential treatment to European-managed farming.

Land, the first essential resource, was already divided in South Africa into areas reserved for European and African occupation, and a similar pattern of land allocation followed colonial annexations in neighbouring territories. In Southern Rhodesia, where Ndebele and Shona were regrouped into new areas after the risings of 1896, and in South-West Africa, where the German administration conducted a particularly nasty campaign against the Hereros, military force secured the transfer of land (and livestock) from African to colonist ownership. This land set aside for European occupation obtained favoured treatment in the provision of transport facilities. The branch lines constructed in South Africa after the Boer War invariably went through European-settled districts, by-passing African reserves, while in the Rhodesias and South-West Africa the new trunk routes served areas allotted, or intended to be allotted, to European-managed agriculture. Settler-farmer politics and practices, beginning in South Africa and spreading into the Rhodesias, then turned towards preventing Africans from leasing land in 'white' areas on any terms other than a labour rent. Such developments, when coupled with the Europeans' preferential access to the technical services of departments of agriculture and to public and private credit institutions, placed African cultivators at a strong disadvantage in the competition for commodity markets and limited their role as commercial producers.

The use of political-administrative mechanisms to ensure that European rather than African farming would be the principal agricultural adjunct of the urban-mining complex was closely connected with the most fundamental process in the structural evolution of Southern African economics—the creation of a labour force for European-financed and -managed concerns. While difficulties over 'labour supply' were by no means unique to the region—they also appeared elsewhere, most notably during the construction phase of transport improvement—the rapid growth of capitalist mining and mining-related activities in Southern Africa from 1870 onwards had as its corollary a demand for labour which was unequalled in its scale and intensity. Some of the region's labour needs were met by immigration from Europe, more especially of skilled artisans, but the indigenous African communities were expected to provide the greater

110

part, particularly the large numbers of unskilled labourers employed in the mining industries. African participation in the colonial economies, therefore, was severely circumscribed by official policies and business practices designed to solve the 'labour question'. At the risk of considerable oversimplification, the 'labour supply' problem may be said to have arisen from the unwillingness of employers to provide the wages and conditions which would attract the labour of Africans whose family holdings supplied them with basic subsistence and for whom a cash income was, at least initially, a matter of 'discretion' rather than 'necessity'. Overt compulsion, in the form of administrative command and private inducement of chiefs to supply labour to employers, was practised but held in check in most territories. Covert compulsion, in the shape of a virtually universal imposition of taxes intended to enlarge the 'necessary' element of cash in African household incomes, had the effect of 'encouraging' the entrance into employment of Africans from areas where other possibilities of income-generation were absent—but had less impact in areas where Africans were in a position to sell grain and/or livestock. To mine owners and other urban employers, therefore, the growth of an African cash-cropping peasantry appeared as much a threat as to European settler-farmers, and these groups co-operated, openly or tacitly, in securing restrictions on African agrarian enterprise. Recent studies suggest a link between the lowering of wage-rates on the Rand in 1896 and in Southern Rhodesian gold mines in 1904, and the onset in these territories of pressures to reduce African opportunities for market production.[5]

From the interaction between the 'cheap labour' goals of the largest European employers and the 'discretionary' character of much of the early African incentive to enter wage-employment, there emerged a system of oscillating migration by which African wage-earners, rather than settling down with their families at places of employment, shuttled back and forth between 'white' areas and their family land in the reserves or 'tribal' territories. Wages, housing and other conditions of employment tended to be geared to the single man, and the costs of maintaining a worker's family did not fall on the employer's wage-bill. Practices varied considerably—from the seasonal movement of Africans seeking temporary harvest-work (in much the same manner as Scottish Highlanders migrated to Lowland farms in the eighteenth and early nineteenth centuries) to the rather longer-term settlement of Africans as squatter-labourers on European estates or employment of mission-educated men in clerical or other semi-skilled posts in the towns. The predominant pattern, however, was that set by the mines, whereby Africans were hired on short-term contracts by recruitment agencies which frequently operated at considerable distance from the centres of mining activity. Union Minière, functioning in a sparsely populated area, obtained most of its work-force from Northern Rhodesia and Nyasaland, through Robert Williams and Company, a labour-recruiting subsidiary of Tanganyika Concessions, but the Rand gold mines were the principal focal point of organized, long-distance labour migration.

As the Rand mines expanded their production after the Boer War, a serious labour shortage developed, caused in the main by the lower wages now being offered to unskilled labour. An experimental importation of indentured Chinese, up to 25,000 by the end of 1905, proved politically unacceptable and was terminated in 1907. The Chamber of Mines, however, solved its labour shortage by erecting a recruiting network spanning the entire region but which gave special attention to the attraction of labour from areas and territories where, in the absence of transport facilities, African opportunities for cash-earnings from agriculture were severely limited and labour migration was virtually the only means by which the tax demands of colonial governments could be met. The Witwatersrand Native Labour Association recruited from the nearby British protectorates of Basutoland, Swaziland and Bechuanaland, from the relatively densely populated Nyasaland, and above all from Mozambique, where an arrangement with the Portuguese government secured administrative assistance in return for a set fee per recruit. Death rates on the mines, from pneumonia and other climatically related diseases, were particularly high among labourers from the tropical north-east—nine to ten per cent among recruits from Nyasaland and Mozambique—and consequently W.N.L.A. recruitment was officially prohibited from Nyasaland in 1907 and from north of the 22nd parallel in Mozambique in 1914. Nevertheless, thousands of labourers from the region's north-east corner continued to make their own way to the Rand.

In the interterritorial flow of labour, even more than trade in food-stuffs or agreements by governments to connect their respective railway systems, the economic interdependence of colonial Southern

Africa is most clearly demonstrated. An informal division into labour-recruiting 'spheres of influence' reduced competition for labour between the mining growth-poles and their settler mixed-farming satellites, but had the effect of spreading migratory labour practices and habits across political boundaries until they penetrated the most remote localities. Only by securing the part-time wage-employment of the region's African populations did European large-scale mining and labour-intensive mixed-farming obtain the quantities of cheap, unskilled labour believed necessary for their commercial success. This in turn rested upon official policies combining neglect with active discouragement of African agricultural potential. Southern Africa would appear to have been characterized to a greater extent than other regions by the phenomenon of economic dualism, in which a dichotomy in economic and social organization is said to exist between the advanced, 'modern' immigrant sector and the backward, 'traditional' indigenous sector. Differences in economic behaviour, however, owed as much to the on-going inequality of relations between the sectors, more especially in the political allocation of resources for market production, as to the earlier dissimilarities in market experience of African communities and incoming European immigrants.

EASTERN AFRICA: THE SEARCH FOR VIABILITY

Broad patterns of regional uniformity were absent from Eastern Africa. Considerable diversity in terrain and climate had long meant the prevalence of strongly differentiated and relatively discrete social formations, and the region's claim to any essential economic unity rested somewhat weakly on the fact that formative external relations had been predominantly with North-East Africa and Western Asia and that slave-exporting had persisted longer than in regions more directly subject to West European influence. A similar ambiguity about the existence of any clearly defined Eastern African entity characterizes its economic history in the period 1896–1914, for at least three distinctly different, and largely unconnected, zones of external exchange activity can be identified.

The first of these, the Horn including Ethiopia, needs little comment since, within the transhumant pastoralism of the semi-arid lowlands and the feudal-manorial agrarian system of the Ethiopian highlands, few significant changes occurred. The area, almost totally

113

lacking in modern transport facilities, continued to export relatively small quantities of hides, ivory and beeswax plus some alluvial gold and coffee (mostly gathered in the wild) from Ethiopia. The second sub-regional unit, the Anglo-Egyptian Sudan, is of interest for the way that its predominantly British administration, uniquely independent from the Colonial Office, obtained inspiration for its policies more from Egyptian experience than from colonial territories in the rest of Subsaharan Africa. Expenditure on railway and steamship communications, partly motivated by military-strategic considerations, facilitated the revival of commerce with Egypt, previously broken by the Mahdist state, and a renewed expansion in Sudanese exports of livestock, gum arabic and raw cotton from riverain localities. In the latter commodity the administration saw hopes both of satisfying British metropolitan desires for the growth of cotton production within the Empire, articulated by the influential British Cotton Growing Association, and of emulating the Egyptian performance in cotton-exporting through large-scale irrigations of canals. It therefore financed and otherwise assisted experimental projects while beginning to plan the vast irrigation scheme for the Gezira lands between the Blue and White Niles. A singular form of bureaucratic-peasant nexus was in the process of gestation.

The third zone, comprising the British colonial possessions of Zanzibar, Kenya and Uganda and German-ruled Tanganyika, generated around two-thirds of Eastern Africa's pre-First World War external commerce. It incorporated the greater part of the sphere of operations of the nineteenth century exchange network linking the Arab-Swahili coast and islands with the African societies of the interior. In this distinctive sub-region forces determining structural change were more evenly balanced, and the interaction between them more open, than in almost any other part of Subsaharan Africa, and the debate in colonial circles about the relative merits of various forms of economic innovation was particularly lively. The absence of major mineral deposits and the early collapse of the chartered-concessionary companies of the Partition period means that Anglo-German East Africa of 1896–1914 does not fully justify representation as a microcosm of trends and issues arising in Subsaharan Africa as a whole. Nevertheless, in its patterns of agrarian evolution it comes close to that situation, for the interplay between colonial policies and market forces resulted in the development of agriculturally based colonial economies dominated neither by the peasant production typical of West Africa, nor by the settler-planter activities of Southern Africa, nor even by the large-scale company plantations beginning to set roots in West-Central Africa. On the eve of the First World War, rather, the economics of the East African mainland comprised a mixture of all three elements, more especially the former two, resting in a state of uneasy relationships amidst tension over resource-allocation.

Space prohibits any detailed examination of the complex developments of this period—a period which began with the 1890s crisis in the plantations of the Arab-Swahili coast and islands, from a combination of depressed commodity prices and colonial proscription of slavery. The cultivation of cloves survived on Zanzibar and Pemba, partly because few employment alternatives existed for liberated slaves, but with Arab-owned land now heavily mortgaged to Indian merchant-bankers. On the mainland, however, the crisis opened the way to the sale of land to incoming British and German plantations. A parallel decline occurred, over a somewhat longer time-span, in Arab-Swahili control of interior long-distance commerce as a result of administrative action against slave-trading and, more importantly, the growth of competition in the ivory trade from European hunters and European and Indian traders moving up-country in the wake of colonial troops and railway lines. From the fluid situation surrounding the break-up of older systems of externally oriented production and exchange a new pattern began to emerge in which European settler-planters and plantation companies, initially established on the coast, pushed into the highlands of north-east Tanganyika and south-west Kenya, and to a lesser extent into Uganda. In Tanganyika, Uganda and along the Kenya coast, typically monocultural plantations, individually and corporately owned, produced coffee, rubber and sisal for export, but in the cooler conditions of the Kenya highlands settlers concentrated on mixed-farming practices rendered highly precarious by the lack of any sizeable local market for food grains and dairy products. The success of European agricultural enterprises, like those in Southern Africa, tended to be heavily dependent upon administrative assistance in the supply of land, the provision of transport and the use of taxation and/or administrative 'persuasion' to secure labour from the African communities. However, lack of numbers, official unease about the socio-political consequences of European-managed agriculture and uncertainty as to whether it alone could underwrite the revenue needs of colonial governments, combined to prevent immigrant farming from obtaining any clear superiority in production for the market.

The rise of peasant cash-cropping in East Africa owed more to political injunction and regulation than did the same process in West Africa because market systems were more weakly developed and colonial governments harder pressed for taxable exports and freight for loss-making railways. Early initiatives in African cultivation for export, therefore, generally involved co-operation between officials and chiefs in the distribution of seed and organization of planting and harvesting on chiefs' land or their subjects' holdings. The best-known case is perhaps the role of the Ganda chiefs in helping to initiate the agricultural innovations which made cotton Uganda's principal export, but parallels can be found in the early origins of coffee-growing by the Haya and cotton-cultivation by the Sukuma peoples of Tanganyika. Such pressures from above were not always successful, since officials sometimes tried to push crops or techniques unsuited to local conditions and practices or tried to work through weak local authorities—thus the failure of the administration's cotton scheme in the Nyanza province of Kenya and the resistance to compulsory cotton-growing which triggered the Maji-Maji rising in south-central Tanganyika. The longer-term development of cash-cropping as a distinctly smallholder phenomenon, moreover, whether in areas where the powers of chiefs secured some initial core of experience, in areas where no such pressures were exerted, or even in areas where people had first responded by rejection and rebellion, ultimately rested upon the evolution of a market network of comparable sophistication, scale and depth of penetration into rural districts to that which already existed in West Africa. In this process Indian traders played a leading part. Indian mercantile capital shared the upper end of the nascent marketing hierarchy—wholesale import-export and crop-processing functions—with European firms, but in pioneering the middle and lower levels of commercial activity, above all in establishing the country stores which offered African smallholders an incentive for cash-cropping beyond the need to pay taxes or obey chiefs, Indian entrepreneurship made a crucial contribution to the emergence of an African peasantry. In this respect at least, strands from the older legacy of Afro-Asian interaction continued to be woven into the fabric of socio-economic change.

By 1914 Subsaharan Africa's connexions with, and role within, the global system of intercontinental production and exchange were considerably stronger and more direct than they had been in, say, 1870. A subcontinent that had formerly exported people had become one of net population-immigration; exporting of raw materials and foodstuffs now involved, directly or indirectly, the energies of a substantial part of Africa's population; modern communications had eroded local self-sufficiency over large areas; currencies interchangeable with those of the rest of the world had become common units of account; imports of capital and capital goods now figured alongside consumer imports in African trade and payment balances; the infrastructural underpinnings of modern 'national' economies had been superimposed upon older politico-economic frameworks. To be sure, remote localities of autonomous economic activity still existed and external forces of demand and supply still had only marginal relevance for a great many Africans, for whom obtaining domestic food supplies from family holdings continued to take precedence over all other pursuits. Nevertheless, to the extent that any single (and necessarily arbitrary) span of years can be said to encapsulate a lengthy historical process, the period between the mid-1890s and the outbreak of the First World War can be claimed with more than a little justification as the one in which Subsaharan Africa as a whole was finally integrated into the operations of the international economy.

The development of these years may be summed up as the use of colonial power to facilitate the penetration of European capital, from its existing peripheral spheres of activity, into the further reaches of the subcontinent. As this chapter has shown, however, the form and socio-economic impact of such penetration differed between and within regions, depending upon whether mining, settler-planting, mercantile or some other type of capital had predominant influence on colonial strategies and policies. Such broad patterns were historically determined to a considerable degree since, by and large, the structures of new colonial economies were variants of those previously shaped by Euro-African intercourse in parts of West and

Southern Africa. Only the Anglo-Egyptian Sudan, oriented towards Egypt, and the Belgian Congo, where, after the 'false start' of concessionary exploitation, there emerged a system of large-scale, company plantations close in style to that of Dutch-ruled Indonesia, can be said to have escaped the influence of West African and Southern African 'models'.

From the interaction between a European capitalism, diverse in goals and methods, and the various indigenous societies, an incipient socio-economic stratification developed. Between the mine or plantation on the one hand and the subsistence smallholding on the other, a variety of proto- or semi-capitalist modes of production arose— such as the quasi-manorial organization of the mixed-farming, squatter-labour estates of settlers in the Rhodesias and Kenya or the land-purchasing, labour-hiring cocoa farms of the southern Gold Coast. In marketing, too, growth in the scale and number of transactions supported layers of mercantile enterprise, from the relative handful of large, oligopoly-tending import-export houses in capitals and ports to the multitudes of local, stranger or immigrant petty traders who bought and sold in the villages. Parallel with, and consequent upon, the shift in the direction of market-oriented production came changes in the mobilization of labour. Slavery disappeared, to be replaced by different forms of wage-labour and share-cropping. In the conditions of low population/land ratios, however, workers supporting themselves and their families solely from labour-hiring were rare, and the political, social and territorial inequalities which generated the 'sale' of labour can be described as elements merely in a process of proto-proletarianization.

Innovation in economic behaviour characterized Subsaharan Africa of 1896–1914 to a greater degree than any previous period in the sub-continent's long economic history. Whether this owed more to the pressures and policies of colonial authorities than to the incentives of world prices remains open to debate and discussion. There can be little doubt, however, that a combination of the two created a situation in which Subsaharan Africa, both as a centre of primary product supply and as a small but rapidly growing market for Europe's industrial goods, more especially its older established lines, played a modest part in the revival of world trade which preceded the First World War. Foundations of economic interdependence between Europe and Africa were now clearly laid.

118

Five

Instability and expansion, 1914–1929

The First World War, a conflict of global dimensions without parallel since the Napoleonic Wars of the early nineteenth century, was highly disruptive of the operations of the international economy. Whether the war acted as midwife at the birth of a distinctly new phase in the evolution of the international economy, or merely exaggerated and intensified certain tendencies already inherent in international economic affairs, is open to disagreement. Nevertheless, the upheavals of 1914–18 clearly had a severely destabilizing effect upon world commerce. The dislocation of existing patterns of trade between belligerents, and between them and their overseas suppliers and customers, the destruction of life and productive capacity in the zones of conflict, the reallocation of resources from peacetime production to the war effort, the build-up of inflationary pressures at the centre of world trade and their transmission to the peripheral economies, the transformation of the major European nations into debtors of the United States, and the break-up of the empires of Central and East European states were among the immediate and direct consequences of the armed struggle. Nor did peace bring renewed stability because the reconstruction of war-torn economies and the liberation of pent-up consumer demands generated a sharp post-war commodity boom which was followed, almost inevitably, by a slump into a short but savage depression in world production and exchange in 1921–2. Not until 1924–5 can the international economy as a whole be said to have returned to an equilibrium approximating that of 1913–14, and even this apparent 'normalcy' masked certain basic shifts which had occurred in the structure of world trade and finance—including the Russian retreat into near autarky and, perhaps more significantly, the passing of monetary and financial power from a relatively impoverished, foreign trade-oriented

119

Western Europe to a highly self-sufficient America. The international conditions of 1914–29, therefore, presented African economies with a contextural framework which differed in many important respects from that of 1896–1914.

THE WAR AND ITS AFTERMATH

The First World War impinged upon material life in Subsaharan Africa both directly, through the colonial powers' mobilization of resources for military purposes, and indirectly, through the wider effects of the conflict on commercial relations between Europe and Africa. The military struggle within Africa had the character of a second colonial Partition, as German colonies became the targets of British, French and Belgian campaigns. The Allied distribution of the spoils was legitimized later by the League of Nations' mandate system under which Britain obtained control of Tanganyika, Belgium of Ruanda-Urundi, and South Africa of South-West Africa, while Togo and the Cameroons were divided into British and French spheres. On the whole, warfare between the colonial powers was spasmodic, involving short campaigns, and the destruction of crops, requisitioning of food supplies and labour, and dislocation of local trade which occurred in areas of military operations were brief, if sometimes serious, interruptions to the normal rhythm of economic life. A major exception, however, was the lengthy resistance of the German forces in Tanganyika, lasting for the entire war, which not only made Tanganyika the most fought-over and economically disturbed territory south of the Sahara but meant that pressures to supply Allied forces with men and materials fell particularly heavily upon the surrounding colonial territories. Porters, food supplies and draught animals were compulsorily acquired from the African populations of Uganda, eastern areas of the Congo, Northern Rhodesia, Nyasaland (where resentment over conscription of military labour helped to spark off the Chilembwe rising of 1915) and above all Kenya, the administration of which conscripted over 166,000 Africans, the greater part of the able-bodied male population, for service as carriers.

If the demands of intercolonial warfare were most disruptive of normal economic activity in East Africa, pressures from the conflict along Europe's 'Western Front' impacted most strongly upon the French colonies of West Africa. France, bearing the brunt of the war in Western Europe, was the only colonial power to use political measures to mobilize the human and material resources of its African dependencies for the military effort in the metropolitan war zone. Conscription of West Africans for the French army, beginning at a rate of 39,000 men in 1915–16, reached a peak of some 63,000 recruits in 1918, and meanwhile the requisitioning of cereals to replace the losses in France's own agricultural output resulted in a tripling in local prices for foodgrains, a sharp rise in imports of rice from Indo-China into Senegal and, in the opinion of several observers, a country-side on the verge of famine. Sporadic revolts against French rule broke out in parts of the northern savanna and in Dahomey.

The destruction of warfare or the drain on manpower and food supplies checked and distorted the externally oriented exchange activities of some territories more than others, but all felt the financial and commercial backwash of Europe's turn to war. The inflow of private and public capital from Europe dried up and expenditure on railways, harbours and other public works ceased (except in the odd case where this could be justified on military grounds). Primary product prices moved sharply upwards, although offset to some extent by higher prices and shortages of imported consumer and capital goods. An import-substitution effect developed, more especially in South Africa where nascent manufacturing industries and new ones springing up during the war took advantage of reduced competition from European industries to supply the domestic market and neigh-bouring mining economies, and where the first tentative steps in establishing an iron and steel industry were taken. Such fragmentary evidence as exists suggests that, with certain localized exceptions, Western Europe's rapid inflation was not fully matched in African economies, where wholesale and retail prices, including foodstuffs, rose more slowly than in Europe, with a consequent lesser pressure on wage rates. To labour-hiring producers of export commodities, therefore, the differentially rising export prices and costs of produc-tion of the war years brought significant gains.

This feature was perhaps most readily apparent in the mineral production of Southern Africa, the output of which continued to grow through the war years. Smaller, less efficient gold mines in South Africa and Southern Rhodesia were kept in, or brought into, operation by the higher prices prevailing in a period of depreciating world currencies, mining of low-grade oxide copper ores in Northern

Rhodesia proved commercially viable for the duration of the war, and Union Minière's investment in Katanga paid off in an expansion of output which by 1919 made Katanga the third largest centre of copper production in the world and enabled the company to pay its first dividend. But agricultural exports from West, West-Central and Eastern Africa, whether produced by plantation or peasant smallholding methods, also rose in volume and value. For some territories and certain commodities, most notably palm kernels, a redirection of trade flows from Germany to Britain and the United States occurred. Towards the end of the war, however, shipping shortages and other restrictions on overseas demand resulted in a generally lower rate of growth in export volume, and during 1918 an absolute decline in exports of many commodities. A gap opened up between productive capacity and export performance which was especially marked in the case of tree crops like cocoa, coffee, rubber and tea planted several years earlier and now coming into production.

The end of the war, removing such bottlenecks to trade, was followed by a scramble for commodities by the world's industrial economies which lasted through 1919 and 1920. Bidding was more intense in British and American markets than in those of continental Europe and consequently the commodity boom was more pronounced in British colonies and the Belgian Congo than in French West and Equatorial Africa or the Portuguese colonies. With demand for tropical agricultural produce now exceeding supply, the export earnings of several African economies were little short of phenomenal —between 1918 and 1920 the quantity of Nigerian palm oil and Kenya coffee exports was virtually static, but their value almost doubled, the Gold Coast's cocoa exports doubled in quantity but rose by over 500 per cent in value, and cotton exports from the Anglo-Egyptian Sudan, doubling in quantity, and assisted by boll weevil infestation of American crops, rose a staggering 800 per cent in value. The collapse in the reaction of 1921–2 was equally abrupt, bringing price levels back towards those prevailing in the mid-war years and leading to a cut-back in the production of annual export crops, a falling-off in new plantings of tree crops and a decline in land transactions and values. The intense pressures on labour supply, which were a feature of the heady boom years of 1919–20, gave way to wage-reductions and the first appearance of unemployment (in the sense of more men seeking employment outside household farming than were able to obtain it) in at least some colonial economies. Price fluctuations varied to some extent by commodity (see Figure 1, p. 149), market conditions being more volatile for the Gold Coast cocoa farmer or the Sudanese cotton cultivator than for the groundnut producers of Northern Nigeria or Senegal, for the coffee-growing settler-planters of Kenya more than for the European tobacco farmers of Southern Rhodesia. The incidence of income instability, both for individuals and governments, therefore differed between and within the various colonial territories.

Although the war and its boom-slump aftermath had obvious short-term effects upon economic activity in Africa, as well as longer-term consequences for former German colonies being integrated into the commercial, financial and administrative system of other metropolitan powers, the upheavals of 1914–22 produced few significant changes in the structures of African economies. On the whole, a process of consolidation may be said to have occurred in which the basic features of the structures laid down prior to 1914 continued through the war years into the mid-1920s, the upward trend in commodity prices to 1920 compensating for the temporary cessation of transport improvement as a spur to the expansion of export-production, and the depression of 1921–2 being too brief to alter established patterns radically. A major exception to this generalization, however, is to be found in East Africa—where the events of 1914–22 had a direct bearing upon the political economy of structural change.

The issue of whether European capitalist or African peasant agriculture should have first priority to land, labour and the technical and financial services of the state, already settled in West and Southern Africa, was finally resolved in East Africa by the particular circumstances of the war and its aftermath, which disturbed the uneasy balance between the two forms of production hitherto prevailing in Kenya, Uganda and Tanganyika, and brought about the relatively clear-cut predominance of one or the other in each of the three colonial economies. In Kenya the drift of official policy even before 1914 tended in the direction of favouring settler-planting activities, but the war years were critical to the achievement of political power by the colony's mainly British settlers, numbering perhaps one-half of the 1914 European population of 5,000. In return for assistance in prosecuting the war against the Germans in Tanganyika, Kenya's settlers demanded and obtained elected representation in the colony's highest governing bodies, enabling them to secure legislative and administrative measures which promoted their farming operations while stifling African smallholding enterprise. The range of measures included the introduction of pass controls on the movement of labour and performance of labour contracts, the closing of African access to land outside the reserves to all but labour-tenants, a Soldier Settlement Scheme to swell the ranks of the settler population, the construction of branch railway lines through areas set aside for European farming, and the prohibition of coffee cultivation, which had emerged as the most lucrative export activity, by Africans. As Kenya's agrarian economy and framework of socio-economic relations moved closer to the South African and Southern Rhodesian paradigm, the high tide of settler-planting penetration ebbed away around it. War and the British confiscation of 'enemy' property broke the back of the numerically stronger German settler-planting complex in Tanganyika, and although some estates began to pass under new (British and Greek) ownership they were barely back into production before the 1921–2 depression brought a further check to the revival of the European-managed agricultural sector. This interruption in settler-planter influence permitted the incoming British administration to formulate policies giving priority to the encouragement of peasant cash-cropping and which, while not hostile to immigrant capitalist farming, denied it the same degree of authority over policy-making as Kenya's settler-planters had acquired. In Uganda, meanwhile, where as a consequence of distance from ports and other local factors European-owned estates were more delicately poised between commercial success and failure, the 1921–2 collapse of commodity prices snapped the fragile thread, undermined merchant and banking confidence in rubber and coffee planting, led to an out-migration of settler-planters and their capital to more favourable locations, including Kenya, and left the Ugandan economy more firmly based upon peasant production than even that of Tanganyika.

The depression of 1921–2 served as the first intimation that the global context for Africa's trade and production had altered since 1914. Behind the replenishment of temporary shortages in primary product stocks during 1919–20 lurked longer-term effects of the war which dampened demand for raw materials and food supplies in European markets and prevented African trade in the 1920s from attaining the rate of growth it had achieved between 1896 and 1914. The war had pushed the international economy out of kilter and reduced the trading propensities of the West European industrial economies at its centre. An accelerated trend to protectionism, with Britain finally abandoning free trade and older centres of manufacturing emerging from the war to meet sheltered infant industries in former markets, the peculiar American role as the world's major source of capital exports which also set highly protectionist barriers against its debtors' merchandise, the European difficulties in returning to the mechanism of the Gold Standard, and the slow-down in the demographic impulse to market expansion in Europe, as a consequence of high death rates during the war and low birth rates after the war, were among the several interrelated factors which produced a more sluggish beat in the former West European heart of the international economy. Conditions for peripheral, primary producing economies in international markets therefore differed significantly in the 1920s from the earlier expansionary years of growing world demand and rising prices which preceded the First World War and continued to some extent through it. Although commodity prices recovered briefly just after the low of 1921–2, the upward trend was not held for long and in the later 1920s a secular down-turn in prices, beginning earlier for some commodities than others, indicated the existence of a gap between total world demand and supply of primary products.

As an enfeebled Europe's trade decelerated, so too did Africa's. Between 1913 and 1929 Subsaharan Africa's foreign trade by value grew by only half as much as it did over the equivalent sixteen-year period from 1897 to 1913, and as the trade statistics (Appendices I–III) reveal the greater part of this slackening in pace occurred in the years between 1919 and 1929. In only a handful of African economies did trade by value grow by a greater percentage in the 1920s than in the period 1913–19, and they were mainly cases where wartime mobilization or neglect by colonial governments had resulted in a lower-than-average growth during 1913–19. Measurement by volume would produce a slightly different result—in that 1929 values reflect the downward trend in commodity prices in the late 1920s—but would not substantially alter the picture of a general loss of momentum in Africa's external commerce. On the other hand, one finds only a few cases of commercial stagnation (Sierra Leone, Gambia and Zanzibar) and at least one colonial economy, Northern Rhodesia, in which the growth of foreign trade was exceptional by any standards. Africa's external exchange as a whole may have lost some pace, but it did not totally lack dynamic qualities.

THE COLONIAL CONNEXION

The policies and practices of colonial governments, formulated in the main by governors and local administrations but receptive to pressures and ideas from metropolitan sources, provided one determinant of the character of Africa's participation in the international economy during the 1920s. After the war, colonial investment in infrastructure, principally railways and harbours, revived. France's post-war colonial minister, Albert Sarraut, in particular devised an ambitious programme of railway construction in French West and Equatorial Africa, as part of a wider scheme for the *mise en valeur* of France's colonial empire, but finance for the Sarraut 'Plan' was severely hampered by the effects of inflation and a depreciating franc on metropolitan and colonial budgets—and in the end little was achieved apart from the completion of the Senegal-Niger line and the commencement of the Congo-Ocean line in Equatorial Africa. The latter, eventually completed in 1934 at the cost of heavy mortality among Africans forced to work on its construction, gave French Equatorial Africa a rail-link independent of the Matadi-Leopoldville line in the Belgian Congo—but of dubious commercial value. Similar considerations of national prestige lay behind the Belgian priority in construction and rating structure for the Katanga-Lower Congo line over the Benguela Railway from Katanga through Angola, which was finished only in 1931. Both these railways, however, had an impact on agriculture in the areas through which they passed, the former unlocking the foodstuff markets of Katanga to African cultivators in Kasai province and the latter facilitating the emergence of maize exporting from the Ovimbundu Plateau of Angola. In British colonies railway construction largely took the form of filling out the sketchy pre-war communications framework—completing some sections of trunk lines, extending others and adding various short feeder branches—with local ramifications ranging from the opening-up of new areas of peasant groundnut-cropping in Northern Nigeria, cotton-cultivation in Uganda and coffee-growing in Tanganyika to the consolidation of settler-planter supremacy in Kenya. Railway-building in the Gold Coast was linked, under the well-known public works programme of Governor Guggisberg, to the construction of a new deep-water harbour at Takoradi which was the outstanding harbour project in Africa of the 1920s (but which was arguably of greater assistance to the newly-opened, British-owned diamond and manganese mines in the western districts than to the Gold Coast's cocoa-exporting farmers).

The wisdom of the continuing emphasis on railways in colonial transport policies may be questioned in retrospect, for throughout Subsaharan Africa signs were now appearing that road transport was of potentially greater commercial significance, for agriculture and its related activities perhaps more than for mining. Rising imports of lorries and cars, and investment in motor vehicles by merchants, traders and wealthier farmers, indicate the growing adoption of transport methods which were more flexible than railways and had greater powers of integrating local markets into wider domestic and external networks, but to which the balance of colonial expenditures between rail and road systems gave scant attention.

The costs of transport and other infrastructural projects fell on colonial budgets and taxpayers—involving substantial increases in public debt and a burden of interest repayments which were relatively heavier in this period of slow growth in administrative revenues— since metropolitan governments continued to insist upon the basic financial self-reliance of colonies. At the same time, however, they expected colonial economies to satisfy the needs of metropolitan economies for raw materials and markets. The First World War, indeed, brought a sharper focus to long-held views about the desirability of 'imperial self-sufficiency' within world trade, both from general strategic considerations and from the point of view of the indebtedness of West European nations to an America from which they imported considerable quantities of raw materials and foodstuffs but to which they had difficulty in selling manufactured goods. Neo-mercantilist attitudes, which had tended to fade in the years between 1896 and 1914, obtained a new lease of life.

Manifestations of the change included the largely abortive Sarraut Plan for 'self-sufficiency' in the French Empire and Britain's adoption of a system of imperial preferences by the Finance Act of 1919. The latter, among its other provisions, gave tobacco from Southern Rhodesia, Nysaland and the north-east corner of Northern

127

Rhodesia, which were within the South African Customs Union, preference over American tobacco in the British market and ensured the success of a hitherto largely experimental line of production in these colonies. Tobacco-cultivation in Southern Rhodesia, the output of which rose from 3,000,000 tons in 1914 to 25,000,000 tons in 1928, was principally the preserve of European settler-farmers who produced flue-cured cigarette tobacco. Achievement of a secure overseas market, giving the settlers an alternative to maize-growing for local and regional markets, broadly coincided with a final transfer of political power to them from the British South Africa Company in the arrangements for internal self-government in 1923. In Nyasaland, by contrast, where settler authority and political barriers to African cash-cropping were weaker, peasant methods predominated, production being mainly of the fire-cured pipe tobacco which required less expensive processing.

In schemes to increase 'imperial self-sufficiency' in raw materials, however, tobacco took second place to cotton. Both saved scarce dollars, but the latter was also the necessary input for the major textile industries of Britain, France and Belgium. Each of these three colonial powers, therefore, took steps to enlarge the output of cotton from their African possessions. British desires to reduce dependence on American sources of raw cotton, in fact, long preceded the First World War, and the British Cotton Growing Association, an organization of textile and shipping interests established in 1902, had already had a strong influence on colonial policies and patterns of agricultural change in Uganda, the Anglo-Egyptian Sudan, and to a lesser extent Nigeria. But renewed concern about cotton supplies after the war led to the formation in 1921 of the Empire Cotton Growing Corporation, a statutory research and promotion body backed by public funds. It also resulted in a quick release of loans promised to the Gezira Scheme in the Sudan, which was the centrepiece of British cotton growing promotion in Africa in the 1920s. The Sudan government, supplied with loans of £13,000,000 between 1919 and 1924, constructed the Sennar Dam and major canal systems which provided water to irrigate the Gezira Plain west of the Blue Nile. The Sudan Plantations Syndicate, a private concern in which the B.C.G.A. had a substantial stake, undertook general management, credit, ginning and marketing functions and supervised the cultivation of cotton by the Gezira's inhabitants. Government reforms of land tenure and the distribution of holdings had converted the latter into tenants of the state. The scheme was a hybrid between peasant and plantation methods of production in which the return to the administration was 25 per cent, to the Syndicate 35 per cent and to the tenants 40 per cent of the harvest. Carefully controlled conditions, placing heavy restrictions on the tenant's freedom of action, permitted specialized production of relatively highly priced, long-staple cotton and resulted in per acre yields which were considerably in excess of those in other cotton-growing areas of Africa.

A comparative measure of the Gezira's significance is the fact that, whereas the Sudan's cotton acreages in 1927 were less than half of those in Uganda, its exports by quantity exceeded the combined exports of Uganda and Kenya by 20 per cent. Rainfall cotton-production in Uganda, despite the growth of acreages as a result of the railway extension to Kampala and the imitation effect by which cultivators continued to join the ranks of the cotton-growing peasantry, could not match the productivity of the Sudan's irrigation methods. Somewhat paradoxically, however, official policy in Uganda in the 1920s gave far less attention to issues of productivity than to plans to regulate ginning and marketing, with the general aim of limiting the competition to established concerns. Administrative intervention helped to impart a rigidity to distributive arrangements which were of dubious merit in raising the economy to productive capacity.[1]

Belgian and French cotton programmes tended to be even cruder variants on the themes of state command and private monopoly. The system which predominated in West-Central Africa, whereby district officers in woodland-savanna zones compelled the African villagers under their charge to cultivate cotton on large 'communal' plots, the harvest then being sold to European ginning and marketing companies with monopoly rights of purchase over a defined area, was first introduced in the Belgian Congo in 1917. Such methods raised the Congo's share of Belgium's raw cotton imports from virtually nil to 5·7 per cent of the total in 1929. From the Congo the system spread into Ubangi-Chari and Chad in French Equatorial Africa where, beginning in 1924, the local administration signed agreements with four companies, three of Belgian or Dutch origin, and set about recruiting the small army of *boys-coton* (instructors) who would enforce the cultivation of the crop. In the Sudanic (savanna) areas of French West Africa, too, pressures on Africans to produce desirable export crops like cotton, long part of the more *étatiste* traditions of French colonial political economy, increased after the First World War—but to relatively little effect. Indeed, increasing numbers of the inhabitants of this zone, still highly deficient in transport facilities, preferred to earn an income by annual migration to centres of commodity-production closer to the coast, becoming share-croppers in Senegal's groundnut fields or labourers in the Gold Coast's cocoa farms. The expectations of the colonial government and interested cotton-purchasing companies began to focus elsewhere—on a plan to develop an equivalent of the Gezira Scheme on the Niger River's inland delta in Niger. Surveys and pilot projects to test the technical possibilities of large-scale irrigation and settlement of population occupied most of the 1920s.

THE ROLE OF 'BIG BUSINESS'

If one dimension to the character of African external exchange relationships at this time is to be found in a heightened European identification of 'national' interests in the raw material and food-stuff production of African dependencies, the rise of business concentration and combination in Europe and Africa provides yet another. To be sure, this was by no means a new phenomenon. Early examples of concentration among firms operating in Africa include, in West Africa, the amalgamations among trading houses which produced the Royal Niger Company in Nigeria and the 'big two' of French West Africa, C.F.A.O. (The French West Africa Company) in 1887 and S.C.O.A. (The West Africa Commercial Company) in 1906; in Southern Africa, De Beers Consolidated's rise to domination of diamond mining and the complicated 'group' arrangement which connected finance and mining companies in Rand goldmining. Nevertheless, the post-First World War decade, with its early boom-slump phase presenting many companies with liquidity problems and its later general slow-down in trade encouraging ideas of spreading risks and sharing markets, proved to be a particularly fruitful period of integration through mergers, takeovers, inter-firm agreements, inter-locking shareholdings and directorships, and promotion of new subsidiaries. Many of the developments apparent in Africa were in turn linked, directly or indirectly, to changes in financial and business organization taking place in Europe under the fashionable banner of 'rationalization'. So complex is the story of business concentration in Africa, and so wide are the gaps remaining to be filled by historical research, that substantive explanation of causation is impossible. Nor is analysis of overall form any easier. There occurred both horizontal integration, bringing together firms engaged in broadly the same type of activity, and vertical integration, through the development of backward and forward linkages, with certain firms developing 'mixed' interests by engaging in both forms of organizational development at the same time.

In West Africa concentration involved expatriate firms undertaking a relatively narrow range of commercial functions—import-export merchandizing, shipping and related activities like haulage and lighterage. Business organization in the British colonies moved closer to the pattern already set in French West Africa, with the elimination of many smaller firms and the rise of one or two huge 'mixed' concerns alongside a somewhat larger number of medium-sized firms. In Nigeria, for example, the number of European firms engaged in trade only, that is mainly the smaller businesses, dropped from 88 in 1921 to 59 in 1929, while over the same period there emerged the vast United Africa Company. The old Niger Company, now shorn of its royal charter, was purchased by Lever Brothers in 1920, one year after its principal British competitors had amalgamated into the African and Eastern Trade Corporation. These two large companies, growing at the expense of smaller firms, finally merged in 1929 into the United Africa Company, which had a share capital of £15,000,000, handled half of Nigeria's external commerce and a large part of the Gold Coast's, collected half of the government's revenues from tin-mining in Nigeria, and traded through subsidiaries in French West and Equatorial Africa. U.A.C. was in turn a subsidiary of the foremost European multinational concern, the Anglo-Dutch Unilever soap and margarine manufacturing organization.

The trend towards concentration in West Africa, which had U.A.C.'s formation at its apex, was one more chapter in the story of conflict and co-operation between the various strata engaged in the distribution of products from West African fields and forests to metropolitan markets. The shift towards fewer and larger firms, strengthening oligopolistic tendencies in the West African export trade, brought a new degree of friction to relations between import-export houses and the predominantly African intermediary or middlemen merchants who bulked up commodities from local markets. These intermediaries came under increasing pressure from the elimination of the smaller European houses which formerly purchased from them, the larger companies' greater reliance on buying-posts and agents in internal trade, and the use of the pool (or cartel) to force down prices paid to the intermediaries (and through them to the producers). Cartelization, a favourite device in the late nineteenth century, re-emerged in the 1920s as a solution to falling commodity prices. In the Gold Coast, for example, a buyers' pool lasting for two seasons followed the short-term collapse of cocoa prices in 1921–2, while in Northern Nigeria the secular decline of groundnut prices from 1925 onwards resulted in the introduction of pooling agreements during 1927–9. Meanwhile, the threat of a challenge from metropolitan industrial capital, to the oligopolistic practices of mercantile capital in West Africa, inherent in W. H. Lever's attempts to by-pass dealers by establishing his own plantations, faded from the vegetable oil trade when Lever Brothers bought into and obtained a dominant influence within the ranks of the West African trading companies. Some manufacturers of cocoa products, including Cadbury's, found a similar, if less exalted, niche in Gold Coast cocoa-buying.

For all that, West Africa was the scene of a classic case of cartel-busting by a metropolitan manufacturing organization wishing to obtain direct control over its supply of raw materials. The West African cocoa and groundnut pools were but local manifestations of a worldwide movement towards cartelization in primary product transactions during the 1920s. Among several such cartels, usually involving producers and production quotas as well as pricing agreements, and therefore much more highly regulated than West African dealers' pools, was the Stevenson Plan of 1923–4 through which British plantation producers of rubber in Malaya and Ceylon attempted to force up prices by restricting output. American purchasers of rubber, consuming 70 per cent of total world output, reacted in the main by switching to Indonesian supplies, but Harvey S. Firestone, founder-president of the Firestone Rubber Company of Ohio, took the singular step of initiating his own raw rubber production in Liberia. Liberia, created around a nineteenth-century settlement of freed slaves, was an informal dependency of the United

States, which periodically assisted the Liberian government out of its recurrent financial difficulties. Firestone's plans were linked to negotiations between the respective governments to clear Liberia's outstanding foreign debts, 'national' interests in raw material supply being evoked to support the drive of a powerful manufacturing concern, and in 1926 Firestone obtained an agreement giving an option on up to 1,000,000 acres of land for rubber planting and the recruitment of up to 10,000 labourers annually by the Liberian government's Labour Bureau. Work commenced on establishing the highly enclavistic plantations at Harbel and Cavalla.

Seen in the context of the economic history of the West African region, however, the intrusion of large-scale plantation methods into Liberia was highly atypical. Elsewhere in West Africa small-to-medium-scale methods of agricultural production prevailed, and established expatriate businesses confined themselves to mainly commercial-financial functions, tightening control over producers' outlets rather than innovating new techniques or initiating diversification into new lines of commodity production. In this respect at least what happened in Liberia was closer in style and content, and perhaps in its connexions with the international manœuvrings of metropolitan concerns, to the pattern of events in West-Central Africa, where foreign investment in plantations and mining generated above-average rates of growth in external trade.

In the Belgian Congo in particular export-production and related service functions were concentrated in the hands of a few large organizations to a unique degree. By 1929, three firms provided at least 60 per cent of the Congo's total exports by value—the Katanga copper of Union Minière being worth 43 per cent of total exports, the diamonds of the Forminière mining organization adding a further nine per cent, and another eight per cent being the palm oil and kernels (one-half of all such exports) shipped out by the Huileries du Congo Belge, a Lever Brothers (latterly Unilever) subsidiary. The origins of 'big business' domination of the Congo's colonial economy antedate the First World War, its roots extending back into the concessionary system allied with state participation which, in a somewhat modified form, was Leopold's legacy to the Congo's political economy. Close co-operation between the state and private enterprise, however, was not the only hallmark of the Congo. A sort of Indonesia of Subsaharan Africa, the Congo was open to investment from all metropolitan sources to an unusual extent, so that British and American capital had a prominent part in company formation and growth, usually if not invariably in association with Belgian capital. One measure of the attraction of the Congo's particular political-economic configuration for overseas investors is the fact that between 1919 and 1929 total private investment in the Congo increased some tenfold in real terms (from the equivalent of 18·8 to 201·0 million gold francs). How much this dramatic increase owed to the activities of the 'big three', now consolidating their breakthrough into profitability during the war years, and how much to the smaller businesses being set up in planting, commerce and services, cannot be adequately estimated—but given the scale of 'big three' operations, and the fact that they supplied many of their own ancillary requirements, a preponderant role may be assumed.

Perhaps the most remarkable investment decision in the Congo's economic history was that taken by Union Minière during the slump of 1921–2 when, rather than taking the obvious course of cutting back production, the board decided to double it. As a first step, Union Minière raised its share capital from 12,700,000 to 70,000,000 francs, which was mostly taken up by the big Belgian financial trust, the Société Générale. (This had the incidental effect of considerably reducing the weight of the Anglo-South African component in the company's ownership and control.) Union Minière then commenced the opening-up of a second major mine, installed new smelting and refining plant, and set up coal-mining and hydro-electric subsidiaries to supply energy needs. With these developments in hand, the organization was strategically placed to take advantage of the recovery in world demand and prices in the mid-1920s.

The Huileries du Congo Belge also undertook new investment in productive capacity during the 1920s, although at a lower level. H.C.B. was established in 1911 as an offshoot of W. H. Lever's shift into raw material supply, pioneering the kind of backward integration which Firestone would subsequently undertake in Liberia. Under the 1911 agreement the Belgium Administration allocated to the H.C.B. five circles of land, each with a radius of sixty kilometres, in the Congo's forest zone, within which the company was empowered to erect mills and select up to a total of 1,900,000 acres for the cultivation of oil palms. Investment in milling and a fleet of steamers preceded investment in planting, and for the first ten to fifteen years

of its existence H.C.B. had less the role of a strictly plantation enterprise and much more that of trading organization, purchasing palm
products gathered by Africans from the wild or 'natural' oil palms in
the forest. It established a subsidiary (S.E.D.E.C.) in 1917 to compete
with smaller European and African merchants in this trade, and
gained an effective commercial monopoly around its mills, a monopoly given partial *de jure* force by legislation in 1926. During the
1920s, however, and in line with developments in South-East Asia,
H.C.B. began to increase its own oil palm-planting, to experiment
with seeds and techniques, and to select land for these purposes.

The third member of the triad, Forminière, was basically a partner-
ship between the Société Générale and the American Ryan-Guggenheim mining-refining group to exploit diamond discoveries in Kasai
province. Its first diamonds came onto the Antwerp market in 1913,
but the principal phase in its growth occurred between 1919 and
1929, when output rose by some 800 per cent. Over the same period,
Forminière diversified into the agricultural sphere, setting up plantation and trading subsidiaries to cultivate and handle such commodities as cotton and palm oil. Forminière also moved into neighbouring Angola, where it formed the Diamond Company of Angola
in 1917 to extract diamonds from the north-eastern Lunda district,
as well as a general mineral-prospecting company and, in association
with Standard Oil of Ohio, an oil-exploration concern. Before the
First World War, Angola's external exchange activities comprised the
exporting of such foraged items as rubber and wild coffee, plus
labourers despatched with some element of administrative coercion
to the cocoa plantations of Sao Thome; but after the war this Portuguese colony began to acquire the characteristics of a lesser Congo,
open to international capital seeking new opportunities in mineral
and raw material production. Quite apart from the Belgian and
American finance behind Forminière's Angolan ventures, British,
Belgian and German, as well as Portuguese, capital moved into the
planting, processing and distribution of coffee, cotton, palm oil and
sugar. Angola's rate of growth in external trade between 1919 and
1929 surpassed even that of the Belgian Congo.

Belgian and American capital created in West-Central Africa what
may be regarded as a new mining 'frontier' separate from, if overlapping with, the older Southern African mining complex, the
financial and organizational connexions of which were through South

Africa to Great Britain. In the interstices between these two sets of centre-periphery relationships lay numerous opportunities for conflict and collusion, which gave rise to a complicated story of international manœuvrings by firms which, among other things, resulted in the highly dramatic opening-up of the Northern Rhodesian Copperbelt. Until 1923 mining regulations in Northern Rhodesia, like those in Southern Rhodesia, were formed with the smaller prospector and mine operator in mind—but in the aftermath of the negotiations by which the British South Africa Company withdrew from its governmental role in the two Rhodesias, the policy was changed to one of granting prospecting rights on terms attractive to large mining-financial concerns. A second attraction to companies capable of raising large sums for capital-intensive mining was the discovery that Northern Rhodesia's surface oxide copper ores gave way at a deeper level to vast deposits of sulphide ores which the technical innovation of the flotation process now made commercially viable (as demonstrated by the growth of Chilean copper output after 1911). Two major mining-financial groups entered the ensuing scramble for new concessions as well as rights to existing, but hitherto barely profitable, mines—first, the Ryan-Guggenheim association of companies, represented by the American Metal Co. of New York, the operational centre of gravity of which lay in copper-mining and refining in America and Chile but which had become involved, through its investment in Forminière and Diamang of Angola, in diamond-mining in West Central Africa; second, the Anglo-American Corporation which, despite its title, was a British-South African holding company of diamond and gold-mining interests put together by Ernest Oppenheimer between 1919 and 1926 as part of the concentration process occurring in South African mining arrangements. Initially, in the early 1920s, the two groups had been in a co-operative stance. Oppenheimer acquired interests in, and made marketing arrangements with, the West Central African diamond producing business which assisted the strategy of breaking into, and eventually dominating, the South African Diamond Syndicate through which world diamond sales were cartelized. From the mid-1920s, however, the two groups were keen rivals in Northern Rhodesia. One factor of uncertain significance in the rivalry was the formation in 1926 of an international copper cartel by the American companies dominant in world copper markets, a cartel which Union

Minière joined, so that Oppenheimer's acquisitions in Northern Rhodesia could be presented to City of London backers as an attempt to safeguard 'imperial' copper supplies by side-stepping the American-led cartel.

Whatever the true state of the business politics in the background, Northern Rhodesia in the late 1920s was the scene of a race between companies controlled by the two groups to bring new copper mines into production, a mushrooming of camps and townships in the Copperbelt bordering Katanga, and an influx into the new mining centres of skilled labour from Europe and South Africa and unskilled labour from the territory's rural African societies. A quadrupling in Northern Rhodesia's external trade by value over the five years between 1924 and 1929 was caused in the main by large imports of machinery, vehicles and construction materials, the rise in copper exports from 108 to 5,808 tons over the same period being a mere portent of the Copperbelt's productive potential.

THE AFRICAN CONTRIBUTION

The outburst of activity in the Copperbelt was one of the final acts in laying down the structural foundations of Subsaharan Africa's colonial economies. By 1929 the last pieces were falling into place to complete the differentiated pattern of economic and socio-political arrangements by which the natural and human resources within the territorial units of colonial Africa were harnessed to overseas demands. Virtually every colonial economy now conformed, to a greater or lesser degree, to one of two ideal types—the peasant export economy of West Africa and most of Eastern Africa, and the mining-plantation export economy of Southern and West-Central Africa, which also had odd extensions into West Africa (Liberia) and Eastern Africa (Kenya). The latter is frequently described as a 'dual economy' and its performance analysed in terms of different behavioural principles in 'market' and 'non-market' or 'alien' and 'indigenous' sectors, and of a lack of linkages between the two sectors. Empirical studies, however, cast such doubt upon the underlying assumptions of 'dualist' theory and analysis that the more neutral description of mining-plantation economy is to be preferred. The peasant and mining-plantation categories merely represent tendency, the dominance of one kind and scale of production over the other in the external exchange arrangements of a given political-

137

economic unit, and no colonial economy which might be placed in one category totally lacked elements of the other. They are nonetheless useful as a guide to the differing roles which colonial governments and expatriate businessmen expected the majority of Africans to perform—small-scale cash-cropping on the one hand, wage-employment in larger-scale, foreign-owned businesses on the other.

In the peasant economies of West and Eastern Africa this decade was part of a continuing story of African initiative and innovation, under colonial policies which ranged from almost total *laissez-faire* in, say, the Gold Coast to more strictly interventionist attitudes of administrators in French colonies. Increases in acreages and exports of peasant-grown groundnuts in Northern Nigeria and Senegal, cocoa in Western Nigeria and the Gold Coast, cotton in Uganda, and coffee and cotton in Tanganyika, all showing signs of responsiveness to price fluctuation, were but the outward manifestations of a process by which millions of African smallholders, spurred on by the example of earlier innovators, reorganized their farming practices to make way for new export crops. They acquired new land for cultivation, increased the amount of time spent by household members in family fields, purchased new seeds and tools (usually hand tools), built shelters and sheds for storage, and invested in carts, bicycles, draught and pack animals and even, though more rarely, in lorries to transport crops to market. Such small-scale rural activity was less spectacular and more diffuse in its impact than the construction of a railway or opening of a mine or plantation, but was nevertheless the bedrock of a considerable part of Subsaharan Africa's expanding external trade.

Of the numerous examples which might be used to illustrate local African enterprise in cash-cropping, space permits reference to only one, slightly outstanding, case—coffee-growing by the Chagga people inhabiting the southern slopes of Mount Kilimanjaro in north-eastern Tanganyika. Chagga cultivation of the mild *arabica* coffee, commanding a higher price on international markets than the *robusta* variety which was the more common peasant-grown coffee in East Africa, began before the First World War when chiefs obtained plants from missionaries and imitated the methods of neighbouring German settler-planters. But during the 1920s cultivation spread from the larger estates of the chiefly 'gentry' to the holdings of 'commoners', on which the banana groves of the staple food-crop provided the

138

shade vital to *arabica* production. The revival of coffee prices from the slump of 1921–2 coincided with, and would seem to have influenced, this process, the number of Chagga-owned coffee bushes rising from 178,000 in 1922 to 1,250,000 in 1925. European settler-planters were antagonistic to Chagga coffee-growing but despite their pressure, and in striking contrast to policy in next-door Kenya, Tanganyika's Governor, Sir Donald Cameron, decided against any full-scale prohibition or discouragement. The only serious administrative restriction was the limitation of Chagga farmers to a maximum of 1,000 coffee bushes each, a measure apparently designed to block the emergence of full-blown capitalist methods which might disturb land tenure arrangements and create a 'middle class' capable of challenging the political authority of the chiefs. Perhaps the most remarkable part of the Chagga story, however, was the formation of the Kilimanjaro Native Planters' Association in 1925, to act as a marketing co-operative through which its members, the great majority of Chagga growers, could obtain better prices by selling directly to import-export houses and by-passing Indian and European middlemen. The K.N.P.A. was the first organization of its kind in Eastern Africa, and its inception was possibly influenced by such purely local factors as a habit of co-operation engendered through associations to regulate irrigation used in Chagga agriculture. But it had counterparts in West Africa (emergent cocoa farmers' associations in parts of Western Nigeria and the Gold Coast, for example) and should therefore be seen as an early expression of a wider phenomenon—a coming-together of African producers of agricultural exports to present a common front in the less buoyant and more restrictive market conditions of the post-First World War international economy. Whether, or how far, this development was a direct response to concentration and combination in the expatriate-controlled distributive system remains an open question.

To this brief account of Chagga initiatives others, stressing slightly different elements, might be added from a growing body of research into African export-oriented agriculture. Still relatively neglected by historians, however, is the production of foodstuffs for domestic or internal markets. Even in the peasant export economies, where food and export crops were normally grown side by side, environmental and transport factors resulted in some degree of local specialization in one or the other, and the rise of urban communities, associated with the commercial and transport sides of external exchange, created new demands for such basic food supplies as cereals, root-crops, vegetables, meat, dairy products and fish which were mostly locally produced. Such domestic markets grew even more rapidly in mining-plantation economies, where a larger proportion of population was employed outside food-production. Here, however, the African smallholder normally faced competition from politically powerful and administratively supported European mixed-farming settlers. The situation was perhaps more favourable in the Congo and Angola—during the 1920s Union Minière killed a scheme to encourage European settlement in Katanga because it feared possible repercussions on labour supply—than in such centres of settler authority as Kenya and Southern Rhodesia. Even in the latter, however, a rise in export crops (coffee and sisal in Kenya, tobacco in Southern Rhodesia) as a proportion of the total output of settler-planting agriculture and the spread of road transport meant that African cultivators and pastoralists obtained some outlet for their produce in domestic markets. Plough-cultivation and other manifestations of a more commercial approach to farming appeared in the reserves during the decade.[2]

But opportunities for an African contribution to food supply in mining-plantation economies, complementing the export-production of foreign-owned concerns, took second place to the task of supplying labour to mines, plantations, settler estates and related service enterprises in government and business strategies for economic change. This is not to suggest that a need for labour arose only in these economies. In peasant export economies, the development of commercial, transport and other distributive functions, the fact that peasant agriculture had periods of seasonal peak, mainly at harvesting, when household labour was insufficient, and the emergence of a minority of near-capitalist farmers as part of a process of increasing socio-economic stratification within rural African societies, all contributed to the growth of a labour market. By the 1920s, the demand for labour from centres of export cash-cropping in West and Eastern Africa began to draw manpower from further and further afield, so that the pattern of long-distance migration of wage-earners, first established in Southern Africa, became a truly subcontinental phenomenon. The trek of men from the interior savanna and steppe of French West Africa to the groundnut farms in Senegal and the cocoa farms of the Gold Coast was paralleled in Eastern Africa by the influx of migrants from Ruanda-Urundi into the cotton-growing areas of Uganda. A combination of colonial taxation, the absence of opportunities for commercial agriculture (usually because of a lack of modern transport facilities), relatively high population densities which resulted in some pressure on land resources, and a different seasonal cycle in agriculture which released labour at a time when it could be employed in cash-cropping elsewhere, underlay the rise of long-distance migration from such localities. A somewhat special category of migrants, West African Moslem pilgrims who stopped off in the Sudan while taking the overland route to Mecca, supplied a part of the labour needed, both on tenant holdings and in the administration's irrigation service, for cotton cultivation in the Gezira.

Demands for labour were none the less more intense in export economies based upon mining, plantations and settler-farming, the proportion of total population engaged in wage-employment in the economies of West-Central and Southern Africa normally being five to ten times greater than West or Eastern Africa (with the exception of Kenya). In the formation of a labour force, the authority of the state continued to exert a stronger influence than the attraction of wages. Coercion, in the shape of recruitment for private employers by district officers, was openly practised in the Belgian Congo, Angola and Mozambique (as well as in French West Africa, where the administration supplied labour to the relatively insignificant numbers of settler-planters in Guinea and the Ivory Coast). British colonial administrations, on the other hand, had abandoned the use of forced labour by the early 1920s, except for public works, and in the Rhodesias and Kenya, as well as in South Africa, enlargement of African wage-earning propensities rested on more indirect methods of control—heavy taxation, limitations on African opportunities to enter the market as independent producers, lack of expenditure on services in African-inhabited rural areas, the restriction of growing African populations with reserve boundaries, and the enforcement of labour contracts and pass laws by police and magistrates' courts —which combined with the operations of labour-recruiting agencies and a growth in the 'necessary' element in African desires for cash incomes to effect a steady increase in the numbers of Africans entering wage-employment.

Oscillating migratory labour remained the principal feature of

141

African employment, a consequence of low wage-levels, unpleasant conditions in towns and other centres of employment, and above all the desire of African wage-earners to retain their links with kin and rights to land in rural homelands which provided 'social security' against ill-health, unemployment and old age. Such a system, rendering lengthy periods of on-the-job training unusual, meant that African labour remained essentially, if not completely, unskilled. In the 1920s most employers (and bureaucrats) regarded this as normal and preferred to import skilled labour, the high price of the latter being offset by the low wages of African employees. Here and there, however, ideas about the desirability of labour 'stabilization' began to gain ground among employers anxious to secure a regular supply of labour and reduce the inefficiencies associated with a high rate of turnover among employees. The best known, although possibly not the first, move in this direction came from Union Minière in Katanga, which relied heavily on labour from Northern Rhodesia (55 per cent of the total workforce in 1920). The opening-up of the Northern Rhodesian Copperbelt, and an apparently related administrative regulation limiting Northern Rhodesian Africans to six-month labour contracts, presented Union Minière with an acute labour shortage—to overcome which it began from around 1925 to recruit from even further afield (from Manyema in the northeast Congo and from Ruanda-Urundi) and to attempt to encourage its employees to spend longer periods in service. Renewable three-year contracts, provision of family housing and the introduction of health, primary education and other welfare services for workers and their families were among the measures which Union Minière used to persuade Africans to break with the land and settle in regular employment under a relatively benevolent company paternalism. Union Minière's labour 'stabilization' scheme was initiated as a result of a set of peculiar circumstances but, more than paying for itself through increased productivity, it established a pattern of labour relations and social control which other large mining and plantation concerns, with the notable exception of the South African gold mines, would adopt in later years.

To regard African wage-earners as purely passive objects of social engineering by governments and businessmen, however, is to overlook the African initiatives in the field of wage-employment. Individual initiatives were to be found among the complex of motivation behind entrance into the labour market—in the calculations of men who saw periods of wage-earning as a means of amassing small savings for subsequent investment in cash-cropping or trading, or perhaps even more in the calculations of the minority who undertook formal education, where available, as a means to higher-paid clerical and other semi-skilled employment. Collective initiatives to defend or improve wages and conditions, by contrast, were very much rarer among African workers who were mainly migrants uncommitted to full-time employment—but the first stirrings of a move towards organized labour movements appeared in the sporadic strike action and formation of trade unions which expressed workers' grievances during the difficult post-war years of 1919–23. The first trade union in the Gold Coast, for example, the Accra Artisans and Labour Union, emerged in this period. Only in South Africa, which had well-established European trade unions, refusing membership to Africans, and a higher level of African participation in urban employment than any other economy south of the Sahara, did a new-born labour organization reach any significant size. The Industrial and Commercial Workers' Union, founded in 1919 by Clements Kadalie, an immigrant from Nyasaland, offered African workers membership of a general trade union, open to all kinds of wage-earners. Against a background of considerable labour unrest, I.C.U. enjoyed rapid growth—it claimed 100,000 members by 1927—but its leadership split into factions favouring political action on the one hand and 'responsible' industrial action on the other, its funds were diverted into unsuccessful, peripheral business ventures, and the entire organization fragmented into quarrelsome impotence in the late 1920s. Despite its eventual collapse, highlighting problems and issues common to the early history of many of the world's labour movements, I.C.U.'s initial appeal to large numbers of African wage-earners helps to illustrate the extent to which a transition from proto-peasant to proletarian life-styles and attitudes had proceeded further among the African population of South Africa than elsewhere in the sub-continent.

LABOUR AND INDUSTRIAL POLICIES IN SOUTH AFRICA
The rise and fall of the I.C.U. formed part of a wider pattern of labour politics in South Africa in the 1920s, revolving around attempts by European workers to confirm and extend 'colour bar'

practices of job reservation, which was in turn connected with a further characteristic distinguishing South Africa's political economy from that of the colonial economies to the north—namely the emergence of a political commitment to state-fostered industrialization.

Terms of trade between African primary product-exporting economies and the world's industrial-exporting economies, which had been broadly to the advantage of the former between 1896 and 1914, turned sharply against the primary producing-economies in the course of the First World War and post-war depression and recovered only slightly in the mid-1920s. Though this might seem to have favoured a greater measure of import-substitution and a growth of manufacturing within Africa, industrialization made little headway in the great majority of African economies. Such limited industrial activity as occurred was confined to a narrow range, principally the processing of raw materials for export (palm oil and groundnut-milling, cotton-ginning and copper-smelting) and of foodstuffs and construction materials for local, mainly urban markets (brewing, flour-milling, sugar-refining, saw-milling etc.). The odd factory manufacturing consumer goods appeared here and there—a soap factory at Lagos in Nigeria, a cotton-textile mill at Leopoldville in the Congo, or a cigarette factory in Uganda, for example—but consumer goods were still overwhelmingly imported. Heavy industries, capable of supporting engineering and capital goods production, were non-existent. The reasons for this slow pace of industrialization lie partly in the policies of colonial regimes uninterested in, if not actively hostile to, the growth of manufacturing, partly in the unwillingness of expatriate firms to invest in manufacturing which would compete with overseas production they owned or to which they supplied raw materials, partly in unfamiliarity with industrial processes among smaller businessmen, both African and immigrant, but mainly it seems in the low per capita incomes of the great majority of the population which meant a limited domestic market for the potential manufacturer.

Such bottlenecks to industrialization were weaker in South Africa, the European-elected government of which had obtained independence from metropolitan political authority in 1910, which earned some 50 per cent of Subsaharan Africa's total income from foreign trade, and which had an income distribution that favoured the country's European population of 1,500,000, resulting not only in a comparatively large domestic market (in Subsaharan rather than world terms) but also some potential for local capital accumulation. The infant industries fostered in South Africa by the disruptions of trade during the First World War, mainly small establishments using simple technology, came under renewed pressure from overseas competitors after 1918 and suffered a contraction of the domestic market during the 1921–2 depression. The South African government intervened, providing selective tariff protection and bounties for certain industries, as well as setting up an Electricity Supply Commission in 1923. But although South Africa, in common with other self-governing Dominions in the British Empire, might be said to have been moving towards a greater measure of state encouragement of infant industries under the Smuts government, the latter's replacement by a Nationalist-Labour coalition in 1924 was an important turning-point in the evolution of industrial policy.

This coalition between the National Party, representing the predominantly rural Afrikaner population, and the Labour Party, representing predominantly urban, English-speaking immigrant workers, brought together the two forces in South African society most concerned to see state action both to create new employment and to reserve higher-paid jobs for workers of European 'race'. Prior to and during the First World War, European miners' fears of competition from 'cheaper' African labour, which added a strong racist dimension to the relationships between capital and labour in South Africa, had resulted in legislation, work-practices and agreements between trade unions and employers to reserve skilled and many semi-skilled occupations for Europeans only. In the immediate post-war years, however, mine owners on the Rand, facing lower prices for gold, attempted to reduce the prevailing European : non-European ratio in the labour force, and the European miners responded with the unsuccessful strike-turned-rebellion of 1922, known as the Rand Revolt. The crushing of the revolt in defence of the 'industrial colour bar', and a high court judgment of 1923 which declared the job-reserving Mines and Works Act of 1911 to be *ultra vires*, led the Labour Party into co-operation with the Nationalists. The latter shared the industrial goals of the Labour Party because falling agricultural prices and drought were pushing smaller Afrikaner farmers, especially the *bywoners* or share-croppers, off the land into the towns, and into competition for wage-employment with African migrants from the countryside. One of the first acts of the newly elected coalition government, therefore, was to pass the Mines and Works Act of 1925, which authorized the government to issue certificates of competence for skilled occupations only to Europeans and Coloureds (mixed race). A powerful legislative device was added to the drawbacks of the migratory labour system to ensure that African workers would remain primarily unskilled and lowly paid.

But the coalition also looked beyond immediate job-reservation to the wider task of creating more employment for European workers and their families, giving new emphasis and assistance to the development of manufacturing industry. In 1925 it raised tariff barriers to new heights, providing effective protection for such emergent consumer goods industries as textiles, clothing, leather and confectionery, and in 1928 it established the state-run Iron and Steel Corporation which, taking over and reorganizing the tiny and struggling private concerns, laid the foundation for a heavy industrial, capital goods sector. This shift from an 'open' to a partially 'closed' economy and towards the use of 'state capitalism' had longer-term rather than immediate significance, its results being most clearly seen in the rapid growth of South Africa's industrial output during the next phase of interaction with the international economy.

Two principal themes emerge from a review of Subsaharan Africa's economic history between 1914 and 1929—instability in the world system of production and exchange to which Africa was now firmly connected, and a continuing expansion in African primary production for world markets. The currents and eddies of an international economy unsettled by global warfare reached Africa in a variety of forms, giving the period the appearance of an inchoate welter of disparate developments, as messy and as difficult to render into coherent shape as, say, the economic history of Europe at this time. Some externally derived forces, like deteriorating terms of trade, strongly fluctuating commodity prices, and a general decline in world demand for raw materials and foodstuffs in the 1920s tended to operate against growth in African export production; others, such as schemes for raw material 'self-sufficiency' within colonial empires, tended to function as a positive incentive; yet others, like a trend to business concentration and attempts at international and intra-African commodity cartelization, had contradictory effects, depressing the expansion of exports in some areas while stimulating it in others. These conflicting propensities, reflecting the uncertainties and confusions of the international economy as a whole, resulted in a generally slower growth in external trade after the First World War than in the period preceding it.

Closer examination of the expansion in foreign trade, moreover, reveals that in the 1920s, as in the period 1896–1914, most of the significant additions came from an initial opening-up of production in new areas—here a new cluster of smallholder cash-cropping activity, there the discovery and exploitation of a new body of ores, elsewhere a fresh influx of settler-farmers or plantation companies—all normally associated with the diffusion of modern transport facilities. Commodity production for overseas markets continued to spread from the coastal or near-coastal sites where it first began in the nineteenth or early twentieth centuries into fresh localities in the interior, bringing into play local resources of land and labour which hitherto had not been used to earn income from external trade or had been only lightly employed by way of foraging. Such innovation permitted striking and rapid gains from trade, gains which were to some extent independent of trends in world markets because, as long as income from sales exceeded local costs of production, new entrants could obtain additions to income even from commodities whose market prices were static or falling. Once the initial process of transition was complete, however, established commodity producers could obtain gains only through rising prices, lower costs or increased productivity, or some combination of the three. They faced a different set of circumstances from those whose decision was whether or not to take the first steps into production for the market.

A division of Subsaharan Africa into centres of older and centres of newer external exchange activity—admittedly one which cannot be made with any great precision—would seem to clarify certain important features of this decade. This division is partly revealed, and partly masked, by regional and territorial trade statistics. Between 1914 and 1929, but most clearly in the 1920s, the trade of West and Southern Africa, which had a longer history of integration into the international economy, grew more slowly than that of West-Central and Eastern Africa where, on the whole, production for overseas markets was a newer phenomenon. Within the former regions, however, the external trade of South Africa was less buoyant than

localities of South Africa, the coastal palm oil and groundnut zones of West Africa, the cocoa-growing belt of southern Gold Coast, the cotton-growing area of Buganda in Uganda, and possibly the clove-plantation islands of Zanzibar and Pemba, where specialized production for overseas markets was already well advanced on the eve of the First World War, and where most of the early gains accruing to new entrants had been made already, experienced stress in the changed market conditions of the 1920s. Lower commodity prices and the absence of any significant cost-reducing technical change resulted in the growth of tensions over the distribution of income from foreign trade—between employers and labour in South Africa, between peasants, middleman traders and oligopolistic mercantile houses in West Africa and Uganda. Only in South Africa, however, did these socio-economic tensions show any sign of leading to significant structural change.

Six

Depression, recovery and war, 1929-1945

The shaky house of cards which was the international economy in the 1920s collapsed into a disorderly pile in the following decade. Beginning with the New York stock market crash of 1929, savagely deflationary pressures spread through the financial institutions of the world's industrial centres, causing a drying-up of foreign and domestic credit, bank failures and bankruptcies, currency devaluations, cutbacks in investment, massive unemployment, social unrest and a spiralling contraction in world trade as manufacturing and raw material-exporting economies alike became locked into mutually reinforcing reductions of demand and price. On the whole, primary producing-economies suffered most acutely from these reverses in world commerce, terms of trade once again moving sharply against them to cause serious balance of payments difficulties. The export-oriented economies of Subsaharan Africa could not be sheltered from these forces, and with the collapse of world markets the expansion in African external exchange came to an abrupt end. Between 1929 and 1932 the value of Africa's commerce fell by some 42 per cent, a decline which was shared more or less equally by all regions and territories. This was slightly less than the approximately 60 per cent fall in the value of world trade as a whole but none the less represented a serious check to African export growth.

Behind these bald figures lay a major loss of income from exporting, rising levels of private and public indebtedness, and a contraction of credit from metropolitan financial and commercial institutions which sent reverberations through every African economy. Bank failures were confined to private banks in the Congo and Senegal (the latter caught in the backwash of the 1931 bank panic in France), but everywhere banks and other credit-advancing agencies restricted lending and tightened pressure on their debtors. Most of the large expatriate mercantile companies managed to survive the worst period of the depression, but numerous smaller European, Asian and (in West Africa) African businesses went into liquidation. (In Nigeria, for example, 19 expatriate trading houses failed between 1929 and 1933.) Many of their clerks and agents, plus those dismissed in the 'retrenchment' programmes of the larger firms, entered petty trading and thereby added to the difficulties of retailers, shopkeepers and petty commodity dealers. A decline in production accompanied contraction in commerce. Large mining concerns, like the copper companies of Katanga and Northern Rhodesia, or the diamond firms in South Africa, the Congo and Angola, reduced output and laid off workers; plantation companies like Firestone and Huileries du Congo Belge ceased new plantings of tree crops, as did African cocoa farmers in the Gold Coast and Nigeria; many tenants in the Gezira Scheme abandoned their holdings to West African immigrant labourers who, anxious to gain a foothold in tenancy despite the immediately unfavourable returns, were also the most willing applicants for holdings on newly opened sections of the scheme. On the whole, reduction in output was a more prominent feature of mining and plantation activities than peasant smallholding production—partly because peasant agriculture tended to be taxed through fixed poll-taxes, the burden of which, unlike taxation of company profits or sales, did not ease with reduced earnings, and partly because, where family members provided a substantial part of the enterprise's labour, there were proportionately less savings to be made on wage bills by ceasing or drastically limiting production. Nevertheless, in both peasant-based economies and economies dominated by mines and plantations, employment opportunities and wage-rates fell sharply between 1929 and 1933. Integration into the international economy commanded a heavy price during the Great Depression of the early 1930s.

Recovery in world trade from the depths of depression in 1932–3 was faltering and slow—as attempts to find international solutions ran up against 'national' proclivities to unilateral action, as formerly externally oriented industrial economies in Western Europe gave greater emphasis to home investment, and as multilateral commerce gave way to trade within 'blocs' organized around the world's major currencies. A hesitant revival in trade and prices through 1934 and 1935 turned into a speculative commodity boom, based upon stock accumulation by industrial economies, during 1936 and the early months of 1937—but this bubble was burst by the 1937–8 recession in America, Britain and France, and primary product prices tumbled again. Subsaharan Africa's external trade mirrored this partial recovery—by 1938 the value of its commerce surpassed the 1929 level by some ten per cent. This contrasts with the position in Europe, where foreign trade in 1938 was still some 59 per cent lower than the 1928 figure—for as Europe's production and investment tended to turn inwards to exploit domestic markets, the weight of official policy and business interests in African economies remained committed to growth through exploitation of overseas markets. Nevertheless, for reasons which will be examined later, recovery in external trade was unevenly distributed between Subsaharan Africa's politico-economic units, most of the rise over 1929 levels being accounted for by the economies of Southern Africa, while the economies of West-Central Africa, West Africa apart from Sierra Leone and the Gold Coast, and Eastern Africa except for Kenya and Uganda, were still in 1938 at lower levels of returns from commerce that they had been in 1929. In the disarticulated international economy of the 1930s, export growth proved an uncertain route to income enlargement and transformation of productive capacity.

GOVERNMENT: FINANCIAL CONSTRAINTS AND POLICY
IMPLICATIONS

The semi-stagnant period, dominated by cyclical depression and recession, was a troubled time for the economies of Subsaharan Africa. Depressed commodity prices, easing only slightly in the middle of the decade, placed severe strains upon systems called into existence by, or created for, external commerce and imposed strong constraints upon the freedom of action of their various component elements, including governments.

For most governments the 1930s meant falling or static revenues and heightened difficulties in servicing public debt. Expenditures on infrastructure and welfare services not already funded by public debt became severely constrained by the fact that repayment of interest to metropolitan treasuries or financial institutions had first claims on budgets. Colonial governments could not default. The incidence of such problems varied from territory to territory, depending upon the scale of debt and the extent of revival in revenues through the recovery of trade. Among British colonies, financial difficulties were perhaps most acute for Kenya and Nyasaland—the former because of debts incurred in railway construction and attempts during the 1920s to provide European settlers with a high level of public services, the latter because the British metropolitan government compelled it in the early 1920s to guarantee the debentures of a railway through Mozambique from Beira to the Zambezi river. In consequence of its involvement with this loss-making railway, Nyasaland's public debt grew by a phenomenal 731 per cent between 1925 and 1935.

The finances of the federations of French West and Equatorial Africa were similarly placed under stress by the Great Colonial Loan of 1931 through which the government of metropolitan France revived Sarraut's ideas of large-scale public works in the colonies, mainly with a view to enlarging overseas markets for French manufacturers. This loan, raised at a time when the French franc, stabilized in 1928, was still strong, and before the full effects of the depression were felt on colonial revenues, released funds for large-scale projects previously planned which held out the prospect of an immediate return for the metropolitan economy. These included transport developments—such as the final stages of the Congo-Ocean railway in Equatorial Africa and a new harbour at its Pointe Noire terminus —and the large-scale irrigation scheme on the inland Niger delta. The *Office du Niger*, the parastatal enterprise set up to manage the latter project in 1932, spent the rest of the decade constructing the Sansanding dam and irrigation canals, laying out farm units and recruiting African settlers, many of whom, like the Mossi recruited from Upper Volta, came to the scheme under administrative compulsion. If the Congo-Ocean line, duplicating facilities available across river in the Belgian Congo, was the white elephant of French Equatorial Africa, the Niger Project, its progress bedevilled by a failure to conduct research into the effects of irrigation on local soils and other technical inefficiencies, and draining funds from other services to repay its interest charges, might be described as the 'white water buffalo' of French West Africa. By the middle of the 1930s, the strain of servicing such large public debts caught up with colonial budgets, calls upon metropolitan loans dried up, and the French government had to step in with subventions to assist repayments of interest. The sums placed by the French state in West and Equatorial Africa between 1931 and 1939, totalling 4,633,000 francs, were ten times greater in real terms than the equivalent for the period 1914 to 1929, but this 'generosity' in a period of commercial and fiscal stagnation gave the French colonies an acute attack of financial indigestion.

The metropolitan-colonial financial connexions of France, Belgium and Portugal—the latter two also being compelled to provide subventions for debt repayment—involved no breach in the orthodoxy that colonies should be financially self-supporting. Britain's Colonial Development Fund, however, introduced a small chink in the wall. The C.D.F. was not a direct response to the depression, having been established in 1929 to help combat the unemployment which had persisted in the British economy after the First World War, but in the course of the 1930s it supplied colonial governments in Africa with £4,200,000. Its principal advantage as a resource-transferring device was the fact that 60 per cent of its allocations were interest-free grants and the rest low-interest loans, so that use of the Fund did not normally involve major additions to debt servicing. Its principal defects were pusillanimity—only £1,000,000 being set aside each year to meet the claims of some fifty British colonies throughout the world—and a requirement that C.D.F. grants and loans be used to cover only the capital costs of any scheme, with colonial governments meeting recurrent costs. Historians are divided over the longer-term significance of the C.D.F.—whether it should be regarded as a limited success, a pioneering precursor of the later, more generous funds established by the British parliament in 1940 and 1945, or an almost total failure, contributing only the negative experience of its deficiencies to later aid-giving mechanisms.[1] Whichever view one takes, it seems clear that in the context of the 1930s, the C.D.F. could do little more than marginally ease the financial constraints on colonial governments, enabling them to undertake small-scale measures (principally in transport, urban services and public health) which would otherwise have been impossible.

In the C.D.F.'s allocative policies, moreover, a tendency to concentrate resources on schemes most relevant to metropolitan industrial interests may be detected. This is illustrated by the fact that the two largest projects financed by the C.D.F., together totalling £1,000,000 or nearly one-quarter of all allocations to Africa, were directly related to the fortunes of the British iron and steel industry. Finance of the Zambezi Bridge, the last link in the construction of the commercially unviable railway from Beira to Nyasaland, secured markets for

British iron and steel, while a low-interest loan supplied to a British company through the Sierra Leone government facilitated the exploitation of newly discovered deposits of high-grade iron ore in that colony.

Financial constraints on governments carried implications for colonial economic policy. It resulted in a search for increased production of export commodities as a means to greater revenues, and to a stronger administrative emphasis on peasant-cropping within that process. Agricultural exporting, it was thought in many colonial circles, could be raised through the peasantry with relatively less cost to government than through plantations and settler-farms which tended to require, or demand, expensive public services. This shift in emphasis was by no means universal, being absent from the policy decisions of governments in Southern Africa and having only faint echoes in British colonies in West Africa, where peasant-production was already relatively highly developed through the market. But it appeared in different forms in a large number of colonial economies.

The introduction of *Sociétés Indigènes de Prévoyance* from Senegal, where they had been established before the First World War, into all the other parts of French West Africa was one manifestation of the trend. The S.I.P.s, in which membership was compulsory for every African cultivator, were organized at a *cercle* or district level and managed by French district officers. They were mechanisms through which the administration could distribute seed for, and supervise the cultivation of, export and food crops. They also acted, by way of membership fees and interest charges on seed, as a device for raising taxes, and in the later 1930s began to be used as marketing organizations, selling produce in bulk to processing and exporting firms. The S.I.P.s gave a co-operative façade to what was in effect a series of local administrative campaigns of enforced cultivation and quality control, principally of palm oil and kernels in the forest zone, groundnuts and cotton in the savanna. In 1937 S.I.P.s were introduced into French Equatorial Africa where coercion of the peasantry was, if anything, more open and extreme than in French West Africa. The central element of the 'peasant path' to financial solvency in Equatorial Africa was the cotton programme in Ubangi-Chari and southern Chad. Although commenced in the 1920s, this acquired a new urgency and a new direction from the completion of, and need to provide revenues for, the Congo-Ocean line. A switch from cultiva-

155

tion on communal plots to cultivation on individual holdings, the introduction of a controlled three-year crop rotation, and legislation permitted supervising staff to fine or imprison those disobeying their instructions resulted in a rise in cotton output in Ubangi-Chari from 220 tons in 1929 to 13,000 tons in 1940. So nakedly coercive was the system that the cultivators, selling their crop to ginning and marketing companies with monopoly rights of purchase, were paid not in cash but in bills of credit towards the administration's head tax.

The Belgian Congo's *paysannat indigène* policy also originated in the financial-commercial difficulties of this period, which persuaded the metropolitan and colonial governments that 'the future belongs to colonies where the exploitation of the land can be conducted in the most economic conditions, and this can only take place through the intervention of the native'.[2] African cultivators were to be cajoled or encouraged into cash-cropping, in a subordinate role to the three or four large mining and plantation concerns which dominated the Congo's export economy, producing both export crops like cotton, coffee and palm oil, and foodstuffs to feed the labour force of the mines and monocultural plantations. Such a policy suited the large capitalist organizations, the labour supply of which was assured partly by continuing administrative direction of labour and partly by labour stabilization associated with capital intensive methods, the trading subsidiaries of which would market the peasant-grown crops, and the wage bills of which would benefit from cheaper domestic food supplies replacing food imports from the Rhodesias and elsewhere. More directly threatened, and less likely to benefit, were the comparatively small numbers of Belgian settler-planters who had entered the Congo in the 1920s. Their objections led to certain limitations on the new policy—the coffee planters of highland Kivu Province, for example, ensured that the removal of a prohibition on African coffee-growing would not apply there—but could not wholly block its introduction. Uncertainties and debate about appropriate means—whether cultivation could be individually or collectively based, whether or not there should be a relocation of villages on sites with better soils or transport connexions—characterized the early years of the *paysannat* programme, the effects of which on levels of production and exporting would be seen mainly during and after the Second World War.

In the British colonies of East Africa, too, a new administrative emphasis on peasant agriculture developed. The Tanganyika government's 'Grow More Crops' campaign, which resulted in increased pressures on African farmers and chiefs, a re-examination of the curricular content of African education and innovations in marketing arrangements, took place in an economy where peasant cash-cropping had always made a significant contribution to export earnings. It was therefore a somewhat less radical shift in policy than that occurring in Kenya where the domination of European settler production began to be questioned, if not yet directly challenged, by government attempts to enlarge the exportable surpluses of the African reserves. Official policy in Kenya, previously wholeheartedly inclined towards settler agriculture, began to develop an ambivalence which is perhaps best illustrated by the fact that while the prohibition on African coffee-cultivation was removed in districts remote from the main centres of settler-planting and mixed farming, so that peoples like the Gusii and Meru could now adopt the crop, it was maintained in the Kikuyu-inhabited districts from which the European estates drew the bulk of their labour.

MARKETS AND MARKETING

Alongside, and frequently linked to, government pressures for increased peasant cultivation, stronger administrative intervention in the regulation of marketing appeared—for collapse and stagnation in commodity prices also placed the marketing arrangements in African economies under stress, and triggered off a search for market security and price stability on the part of producers, dealers and governments. The erection of bureaucratic controls over internal and external commerce formed part of a complex pattern of manœuvring over the allocation of shares of contracted markets, and over the distribution of income from these markets, which was a dominant element in Subsaharan Africa's economic history during the 1930s. This involution of commercial politics meant a clash of interests on a grand scale—between different colonial and metropolitan governments, between the various producers of the same commodity or types of commodity, and between producers and merchants—in which there were 'losers' as well as 'gainers'. Differential access to the authority of the state usually, if not invariably, determined 'success' or 'failure'.

The search for market security took two distinct forms—the

157

development of market-sharing arrangements by producers' organizations, backed by government, and the erection of tariff and other protective devices around colonial empires, encapsulating their commerce within relatively closed trading 'blocs'. The former applied to internal as well as external marketing arrangements, most notably in the measures by which European settler-farmers in mining-plantation economies strengthened their control of, and returns from, domestic markets for foodstuffs, largely at the expense of the African peasantry. The switch to a *paysannat* policy headed off any tendencies in this direction in the Belgian Congo, and ensured that the mining-plantation export sectors would be supplied by 'low-cost' African production, but in South Africa, Southern and Northern Rhodesia and Kenya, where settler-farming interests were more strongly entrenched and more favourably regarded by policy-makers, the export sectors had to carry, at least indirectly, the burden of price stabilization programmes for settler produce. During the early 1930s, when prospects for exports were most bleak, the domestic urban, mining and plantation markets for food assumed even greater significance for the European farmers of these territories (some of whom switched from tobacco, coffee and other export crops to maize). They obtained government support for schemes to maintain domestic prices for maize, livestock and dairy produce at higher levels than prevailed in world markets. Statutory commodity control boards to establish quotas and fix prices were set up in South Africa and the Rhodesias, while in Kenya two settler co-operative associations obtained monopoly control over maize and dairy-produce marketing. Output beyond the needs of the domestic market was dumped outside the country at whatever price could be obtained. In the Rhodesias and Kenya, however, although the situation in South Africa was less clear, sales of foodstuffs by African peasant farmers had been growing through the late 1920s and early 1930s, thanks in part to the spread of road transport, and threatened to upset price stabilization for settler commodities. African-produced foodstuffs were therefore brought within these schemes but suffered discrimination by quota or price, usually justified on the grounds of 'poor quality'. The measures did not result in a complete check to African sales to domestic markets, partly because the mining-plantation sectors of these economies recovered relatively quickly from the depression and domestic markets expanded accordingly (in Northern Rhodesia in particular, demand for food supplies in the later 1930s outstripped internal sales by European and African farmers). Nevertheless, the African peasantry operated from a position of disadvantage in producing for the market.

Price stabilization through limitations on output was less easily achieved for export commodities since this normally required international co-operation. The principal international agreements for agricultural commodities—sugar (1931), tea and wheat (1933) and rubber (1934)—covered produce which was relatively unimportant to Subsaharan Africa as a whole but, as in the commencement of Firestone's tapping of its rubber plantations in Liberia in 1934 or the growth of tea-planting in Kenya and Tanganyika, the size of the quota allocated to producers in Africa could have a significant bearing on developments in particular economies. Mineral exports were subject to the tin agreement of 1931 (which resulted in some restriction of Nigerian tin-mining) and the unofficial producers' cartels in diamonds and copper. Here, as in all other quota-based schemes, difficulties arose in reconciling the interests of the longer-established producers, who had to bear the brunt of restrictions, and those of newer producers whose capacity for expanding their output might endanger any market-sharing scheme if their quotas were not sufficiently 'generous'. Thus the diamond cartel, centred upon De Beers in South Africa, had to come to terms with the Consolidated African Selection Trust, whose discovery of, and monopoly concession to, diamonds in Sierra Leone added yet a further element to the remarkable growth of mining in that West African colony. The American-led copper cartel, by contrast, broke down completely in 1932, partly as a consequence of strongly protectionist measures by the American government but also because the copper companies in Katanga and Northern Rhodesia refused to accept the quotas allotted to them and threatened a price war. When an officially backed copper control scheme was set up in 1936, the companies mining in Africa obtained better terms than those offered by the original cartel.

Most of the price stabilization programmes of the 1930s proceeded on the basis of quota controls on produce normally coming from expatriate-owned mines and plantations (and contrasts with the absence of such arrangements for peasant-grown export crops, which colonial administrations attempted to enlarge despite the possible risk of further price reductions). An interesting variant, however, was the French experiment with compensation funds by which levies on foreign imports of certain commodities into France were repaid as subsidies to producers in West and Equatorial Africa. This scheme was an outgrowth of the French version of the accelerated drive to protectionism within colonial empires, which was the most common means by which metropolitan governments attempted to provide market security for producers in African and other colonial dependencies.

A move towards giving colonial commodities favoured access to metropolitan markets had been a feature of the 1920s, with Britain and Belgium adopting a system of imperial preferences in 1919 and 1924 respectively and France revising its older imperial tariff system in 1928. But the depression took these mercantilist tendencies to new heights through increased duties, import quota controls, prohibitions and other restrictive devices, and the adoption of an imperial preference system by the British Empire as a whole under the Ottawa Agreements of 1932. The new arrangements included favoured treatment for metropolitan manufactures in African markets. Most of French West Africa already gave such preferences, but in 1936 the French unilaterally revoked the agreement with Britain covering 'free trade' in the Ivory Coast and Dahomey and extended preference for French manufactures into these colonies. In British West Africa, imperial preferences were imposed on Gambia and Sierra Leone in 1932, and textile import quotas were introduced in Nigeria and the Gold Coast with the object of preventing cheaper Japanese cotton from driving out more highly priced British goods. Portugal, too, imposed preferential arrangements on the trade of Angola and Mozambique. Large parts of the subcontinent, however, comprising most of French Equatorial Africa, the Belgian Congo and the British colonies in East Africa, were precluded by the Congo Basin treaties of 1885 and 1890 from applying discriminatory tariffs or quotas, and remained open to imports from any quarter. The burden of meeting metropolitan needs for market security, and the additional costs which this involved for African consumers, particularly peasant-farmers and wage-earners, fell more heavily on West Africa than West-Central or Eastern Africa.

Colonial preference for metropolitan goods was the *quid pro quo*, unequally distributed, for privileged access to metropolitan and other imperial-colonial markets. From the evidence, it would appear that agricultural producers in French and Belgian colonies obtained an advantage from preferences in metropolitan markets which had hitherto taken large quantities of agricultural commodities from outside their respective colonial empires. The Congo's share of Belgium's raw cotton imports, for example, rose from 5·7 per cent in 1929 to 23·5 per cent in 1934, while French preferences fostered growth in African cocoa-farming and European coffee-planting in the Ivory Coast and settler banana-cultivation in Guinea (the latter also benefiting from new shipping subsidies). The effects of protection on agriculture in British colonies was, on the whole, more uneven. Some producers, more especially in British West Africa which exported a broadly similar range of commodities to that of French West and Equatorial Africa and the Belgian Congo, seem to have lost more from the closing of French, Belgian and possibly Dutch markets than they obtained from preferential access to British and Dominion markets. The latter afforded protection to commodities in the dutiable food and tobacco category, which included the coffee, tea and tobacco produced partly by plantations and settler-planter estates and partly by peasant smallholdings in Eastern and Southern Africa. Of the purely African-grown crops in British colonies, Nigerian and Gold Coast cocoa was the only important recipient of preferential treatment, but it gained little new advantage because the British market was already fully supplied with cocoa from the colonial empire, and West African cocoa was excluded from a Canadian market which gave protection only to West Indian cocoa. Agricultural commodities which were industrial raw materials had no preferential access to British or Dominion markets, because this would add directly to the costs of metropolitan manufactures. The industrial raw material category included some settler-planter crops —like sisal from Tanganyika and Kenya—but the great bulk comprised peasant-grown crops like cotton from Eastern Africa and the groundnuts, palm oil and palm kernels of British West African colonies. The distinction between dutiable food and tobacco items and non-dutiable raw materials, with its consequent differential impact on prices, did not discriminate against peasant agriculture per se. Indeed, where local circumstances were favourable it fostered some degree of diversification in peasant agriculture—as in the perceptible shift of African smallholders in Uganda from cotton to coffee in the course of the 1930s. Nevertheless, whether by accident or design, the weight of the protectionist system drawn round the British Empire in 1932 tended in the direction of favouring plantation and settler-planter more than peasant enterprise.

The export commodities least sheltered by formal measures for security in overseas markets, and most open to world price trends, were the peasant-grown staples of certain British colonies—cotton from Uganda and Tanganyika, and the cocoa, palm produce and groundnuts from Nigeria, the Gold Coast, Sierra Leone and Gambia. In these economies, therefore, the long-standing cycle of competition and combination between and within the three interest groups concerned with the distribution of smallholder crops—the farmers, the middlemen or brokers, and the expatriate mercantile houses—entered a new and more bitter phase. Colonial governments, for their part, took a greater interest in ideas of market 'stability' and 'rationalization', which tended to mean the evolution of policies antagonistic to middlemen operations and favouring the mercantile houses.

The erection of bureaucratic controls over marketing in British-ruled peasant economies began earlier and proceeded further in East Africa than in West Africa, partly because laissez-faire traditions of government were weaker there and partly because administrative programmes to increase peasant output spawned governmental desires to regulate local level marketing. The 'quality control' legislation introduced in Uganda, Tanganyika and Kenya in the early 1930s—requiring African produce to be brought to certain centres for inspection and grading—was equivalent to, if somewhat more extensive than, similar controls in West Africa. But the same legislation also instituted the licensing of traders with a view to eliminating large numbers of small dealers. Established traders, principally Indians, obtained such licences more easily than newer entrants to commodity dealings, who were principally Africans. A squeeze on middlemen, openly undertaken to assist the market dominance of expatriate firms, also followed the cotton-zoning arrangements of 1933 whereby the colonial governments of Uganda and Tanganyika, in moves reminiscent of marketing arrangements in the cotton-growing areas of the Belgian Congo and French Equatorial Africa, gave expatriate-owned (European or Indian) ginneries statutory monopolistic rights over raw cotton-purchasing in surrounding

162

localities. These measures, eliminating competition between ginners, encouraged the growth of pricing pools and ensured the profitability of ginning companies at the cost of lower prices to producers.

Expatriate firms in British West Africa lacked such open support for the pooling arrangements by which they attempted, sometimes periodically and sometimes consistently, to reduce prices paid to middlemen and producers. These combinations (like the pre-cotton zoning pool in Uganda) were not particularly stable or enduring—the longest running, the groundnut buyers' cartel in Northern Nigeria, was eventually broken in the late 1930s by the competition of an aggressive 'outsider', the Lebanese businessman, S. Raccah. Nevertheless, expatriate mercantile houses in West Africa resorted to price agreements with greater regularity and effect, arousing a greater measure of African discontent, than at any time since the late nineteenth century. Producers' discontent took several forms, including the spread of farmers' co-operatives and associations (which administrations tried to use to promote 'quality control' and organize small-scale processing), but its most spectacular eruptions came in the Gold Coast cocoa hold-ups of 1930–1 and 1937.

Commodity hold-ups, relatively common in periods of trade depression throughout West African history, were not confined to cocoa—a little publicized hold-up of groundnuts, for example, took place in the Gambia in 1931—but the Gold Coast's cocoa farmers were more inclined, and perhaps better organized, to use this technique in the 1930s than any other equivalent group. Theirs was the most highly capitalized of all African cash-cropping ventures (the average size of cocoa holdings in the Gold Coast being seven acres as against 2·6 acres in Western Nigeria) and might be more accurately described as 'small capitalist' rather than 'peasant' enterprise. With their crops and land pledged to various sources of credit, including brokers, Gold Coast cocoa growers tended to be more heavily over-extended and more susceptible to price falls than most other African cultivators of export crops. Their first produce hold-ups in 1930–1, organized by the Gold Coast Cocoa Farmers' Association with the assistance of many chiefs, failed to secure better prices, but when, in 1937, the collapse of prices from the brief commodity boom of 1936 coincided with a revival of dealers' pooling arrangements, they returned to the attack with a hold-up combined with a boycott of imported manufactures. This second 'trade war' led to the appointment of the Nowell Commission of 1938, which recommended the creation of statutory marketing bodies for Gold Coast and Nigerian cocoa. Although no administrative action was taken before the outbreak of the Second World War, the drift of events in British West Africa appeared to be leading colonial governments towards intervention in and regulations of marketing, a development which, tailored to differing local circumstances, was already well established elsewhere in Subsaharan Africa.

RECOVERY IN EXPORT GROWTH

The arrangements made for the overseas marketing of export commodities, favouring certain lines of production and particular African economies more than others, had an important bearing upon the differentiated pattern of revival of export growth which occurred in Subsaharan Africa in the middle and late 1930s. By 1938, only a relative handful of African economies—principally South Africa, Southern and Northern Rhodesia, Kenya and Sierra Leone—enjoyed levels of commerce significantly above those of 1929 (see Appendix II), while the remainder were at or below 1929 levels. With the partial exception of Sierra Leone, where an entirely new wedge of expatriate iron ore, diamond and gold mining enterprise intruded into an economy hitherto dominated by African palm produce-exporting (raising minerals from four per cent of exports in 1931 to 71 per cent in 1939), above-average rates of export growth resulted from the impact on existing structures of two principal factors—special advantages obtained from preferential access to metropolitan and other markets, and rising prices for gold.

The advantages of market protection through the enlarged British Empire preference system of 1932, as we have seen, accrued more to plantations and settler-planter estates in the Rhodesias and Kenya than to peasant holdings in, say, Nigeria. European producers of arabica coffee in Kenya made especially significant gains through obtaining preferential access to an expanding South African market—South Africa, which took only 2·5 per cent of coffee exports from Kenya and Uganda in 1931 took nearly 20 per cent in 1938.

Imperial preference was also extremely important for the copper companies of Northern Rhodesia. When the Ottawa Agreements of 1932 imposed a duty on non-Empire copper the Northern Rhodesian Copperbelt acquired a secure market in Britain, where expansion of electrical and automobile manufacturing stimulated a demand for copper. The Rhodesian Selection Trust and Anglo-American Corporation together raised the output of their mines from 6,000 tons in 1930 to 213,000 tons in 1938, and Northern Rhodesia experienced the highest rate of export growth of any African economy in this decade. During this expansionary phase, Northern Rhodesian copper production overtook and surpassed that of Katanga. Union Minière, secure only in the comparatively small Belgian market, compensated for slower market growth by an emphasis on cost reduction, raising productivity by investment in mechanization and labour-stabilization policies which facilitated the replacement of expensive European skilled and semi-skilled labour by less highly paid Africans trained by the company. The number of European to African workers in Union Minière's operations declined by nearly a half between 1930 and 1939 while on the Northern Rhodesian Copperbelt, where European trade unions were imbued with ideas of job reservation originating in South Africa, ratios remained virtually unchanged.

If a protected market for copper was the key to Northern Rhodesia's rapid export growth, the emergence of a free market in gold had an important bearing on the export performance of a number of other economies. Gold was the only African export to escape the low prices prevailing throughout the 1930s, and to appreciate strongly against world currencies and other commodities. Abandonment of the Gold Standard by the world's major economies—led by Britain in 1931 and the United States in 1933—resulted in a rise in gold prices from 85 shillings per ounce in 1931 to 140 shillings per ounce in 1939, and resources were redeployed into gold mining wherever deposits existed. In West Africa, peasant farmers and labourers in several localities found some compensation for lower incomes from agriculture in working small alluvial deposits, and expatriate company operations, centred principally on the Gold Coast and Sierra Leone, obtained a new lease of life. The number of companies at work in the Gold Coast, for example, rose from four in 1936 to 15 in 1941, output quadrupled over the same period and, thanks to the depressed state of cocoa markets, gold became the most valuable single export. In Kenya and Tanganyika, too, settler and expatriate capital and African workers were attracted to newly discovered or newly profitable alluvial and reef deposits, although in neither of these territories did the gold rushes of the 1930s reach the scale of the boom in Southern Rhodesia which was the centre of operations *par excellence* for the smaller European-owned mining company. In Southern Rhodesia, where gold was already the leading export, rising prices brought some 1,300 new producers into gold mining between 1931 and 1935, and the share of small mines in total output grew from 31 to 61 per cent. Exports, increasing from £2,100,000 in 1931 to £5,900,000 in 1939, were roughly on a par with those of the Gold Coast.

The principal beneficiary of the disruption of the world's monetary arrangements, however, was the South African gold mining industry, the output of which greatly surpassed the combined production of the rest of Subsaharan Africa. Rising prices and a change in tax regulations in 1935 encouraged extraction of the vast bodies of low-grade ores in the Rand reefs, company dividends doubled, the labour force grew from 232,000 in 1931 to 364,000 in 1939, and exports of gold rose from £48,400,000 in 1931 to £71,600,000 in 1938. The boom also stimulated a new wave of prospecting and surveying which led, in the late 1930s, to the discovery of a second major complex of goldfields, in the Orange Free State. Gold mining, which rescued the South African economy from the 'Great Depression' of the late nineteenth century, once again came to its assistance in the more difficult conditions of the 1930s. Its rapid expansion impacted upon a domestic economy which government action had been preparing for industrialization, and nowhere else in Subsaharan Africa did the multiplier effect of buoyant export earnings have a more profound stimulus. The nascent manufacturing sector, sheltered behind tariff barriers and enjoying a close proximity to growing markets in Southern and Northern Rhodesia, more than doubled its output between 1932 and 1939. The most rapid growth occurred in the heavy industries (metals and machinery), led by the new state-run Iron and Steel Corporation, but food and tobacco, textiles and chemicals also advanced their output and employment. The construction industry expanded, too, to meet the increased demand for plant and housing in the mining and urban areaas. The South African 'drive to industrialization', initiated in the mid-1920s but held up by the depression of the early 1930s, obtained a powerful new momentum.

South Africa's rapid economic growth influenced official policy in neighbouring territories. Its example of state-sponsored diversification around exports encouraged a similar trend towards state intervention in Southern Rhodesia. New parastatal bodies set up in Southern Rhodesia in the late 1930s and early 1940s, in conscious imitation of organizational innovations in South Africa, included commissions for Electricity Supply (1936), Gold Ore Roasting (1937), Cold Storage (1937) and Iron and Steel (1942). In this, as in other aspects of economic policy, Southern Rhodesia's settler-politicians continued to draw inspiration from the South African paradigm.

In Nyasaland, by contrast, a colonial government struggling with a heavy burden of debt servicing was drawn into an entirely different relationship with the South African economy. The competition for labour which developed in South Africa between the gold mines and the other expanding sectors placed the mining companies in a situation analogous to that which faced Union Minière from the growth of the Northern Rhodesian Copperbelt. However, rather than follow the Union Minière lead in abandoning reliance on migratory African labour and moving towards the creation of a settled and permanent labour force, the South African gold-mining companies widened their recruiting network to bring in migrant workers from further afield, including Nyasaland. From the time of the 1907 prohibition of W.N.L.A. recruitment of Nyasas for the South African mines the Nyasaland government had taken the view that the labour of the colony's African population should be employed within its boundaries and, despite a continuing outmigration of men seeking temporary wage-employment, this remained the official attitude until 1934–5, when the government sanctioned recruitment for the gold mines of Southern Rhodesia and South Africa. Unable or unwilling to resist the attraction of labourers' remittances as a support to its sagging finances, it eschewed any major attempt to raise the output or productivity of agriculture and finally accepted for Nyasaland a similar role to that of Mozambique—a labour reserve for the mining and settlement economies of the rest of the region.

LABOUR, POPULATION AND LAND

As a consequence of differential recovery in export growth, demand for additional labour arose unevenly across Subsaharan Africa. Yet even in economies experiencing above-average rates of export growth, where the aggregate demand for labour grew most rapidly, employers' complaints about labour shortages were less frequently

167

heard during the 1930s than in earlier decades. Furthermore, although forced labour, regressive taxation and other administrative devices to coerce Africans to take up wage-employment did not completely disappear, lingering on most openly in Belgian, French and Portuguese colonies, such measures were relied upon progressively less and less in Subsaharan Africa as a whole. The 1930s, therefore, was a period in which the 'labour supply' problems of employers eased considerably.

Three principal factors appear to have been at work to cause this novel situation. The first, essentially short-term, was the depressed state of incomes in smallholding agriculture, which in many localities lasted for most of the decade, and led to a redeployment of labour from peasant households to wherever wage incomes could be obtained. The second was part of a longer-term trend which began in the previous decade—a gradual improvement in conditions of employment, in the availability of housing and health facilities at the place of employment, and in transport to take the migrant worker to and from centres of employment. Naturally, conditions varied enormously between different localities and different types of employers, but there was an appreciable trend on the part of such large employers as mining and plantation companies or public and private railways to move towards a benevolent 'welfare' approach to industrial relations. Governments, too, increasingly laid down and attempted to enforce minimum standards of housing, work safety, rations and so on, although small employers could usually escape such controls quite easily. These general, if patchy, improvements in workers' welfare were possibly more influential than trends in wage rates, especially real wages about which little is known, in changing attitudes to employment among Africans.

The third factor was the pressure of population on land. The demographic history of Subsaharan Africa in the first half of the twentieth century remains almost as much a mystery as that of earlier centuries, and little can be said about its overall dimensions. Estimates that the population of Africa increased at an annual rate of 0·6 per cent from 1900 to 1930 and 1·3 per cent from 1930 to 1950 have little claim to accuracy,[3] and merely reflect an impression that sometime between the turn of the century and the Second World War the hitherto slow rate of growth of African population gave way to a pronounced, if still relatively modest, upturn. This impression is

168

confirmed by a few case-studies of particular rural societies which point to a continuous expansion in population numbers, at a rate of about one per cent per annum, from at least the First World War years. But if the distribution, timing and causes of this increase in population are little understood, its consequences were becoming apparent in several areas during the 1930s.

Agronomic difficulties of adjustment to higher rates of population growth were by no means universal—large parts of Subsaharan Africa, more especially in the West-Central region, still had low population/land ratios and additional numbers could be accommodated easily. And although evidence of population pressure on land can be found in certain pockets of the West African savanna, the phenomenon appeared in most acute form in those parts of Africa, principally South Africa, Southern Rhodesia, and Kenya, where official land policies had set aside extensive areas for exclusively European occupation and had allocated land to African agrarian communities with little or no consideration for population dynamics. The South African government, for example, established a clear-cut division between European and African land as early as 1913, through the Native Land Act of that year; similar legislation came later in Southern Rhodesia and Kenya—in the Land Apportionment Act of 1930 and the Native Lands Trust Ordinance of 1938—but in practice these measures merely gave a final statutory definition to a division of land-holding which had been administratively enforced since before the First World War. The situation of a growing African rural population hemmed in behind fixed land boundaries was further complicated by the fact that African production for the market in these economies proceeded primarily through land-extensive techniques—plough-cultivation of maize and livestock herding—so that the activities of a commercially oriented minority further diminished the amount of land available to support an increase in human and livestock numbers. By the 1930s, fragmentation of holdings, a breakdown in the cycle of natural fallowing, overcropping and overgrazing, soil erosion and a spate of land litigation were spreading, with varying degrees of incidence, through the African-inhabited areas of immigrant-dominated Southern and Eastern Africa, from Basutoland to the Kikuyu reserves of Kenya, and for a growing number of individuals and households, caught in a rising tide of rural deprivation, the labour market offered the only certain avenue to secure incomes.

169

THE SECOND WORLD WAR

From the stresses and strains of the 1930s—commercial, financial and social—the Second World War brought only slight relief, while at the same time adding further complications to Subsaharan Africa's relations with the rest of the world economy. War, and preparations for war, brought a return to reflationary conditions in the international economy as a whole and to an expansion of demand for Africa's primary products—more especially commodities of military-strategic significance like vegetable oils, metals and industrial diamonds. From 1942, the Japanese occupation of South-East Asia rendered Africa's productive capacity even more important to the war effort of the Western Allies, the palm produce and groundnuts of West and West-Central Africa and the tin mined in Nigeria and the Congo being among the commodities formerly supplied by South-East Asia, while the loss of Malayan and Indonesian sources of rubber gave a boost to Firestone's rubber planting in Liberia and led to a recrudescence of wild-rubber foraging in Nigeria, French Equatorial Africa, the Belgian Congo and Tanganyika. This buoyant demand for African commodities, however, was not fully matched by an upward shift in prices, and African economies gained less from export earnings than they might otherwise have done, because Africa's external commerce became subjected to a series of wartime marketing controls which transformed African production and distribution into an extension of the Allied, and more especially the British, 'siege economy'.

The intervention of the British metropolitan government into African commodity transactions initially began in 1939–40 with guaranteed sales for colonial produce—West African cocoa or Uganda cotton—which were particularly susceptible to dislocations of trading arrangements or shipping shortages, but gradually desires to secure primary produce for Britain, and through Britain for the other Allies, and conversely to deny commodities to the Axis powers, led to arrangements by which the British government became the monopoly purchaser of exports from British colonies. During 1940–1, the administrations of the Belgian Congo and French Equatorial Africa instituted similar arrangements with Britain, leaving only French West Africa, the commerce of which slumped savagely after the fall of France, and the Portuguese colonies, which were obliged to send designated commodities to metropolitan

Portugal, outside the British-controlled system of commodity allocation. Although details of the latter's pricing policy are obscure, the evidence suggests that, in line with wartime price controls in Britain and America, the second most important market for African produce, the generally low prices prevailing in the late 1930s were used as a guide in the early years of the war and that only between 1943 and 1945 was Africa's changed position as a supplier of primary produce reflected in higher prices.

Alongside, and primarily in response to, the metropolitan monopoly of purchasing, statutory or administratively based organizations with a monopoly of exporting emerged in British colonies. While some of these were producers' associations, representing mining, plantation and settler-farmer interests, the West African Cocoa Control Board of 1941 and its successor, the West African Produce Control Board of 1942 which handled all West African peasant-grown agricultural commodities, were state bodies which employed the expatriate mercantile companies as their agents. Rather than the statutory producers' monopoly recommended by the Nowell Commission, therefore, the wartime marketing boards of British West Africa were effectively dealers' monopolies over which African farmers had no control. Apart from the administrative convenience of negotiating with Britain, the Produce Control Board was justified on the grounds that it facilitated price stabilization, which involved withholding part of the producer's earnings and setting it aside in reserve funds for use as price support in times of slump. This aspect of the Board's functions, however, had more the character of a forced levy, to bolster the currency reserves of the metropolitan government for the duration of the war, and should be seen against broadly similar strategies applied to smallholders' incomes elsewhere. In Uganda, French Equatorial Africa and the Congo, for example, state pricing or fiscal measures held back African agricultural incomes and created reserve funds without resort to formal produce-control boards.

The great majority of Subsaharan Africa's peasant producers, it seems, experienced static or falling money incomes during the war years, while real incomes were sharply eroded by the lack, or relative weakness, of controls over import and domestic prices. The colonial state, abjuring price incentives as a means to higher output from African holdings, employed injunction, ranging from exhortation in British colonies to open compulsion, an intensification of the regi-

171

mentation of the 1930s, in French West and Equatorial Africa and the Belgian Congo. The administrations of the latter territories were especially prone to coercive direction of peasant cash-cropping, and the allocation of labour to expatriate concerns, as one of the few ways in which they could directly assist their metropolitan governments-in-exile.

Mining and plantation activities tended to escape the thinly disguised taxation imposed upon peasant production and, represented by their producers' organizations, were in a position to obtain better terms for their commodities (although the extent to which they were more successful in this respect is unclear). On the other hand, they experienced labour shortages and/or labour unrest associated with the effects of rising import prices on real wages, as well as a scarcity of imported capital goods.

The disruption of normal trading patterns meant that imports into Africa were both more scarce and more highly priced. New overseas suppliers appeared to fill the gap partially—India replacing Japan as a source of cheap cotton textiles or the United States replacing Western Europe as a source of machinery and other capital goods—but the import-substitution effect of trade dislocation was nevertheless more pronounced during the Second World War than during the First. Small-scale food processing and the manufacturing of soap, clothing, furniture, household utensils and other simple consumer goods developed in many urban centres in the course of the war, but only in South Africa, and perhaps to a lesser extent in Southern Rhodesia, can this be said to have been an additional stimulus to an already incipient industrialization. South Africa, in which was located the only well-established iron and steel industry south of the Sahara, was not only in a position to supply the metals and machinery needs of mining and engineering operations as far north as Katanga and for consumer goods industries in South Africa itself, but temporarily became an exporter of manufactured goods to overseas markets (in the shape of armaments, clothing and footwear sent to the war zones of the Middle East and South-East Asia). Its transition from a purely mining and agricultural economy continued through the war years, the role of the state in this process being further emphasized by the creation in 1940 of an Industrial Development Corporation to finance new industries.

Constraints on government finance eased somewhat between 1939 and 1945, as the expansion of exports and higher rates of taxation brought increased revenues and the Colonial Development and Welfare Act of 1940 offered the administrations of British colonies a slightly more generous supply of metropolitan funds. Against this, however, projects in support of military-strategic requirements took first priority in official expenditures, and shortages of technical and managerial manpower prevented governments from making full use of the revenues at their disposal. Infrastructural and welfare programmes planned before the war were either abandoned or operated at a reduced level, while new needs emerged. A particularly critical situation arose in the area of urban housing and sanitation as immigrants from the countryside, responding to the labour needs of growing service and manufacturing sectors and escaping from low rural incomes, administrative coercion or (in certain localities) the stresses of population pressure on land, flocked to the towns and cities and placed additional burdens on overstretched urban facilities. Deterioration in conditions of urban life was only one facet of the restrictions on distribution of income from exporting activity through which Subsaharan Africa, and more especially its peasant farmers and wage-labourers, contributed to the eventual Allied victory in 1945.

Between 1929 and 1945 the external commerce which historically provided the principal propulsion to economic change in Africa staggered and stuttered through depression, recession and war. That Subsaharan Africa's total trade by value in 1945 was only some 69 per cent above the 1929 level meant that during this period Africa's commerce grew more slowly than over any equivalent period since 1897 (see Appendices I–III). Certain regions and territories, it is true, fared better than others. Southern Africa's external trade, thanks mainly to South Africa's gold exports, actually rose more during 1929–45 than during the period 1913–29, while its share of African commerce, which had been falling consistently since 1897, increased slightly. The slow-down in the rate of growth of trade was most pronounced in West, West-Central and Eastern Africa, and most of the economies of these regions became locked into a virtual impasse, denied significant gains from trade by the severely disturbed state of the international economy but equally denied the opportunity to shift to a more autarchic path by official policies which favoured

173

export production. Structural change in response to overseas market opportunities was confined to a mere handful of African economies.

The period, however, was something more than a brief unfortunate interlude in African economic history. For Subsaharan Africa, in common with other parts of the world, had passed through a decade and a half in which the self-equilibrating market and monetary mechanisms of the classic 'liberal' international economy had finally broken down and regulation of the market by the state had emerged as the accepted means by which a new set of domestic and inter-national economic relations could be forged. In Subsaharan Africa, as in Western Europe and America, the most discernible trend of the 1930s and early 1940s was the growth of government direction of economic activity, initially in attempts to deal with the problems of the depression but culminating in the widespread controls over the allocation of goods and services during the Second World War. *Laissez-faire* capitalism had always had shallow roots in African soil but, whether in the Congo government's nationalization of the Matadi-Leopoldville railway line, the South African government's creation of an Industrial Development Corporation, or the trans-formation of British West African commodity-exporting from private oligopoly to public monopoly, the drift of official policy between 1929 and 1945 was clearly and unmistakably away from arbitration between conflicting private interests towards an expan-sion of the public sector and the adoption by the state of responsibi-lity and powers for management of the economic system. This trend, coalescing with and influenced by new attitudes to relations between the economy and the state in metropolitan Europe, would have a lasting legacy for the next phase of African interaction with the world economy.

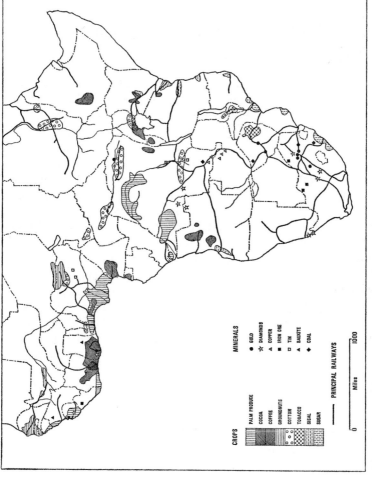

CROPS

PALM PRODUCE
COCOA
COFFEE
GROUNDNUTS
COTTON
TOBACCO
SISAL
SUGAR

MINERALS

● GOLD
☆ DIAMONDS
▲ COPPER
■ IRON ORE
□ TIN
▲ BAUXITE
✦ COAL

PRINCIPAL RAILWAYS

Miles

0   1000

Map 4. Principal Centres of Export Production, 1960

Seven

Post-war growth and terminal colonialism, 1945–1960

The Second World War, in stark contrast to the First, gave way to the most expansionary and buoyant phase in the long history of the Western-centred international economy, surpassing even such earlier periods of global boom as the mid-nineteenth century and the first decade and a half of the twentieth century. The reconstruction of war-torn economies and the abandonment of war-time controls on the movement of commodities and convertibility of currencies, substantially completed by 1950, was followed by a decade of rapid growth in world output and exchange. Cyclical downturns comparable in scale or intensity to the depressions of 1921–2 or 1929–30 vanished from the world scene, and the international economy, which in the early 1930s appeared to be heading for imminent collapse, seemed from the vantage of the late 1950s to have been placed upon a new and more solid footing.

The proximate causes of this revival of the global capitalist system from the set-backs of the inter-war years are well known. The recreation of a world monetary system, effectively a dollar standard, by the Bretton Woods Conference of 1944 which set up the International Monetary Fund and the World Bank, the Marshall Plan by which the United States of America assisted Western Europe's recovery from war, the General Agreement on Tariffs and Trade which partially liberalized commercial relations between states and the trend towards economic and political co-operation in Europe which culminated in the establishment of the European Economic Community in 1956, were all part of a broad strategy through which, under American leadership and against the background of the Cold War, the principal Western economies undid the 'mistakes' of the inter-war years and re-equipped the international economy with a new institutional framework. At a deeper level, it is frequently

176

argued that the post-war era saw the evolution of a vigorous 'new capitalism' in the international economy's North Atlantic heartland, although opinions differ about the form that this took. To one school of thought, the 'new capitalism' involved the advance of state power, regulating and controlling private enterprise, employing Keynesian theories of economic management to maintain high levels of employment and rates of economic growth, and expanding social services through the creation of the Welfare State. To another school of thought, principally if not exclusively Marxist, the distinctive feature of post-war capitalism was the rise of corporate power, a further flourish of business concentration leading to oligopolistic domination within national markets and the spread of vertically integrated multinational firms which operated across political boundaries. Whatever the true explanation of the course of events, the industrial economies at the centre of world trade and finance experienced a rapid growth of output, with rates of growth of Gross National Product ranging from $2 \cdot 5$ per cent for the United Kingdom to $7 \cdot 6$ per cent for Germany in the 1950s, high levels of investment in new processes, a speeding-up in technological innovation, and a substantial increase in real incomes for all social classes. World trade, increasing at a rate of six per cent per annum from 1945 to 1960, grew even faster than world output.

For the African economies at the periphery of the resurgent international economy, the end of the war meant the entry into the most pronounced export boom they had ever experienced. Initially this was overshadowed and somewhat distorted by the maintenance of wartime controls over trade, shortages and high prices of imports and an unsettled currency situation in European metropolitan economies. The years between 1945 and 1949 were consequently a time of considerable labour, and to a lesser extent agrarian, unrest. But from approximately 1948 onwards, the prevailing atmosphere of uncertainty gave way to a mood of optimism and expectation as world demand for African commodities continued to expand strongly and to bring release from post-war austerity. The reconstruction and re-equipment of Western industrial economies, the gradual removal of restrictions on consumer demand and the growth of real incomes there, and the commodity stockpiling engendered by the outbreak of the Korean War in 1950 resulted in prices for Africa's produce rising to unprecedented heights. For the first time since at least before the

First World War, the barter terms of trade ran strongly in favour of the African economies over a period of several years. On an index for which 1948 = 100, for example, Nigeria's net barter terms of trade reached 139 in 1954, Kenya's 150 in 1953 and Angola's 218 in the same year. Various commodities arrived at their post-war price peaks in different years—cotton, rubber and tin in 1951, cocoa and coffee in 1954, and copper in 1955—and the improvement in terms of trade therefore ended somewhat earlier for some economies than for others. In general, a slow secular fall in export prices occurred from the mid-1950s onwards which, unaccompanied by any corresponding decline in import values, resulted in a gradual deterioration in the terms of trade and a slow-down in the rate of growth of external commerce by value. The volume of exports, however, continued to expand as investment conducted during the years of high prices in the late 1940s and early 1950s created additional output.

Although shadows were beginning to hover over African commerce in the late 1950s, the years between 1945 and 1960, at which latter date colonial regimes were in the process of transferring authority to popularly elected governments in all but Southern Africa, can be fairly represented as a period in which the producers and administrations of Subsaharan Africa made unparalleled gains from participation in international trade. Over these years, Subsaharan Africa's total trade by value increased from £603,000,000 to £3,782,000,000 (see Appendix I). This massive 526 per cent rise contrasts with a growth of 164 per cent between 1897 and 1913, and a further 221 per cent over the longer time-span from 1913 to 1945. Admittedly, measurement in current prices, reflecting the inflation which was a constant element after 1945, somewhat overstates the increase of 1945–60, but even so the period remains an outstanding one in the history of African participation in global exchange. Table 5 provides some indication of the scale of growth in commodity production over this period, the figures being arranged for convenience on a regional rather than a territorial basis. Although increases in output varied by commodity and by region, the overall perspective is one of sizeable growth, especially marked in the case of groundnuts in West Africa, coffee in West, West-Central and Eastern Africa and cotton in all four regions, while the rise in mineral production was, if anything, even greater than in export crops. Whether measured by figures for production or exchange, the pace of economic change speeded up

TABLE 5 Production of Selected Commodities by Region, 1947 and 1957 (thousand metric tons unless otherwise stated)

	WEST			WEST-CENTRAL			EASTERN			SOUTHERN		
	1947	1957	% Change	1947	1957	% Change	1947	1957	% Change	1947	1957	% Change
Groundnuts	1,410	2,844	101	274	177	−35	192	182	−5	76	138	81
Palm Kernels	666ᵃ	631	−5	148ᵃ	238	60	—	—	—	—	—	—
Cocoa	356	442	24	n.a.	8	—	—	—	—	—	—	—
Coffee	55	133	141	81	149	83	60	160	166	—	—	—
Cotton	13	56	330	67	91	35	83	155	86	24	39	62
Sugar	—	—	—	59	84	42	75	131	74	545	1,035	89
Tobacco	—	—	—	—	—	—	—	—	—	72	118	63
Tea	—	—	—	0·1	2	1,900	8	17	112	8	16	100
Sisal	—	—	—	21ᵃ	46	119	165ᵃ	406	146	18	31	72
Copper	—	—	—	150	244	62	—	—	—	230	497	116
Iron Ore	70	2,180	3,014	—	—	—	—	—	—	1,118	1,390	24
Manganese	311	305	−2	5	194	3,780	—	—	—	121	310	75
Bauxite (crude ore)	131	540	312	—	—	—	—	—	—	—	—	—
Diamonds (carats 000's)	1,520	4,094	169	6,380	16,620	160	92	391	325	1,421	3,576	151
Chromite	n.a.	7	—	—	—	—	—	—	—	246	610	147
Tin	9,383	9,766	4	12,610	14,510	15	250	55	−78	786	2,133	171

NOTES: ᵃ 1950

SOURCES: U.N., *Review of Economic Conditions in Africa* (1951); U.N., *Economic Survey of Africa since 1950* (1960)

dramatically in Africa after the Second World War and the sub-continent entered a new era of interplay with the wider world economy.

GOVERNMENT: FINANCE AND 'PLANNING'

If one external dimension to Subsaharan Africa's post-war economic history was the unusually high overseas demand for African produce between the late 1940s and early 1950s, a second was a new commitment by governments in metropolitan Europe to the 'development' of their African dependencies, more especially by abandoning the doctrine of financial self-sufficiency for colonies. This adoption of what came to be known as 'responsible colonialism' was born out of a mixture of genuine humanitarian concern about poverty in Africa, a sense of moral obligation for wartime assistance, and a very large dose of self-interest. World commerce emerged from the war firmly concentrated into the trading blocs of the dollar and sterling areas and the franc zone, and to a dollar-scarce Europe the possibility of enlarging African exports, as a means both of savings on imports and earning currency from the dollar area, had a powerful appeal. Britain's Colonial Development and Welfare Act of 1945 and France's *Fonds d'investissement pour le développement économique et social* (F.I.D.E.S.) of 1946 must be seen against these immediate post-war goals. As time passed, and as Europe's dollar shortages eased, the metropolitan 'aid' programmes assumed a different rationale, being justified by statesmen on the grounds that they provided markets for metropolitan goods as well as finance for colonial 'development'. Assumption of responsibility for supplying grants and low-interest loans also secured for metropolitan governments a greater measure of control over, and ability to coordinate and influence, the investment policies of colonial administrations. France in particular, unlike Britain or Belgium, had espoused the goal of 'assimilating' colonies to the metropolis, as evinced in the constitution of the new French Union in 1946, and its colonial 'aid' was linked to the public investment programmes through which the *polytechniciens* in the French bureaucracy conducted their Plans of Modernization for France itself.

But whatever the motive or intentions behind the growth of metropolitan 'development' funds and agencies, the fact remains that sums considerably in excess of and on more generous terms than anything

180

which had gone before, were made available to the administrations of colonial Africa after 1945. In French West Africa, for example, more than twice as much public investment took place in the ten years from 1946 to 1956 than in the entire period from 1903 to 1946. Strictly comparable figures on the flow of metropolitan financial assistance over the years from 1945 to 1960 are not available, but some indication of its dimensions is the fact that during 1954–8 Britain supplied the equivalent of $143,700,000 to its colonies in Eastern Africa, $62,600,000 to West Africa and $58,200,000 to Southern Africa, while France provided the equivalent of $346,500,000 to French West Africa and the Cameroons, and $111,200,000 to French Equatorial Africa. Belgium and Portugal, on the other hand, supplied little or no direct financial aid to their African possessions, although the former at least was prepared to guarantee loans from the World Bank.

External finance was one bulwark of an expansion in state activity, a growth of the public sector and a close regulation of the market which characterized the political economy of post-1945 Subsaharan Africa. This trend was both a legacy of earlier intervention during depression and war and a reflection of parallel metropolitan shifts in the direction of the managed economy. To be sure, governments in Africa, with the exception of South Africa, lacked the full panoply of regulatory controls, more especially in the area of money supply, and were therefore unable to undertake the same kind of counter-cyclical measures engaged in by European governments, but although managerial goals might differ, the concept of the managed economy seems as applicable to post-1945 Africa as to post-1945 Europe. Central to the advance of state regulation and direction were the 'Development Plans' instituted by virtually every administration in Africa between 1945 and 1950, a few of which, like those for Angola and Uganda, were already in the pipeline but the great majority of which were responses to post-war requests for 'plans' to which metropolitan finance might be supplied. Revised or second 'plans' appeared during the 1950s. None were growth plans in the sense of setting targets for levels of production or employment and allocating resources to that end, but were, rather, long-term public expenditure programmes which brought a greater degree of co-ordination to the functions of government departments and the various boards, commissions, corporations and other agencies which sprang to life as arms of the

181

state. Only South Africa lacked a 'Development Plan' giving formal expression to political and bureaucratic command of structural change in the economy, but here a handful of powerful public corporations, principally I.S.C.O.R. and the Industrial Development Corporation, took a central role in co-ordinating state activities (rather along the lines of E.N.I. and I.R.I. in Italy).

Finance for the 'Development Plans' came partly from metro-politan aid, partly from borrowings from external sources of capital, including the World Bank, and partly from local revenues. The relative importance of each varied considerably, from the 'plans' of the Belgian Congo or Angola which relied almost totally on the latter two sources of capital, through an intermediate position occupied by most British colonies, to French West and Equatorial Africa which relied heavily upon metropolitan public finance from F.I.D.E.S. and C.C.F.O.M. (*Caisse Centrale de la France d'Outremer*). Increases in local revenues, and in turn the ability to raise commercial loans, were a consequence of buoyant world demand for African commodities and the growth of external trade, and among the fiscal devices intro-duced to tax the latter the statutory marketing boards of British colonies held a special place.

The marketing boards established throughout British colonies between 1945 and the early 1950s were lineal descendants of wartime produce control agencies, being set up to administer the accumulated reserves, to continue monopoly export and sometimes internal trade in particular commodities, to provide supporting services and to operate price-stabilization schemes. The West African Produce Control Board, for example, was succeeded by marketing boards for cocoa, palm produce, groundnuts and cotton in Nigeria, cocoa in the Gold Coast, palm produce in Sierra Leone and groundnuts in the Gambia, while in Uganda a Cotton Lint Board was created in 1949 and a Coffee Industry Board in 1953. The system perhaps reached its apex in Kenya where, by 1953, marketing boards had been established for almost every conceivable agricultural commodity. Considerable controversy surrounds the operations of these boards, in particular their price-stabilization goals. Critics point out that stabilization of prices could mean destabilization of incomes in situations of fluctua-ting output and there is debate as to whether or how far 'stable' prices influenced the allocative decisions of producers.[1] It is generally agreed, however, that the marketing boards, more especially in

182

economies where export earnings accrued principally from small-holder cash-cropping, had a highly significant fiscal role, and indeed served as the principal regulatory device employed by the state. High world prices for primary produce meant that marketing boards did not have to intervene to support farm prices until the late 1950s, and in the meantime they accumulated sizeable funds from withholding part of the producers' price. Some of the funds were held in reserve for future price support and, banked in London, made an important contribution to Britain's sterling balances—African holdings of sterling, including the reserves of marketing and currency boards, rose from £204,000,000 in 1946 to a peak of £720,000,000 in 1956. The boards' revenues, however, were also allocated to aspects of the colonial 'Development Plans' deemed relevant to their particular commodity and in this respect their operations may be regarded as a form of forced saving, holding back private consumption and chan-nelling export earnings towards the expansion of 'social overhead capital'.

Arrangements for public marketing and 'price stabilization' in French, Belgian and Portuguese colonies took different administra-tive forms from those in British colonies, coming closest to the latter perhaps in the organization of cotton-marketing in the Belgian Congo and A.E.F., and no easy comparisons of tendencies to limit private consumption by such means can be made. On the whole, French administrations reintroduced 'price stabilization' mechanisms some-what later than British colonial governments, the *caisses de stabilisa-tion* which levied additional export duties being set up in the mid-1950s, towards the end of the phase of rising commodity prices, and therefore failing to accumulate funds on the scale of the British marketing boards.

Of the three broad categories into which the expenditures of the colonial 'Development Plans' are conventionally divided—namely infrastructure, social services, and agriculture and other production—the last normally had lowest priority. The First Plan for the French Colonies (1946–56), for example, allocated only 18 per cent of its available finance to 'production' while the Ten Year Plan for the Belgian Congo (1950–60) allowed, even when revised in 1953, only 4·3 per cent for agriculture. Social services, including education, health and urban housing, fared somewhat better and despite their limitations, particularly the tendency to concentrate resources on the cities rather than the countryside, the 'public welfare' programmes of colonial governments were substantially better funded after 1945. This reflected not merely the shift to 'welfare capitalism' in European thinking about the appropriate role of the state but also the growth of African political organizations which demanded more and better social services.

Enlargement of infrastructure, however, had pride of place in colonial 'planning' priorities since this was regarded as the principal means by which government could contribute to the expansion of export production and reduce physical and environmental constraints on exploitation of the commodity boom. Investment in port improvements—in dredging, providing new berths and constructing larger handling and storage facilities—went on in such places as Mombasa, Dar es Salaam, Lourenço Marques and Lagos, while in West Africa, notoriously deficient in natural deep-water harbours, the construction of two entirely new ports, Tema in the Gold Coast and Abidjan in the Ivory Coast, brought major additions to capacity to handle shipping. In strategies for internal transport, railways now tended to take second place to roads. Although the track, rolling-stock and other equipment of railways were modernized, only a few, relatively short sections of new line were built between 1945 and 1960, most of them, like the Kampala-Kasese extension in Uganda or the Conakry-Fria line in Guinea, built to serve newly discovered areas of mineral production. The road networks of most economies, by contrast, were considerably enlarged and, although still deficient in all-weather surfaces or bridges, facilitated a shift to the more flexible lorry and bus transport for goods and passengers, a closer integration of rural and urban markets, and a new, if highly competitive, field of enterprise for the small businessman.

Electrification, and more particularly the development of hydro-electric sources of energy, was another major item of public expenditure, for the harnessing of waterpower had come to be seen as a means of overcoming the shortage of fossil fuels which existed everywhere outside South Africa. The great majority of post-war hydro-electricity schemes were relatively small-scale, but at least four outstanding dam and power-station complexes were built between 1945 and 1960—at Owen Falls on the Nile in Uganda (1948–53), the Zilo-Le Marinel complex on the Lualaba river in the Belgian Congo (1948–56), the Edea scheme on the Sanaga river in the Cameroons (1950–3), and the Kariba dam on the Zambezi between Northern and Southern Rhodesia (1955–60). Le Marinel was a Union Minière project while the others were publicly financed and managed, but all were associated with plans to provide power for existing or new mineral refining-smelting concerns which made heavy demands on energy, as well as for more general urban and industrial consumption. The Owen Falls project, for example, made possible the erection of a copper-refining plant at the town of Jinja to process ore from the newly opened Kilembe mines; the Edea scheme was influenced by the demands of the French aluminium industry for additional sources of energy and a French consortium, led by the Sociétés Pechiney et Ugine, installed an aluminium-smelting factory which from 1957 drew its bauxite from mines in Guinea.

The large government expenditures of this period, and the growth of the bureaucracy itself, meant a considerable expansion in the need for technical and managerial manpower. The great majority of such posts which opened up, however, although the incidence varied from territory to territory, were filled by incoming Europeans, for although colonial governments did not totally neglect the provision of technical education for local people, their efforts were comparatively modest and could not match the requirements of their 'development plans'. This feature, plus the growth of equivalent opportunities in the private sector, resulted in a fresh influx of Europeans into Subsaharan Africa in the post-war years, an immigration which was by no means confined to such historical centres of European settlement as South Africa, the Rhodesias or Kenya. In French West Africa, for example, where reliance on immigrants from the metropolis was more extreme than in neighbouring British colonies, the European population rose from 32,000 in 1946 to 90,000 in 1956, while in the Belgian Congo a European population of 56,000 in 1950 swelled to 110,000 by 1960. Many of the newcomers were on short-term contract, and therefore differed in their social and political ambitions from those who intended to settle permanently in Africa, but their presence contributed to 'leakages' from the local economy in the form of repatriated savings and high levels of demand for imported luxury consumer goods.

AGRICULTURE AND AGRARIAN SOCIETY

Although agriculture had a lower priority than infrastructure or social services in official allocations of financial resources, it did not remain free from government intervention and control. Indeed, the post-war trend was in the opposite direction—towards a more constant official supervision of every aspect of agricultural production and distribution. African smallholders in particular came under increasing administrative pressure to introduce what were regarded as 'scientific' and 'rational' methods of production for, although colonial governments continued to supply company and settler-planter estates with a wide range of supporting services and facilities, they tended to avoid interference with day-to-day management of these undertakings. Such restraint was weaker in official attitudes to African farming. Practices varied from territory to territory, administrative direction of agricultural change being a more pronounced characteristic of the Eastern, Southern or West-Central regions than of West Africa, but even the governments of the Gold Coast and Nigeria employed compulsory measures to eradicate swollen shoot disease from African cocoa farms.

A wide range of state organizations existed, or were brought into being, to formulate and apply policy towards agriculture and African agrarian societies. Some were purely research institutes, conducting investigations into seed varieties, crop rotations, pest control and other aspects of arable and pastoral technique, and diffusing their findings through government agricultural departments and related bodies which attempted to put research findings into practice. Others, like the *Institut National pour l'Étude Agronomique du Congo Belge*, carried out both functions. So diverse were agrarian conditions, so many were the official organizations concerned with promoting change, and so numerous were the projects launched that any comprehensive assessment of the impact of the state on agricultural practice and performance is beyond the scope of this chapter. In broad terms, however, three principal and partly interlocking sets of ideas seem to have dominated the thinking and engaged the greater part of the energies of colonial agricultural officers between 1945 and at least the mid-1950s. The first was the need to combat soil erosion, whether caused by over-concentration on cash-crop production or the pressures of human and animal populations on land, the second to raise output through the mechanization of agriculture, and the third to resettle African populations in new areas as a means both of achieving the first two goals and of facilitating the exercise of closer control over the agricultural practices of the resettled people. In the main, these ideas applied more to savanna than to forest agriculture, and colonial pressures were exerted more strongly upon the inhabitants of the former zones.

Official concern for soil conservation is exemplified in West Africa by the French introduction of a new three-year rotation of crops to overcome the soil exhaustion which emphasis on export production was bringing to the groundnut fields of Senegal, while in parts of Eastern and Southern Africa, where a combination of hilly or mountainous terrain, concentration of population into relatively dense pockets, irregular rainfall and land-extensive farming practices rendered soil erosion a more prominent feature of the rural scene, agricultural officers initiated soil conservation programmes with considerable zeal.

If new crop rotations and contour-terracing were regarded as the key to halting the trend towards agronomic deterioriation, the tractor was seized upon with even greater enthusiasm as the technological mainspring for a transformation of productivity in savanna agriculture. The story of bureaucratic muddle and planning inefficiencies which surrounded British projects to promote mechanization, more especially in the notorious groundnut scheme in southern Tanganyika and the smaller-scale project in the Niger Province of Nigeria, is perhaps too well-known to bear repetition. The enthusiasm for mechanized clearing of land which proved to have intractable root growth or became liable to erosion when stripped of natural vegetation, and for which labour-intensive hoe cultivation was therefore better suited, was not a peculiarly British disease, however. Even when British ardour began to cool in the early and middle 1950s, the French persisted with similar programmes in the Casamansce area of Senegal and the Niari Valley of Middle Congo in Equatorial Africa.

Both soil conservation and mechanization schemes involved some relocation of villages and settlements and government-directed colonization of new localities. But possibly only in the Belgian Congo can the resettlement of African populations be said to have been the central element of government policy towards smallholder agriculture. Here I.N.E.A.C., established in 1933 to operate the *paysannat indigène* programme, decided from 1948 onwards to concentrate its efforts upon the creation and management of new village communities, on the grounds that a physical and psychological break with 'traditional' farming and social systems was necessary for the successful commercialization of African agriculture. By 1958 some 200,000 households (representing a little under 20 per cent of the Congo's agrarian population) had been resettled in these *paysannats*, principally in Orientale and Kasai provinces, and produced cotton, groundnuts and other commodities under carefully controlled rotational methods.

Such brief descriptions do not fully exhaust the broad spectrum of official 'planning' and action. The continuing commercial success of the Gezira Scheme, which in 1950 became a fully state-run project with the exclusion of the Sudan Plantations Syndicate, and the further expansion of irrigated acreages under its aegis, meant an on-going interest in irrigation projects, both large and small, elsewhere. The French equivalent, the *Office du Niger*, on the other hand, remained singularly unsuccessful in securing a return for the heavy investment in dams and canals both before and after the Second World War (investment which amounted to the equivalent of $175,000,000 by 1960). At an entirely different level of official activity, encouragement of African smallholders to form co-operative organizations, both as marketing agencies and to conduct primary processing of crops, was much more clear-cut, and far less ambivalent, in the post-war years than it had been in the 1930s. The spread of peasant co-operatives was especially pronounced in British colonies, for the Belgian *paysannats* operated without such institutions and French administrators were slow to abandon the authoritarian traditions of the *sociétés de prévoyance*.

An increased intensity in state direction of agricultural practices was undoubtedly a major characteristic of post-war Africa. What is less certain, however, is the extent to which the growth in acreages under export crops, and to a lesser degree in food crops, and the rise in per-acre yields which occurred in at least some long-established centres of export production—the Northern Nigerian groundnut zone or the Uganda cotton belt—owed to direct government intervention and command, as opposed to the more 'permissive' administrative role in building rural roads and distributing better seed. The interaction between the colonial state and African agrarian societies varied so much from locality to locality that the relative weight of the forces for agricultural innovation is not immediately discernible. There is some reason to believe, however, that the striking advance in production for the market resulted more from 'private' enterprise and initiative, responding to exceptionally high world prices and the growth of internal urban and mining demand, than from the managerial expertise of the state.

A focus on coffee production provides some indication of the diversity of agrarian circumstances and the difficulties of generalization. Coffee may be described as the export crop *par excellence* of post-war tropical Africa, just as cocoa had been up to the early 1920s. It was capable of cultivation both by small- and large-scale methods and experienced conditions of buoyant demand related both to a growth of consumption in the industrial economies up to the mid-1950s and to the fact that *robusta*, the most common variety grown in Africa, was suited to the manufacture of instant coffee. One of the new centres of production was Ethiopia, where the Italian occupation of the late 1930s left a legacy of improved roads which permitted the exporting of agricultural commodities from the highlands. Coffee exports, rising in value from \$8,900,000 in 1949 to \$40,000,000 in 1953, quickly surpassed those of cereals, oilseeds and hides. The greater part of the output, however, was gathered from natural coffee forests in the western and south-western areas of the country which, nominally under government ownership, passed into the hands of members of Ethiopia's landowning aristocracy. A small class of landlords, who brought in labour from other areas to pick the berries, were the principal instigators and beneficiaries of Ethiopia's post-war coffee boom. Large estates were also responsible for a virtual doubling of Angola's coffee output, from 44,000 tons in 1947 to 80,000 tons in 1957, the principal differences from the Ethiopian situation being the fact that the owners were immigrant settler-planters from Portugal and that production involved investment in planting. Coffee-planting in Angola was therefore bound up with the colonization goals of Portugal's Salazar regime which resulted in a 400 per cent increase in Angola's post-war European population and in pressures on African communities to provide labour for the European estates which were reminiscent of the more crudely coercive labour policies employed by the colonial administrations before the 1930s.

Small- to medium-scale proprietorship, on the other hand, under-lay the increase in coffee-exporting from the Ivory Coast in West Africa and from Kenya and Uganda in Eastern Africa. In the Ivory

189

Coast, this development took the form of an expansion in cash-cropping in African agrarian societies, mainly the Agni and Boualé of the eastern and central districts, the export production of which had been slight before 1945. Improvements in transport facilities, especially the new port at Abidjan, made an important contribution but equally significant was the termination of the cumpulsory labour system in French West Africa, a system which had previously diverted the Ivory Coast's manpower towards the small coterie of French settler-planters. In Kenya, too, an easing of colonial restrictions on African agricultural enterprise, including a final lifting of the notorious ban on coffee-growing, and a closer government attention to the needs for services in the African-inhabited rural areas, accounted for a dramatic increase in smallholder coffee-production. Whereas, between 1950 and 1960, the coffee acreages of European-owned estates rose from 59,000 to 67,000, the acreages under African ownership increased from 5,000 to 26,000. Perhaps the most striking episode in the story of African reaction to the post-war coffee boom, however, occurred in Uganda and took the form of a conscious switch by many farmers from the established export staple, cotton, to a coffee crop which, for most of the 1950s, gave a much better return per unit of land. From 1945 to 1960, the area under cotton in Uganda rose by only 31 per cent, while that under coffee increased by a massive 264 per cent, and coffee overtook cotton as the principal export by value as early as 1955. This transformation, almost entirely the result of African market responsiveness, was located mainly in the Buganda area, where environmental conditions favoured the cultivation of either crop.

The range of socio-political settings within which coffee cultivation increased was exceptionally broad, from the manorial landlordism of Ethiopia to the nascent petty capitalism of the Ivory Coast country-side, and other export crops lacked this association with a diversity of social formations. Groundnuts, for example, remained very much a crop for the small peasant proprietor, and the post-war expansion of production in French West Africa and northern Nigeria is to be explained principally by an ever-growing number of cultivators who added a few acres to their foodcrop production. The tea and sisal of Kenya and Tanganyika, or the virginia tobacco of Southern Rhodesia, on the other hand, continued to be associated with larger-scale, and progressively more capital-intensive, methods of production,

190

usually metropolitan-financed company plantations in the case of tea and to a lesser extent sisal, and settler-planter estates in the case of virginia tobacco. The post-war growth of output of such crops normally involved increases in productivity through investment in new techniques. Nevertheless, one can detect a certain erosion in the former demarcation in cropping-patterns between estate and smallholder units, perceptible not only in the spread of coffee from European to African land in the Ivory Coast and Kenya, but also in the smallholder planting of rubber trees and oil palms alongside the Firestone estates in Liberia and the Huileries du Congo Belge plantations. A fluid state seems to have been developing in West, West-Central and Eastern Africa in which African production was becoming an acceptable alternative to official policy makers and metropolitan firms previously committed to the foreign- or expatriate-owned plantation.

African agriculture was also becoming progressively less and less a matter of purely 'peasant' activity. To be sure, the great majority of those involved in agrarian pursuits remained smallholders whose production for the market was balanced by production for household subsistence, but in most parts of Subsaharan Africa a growing minority of African farmers were engaged in a more commercially oriented, larger-scale agriculture. The rise of this minority, variously described as a rural élite or petty bourgeoisie, was part of a process of stratification in African societies in which opportunities to supply overseas or domestic markets interacted with and reinforced other forces making for social differentiation, including enterprise in local commerce and services, access to local political authority, the availability of formal education, and competition for land as a result of population growth and the spread of commercial agriculture. The trend differed in intensity and timing across the subcontinent, being well established in the cocoa-growing localities of the Gold Coast by the 1920s, but in Eastern and West-Central Africa, areas like the Ivory Coast in West Africa, and at least some territories in Southern Africa, it coincided mainly with the boom years of the late 1940s and early 1950s. Associated with the emergence of the labour-hiring, profit-oriented rural strata were changes in land tenurial arrangements and the development of a market in land. Concepts of individual proprietorship gained ground over kinship rights to land, and were gradually reflected in official legislation.

On the whole, colonial administrations trod warily on the land issues lying at the heart of social stratification in the rural areas, but during the 1950s the governments of at least three territories were prepared to intervene directly and attempt a restructuring of African rural societies through land reform programmes. All three ruled territories where earlier allocations of land to European immigrants had disturbed African methods of land use and where the African reserves or 'homelands' had been treated primarily as reservoirs of migrant labour for European-run agricultural, mining, manufacturing and commercial enterprises.

In Southern Rhodesia and Kenya, the principal centres of European settlement outside South Africa, rights to land had always been a particularly sensitive issue of political economy. By the late 1940s, years of demographic growth and official neglect had led to serious congestion of human and livestock population and a falling per capita production in many of the reserves set aside for African habitation. Developments within European settler agriculture, essentially a turn to more capital-intensive methods of farming which began in the late 1930s and continued through into the early 1950s, further exacerbated the African land shortage by reducing the need for 'squatter labour', the quasi-manorial practice by which Africans had hitherto obtained access to land in European-settled areas. The government of Southern Rhodesia made some provision for 'squatter' families being squeezed out of European farming localities by the Land Apportionment Amendment Act of 1950, which set aside some 9,000,000 acres of hitherto 'unassigned' land as Special Native Areas, but the administration of Kenya, where cultivatable land was in shorter supply, reacted more slowly and faced the revolt of the Kikuyu 'squatters' and landless men commonly known as 'Mau Mau'. The Emergency forced colonial officials in Kenya into a fundamental reappraisal of their policies towards African agriculture, paralleling a re-examination also under way in Southern Rhodesia as a consequence of recognition of the political 'dangers' of a disaffected rural African population and the need to create a 'middle class' of small-to-medium-scale African commercial farmers. Southern Rhodesia's Land Husbandry Act of 1951 and Kenya's Swynnerton Plan of 1954, therefore, were broadly similar in goal. They sought to alter the agrarian conditions in the reserves by a clear-cut, legally enforced division of African rural societies in to a landed, cash-

192

cropping stratum and a landless, labour-hiring stratum. The consolidation of holdings, their re-organization into 'planned' farm layouts and a registration of titles to land were the principal elements in the enforced land reforms.

Of the two programmes, however, the Swynnerton Plan was more vigorously prosecuted, was more generously backed with funds to assist an expansion of African cash-cropping, and represented a more complete break with earlier official neglect. The reasons for this would appear to lie partly in the fact that Southern Rhodesia's settler farmers, more solidly entrenched in political power than their counterparts in post-Emergency Kenya, were reluctant to see any too-successful application of a policy which, if carried to its logical conclusion, would render the productive capacity of the African reserves a powerful competitor to their own sector of the economy. Perhaps more significant still were the different perceptions of where the men created legally landless might find employment, for the Kenya authorities believed that such individuals should obtain their livelihoods in a more highly commercialized African agriculture while the Southern Rhodesian officials regarded them as potential recruits to the urban-industrial work force.

That industrialization would solve the problems of population pressure and agronomic deterioration in the countryside was also the crux of official policy in South Africa. Nowhere else on the sub-continent could contrasts be drawn more sharply between, on the one hand, a European-managed agriculture profitably engaged in meeting overseas demand for wool, sugar or fruit and a domestic urban-industrial demand for foodstuffs, and reinvesting in new technology, and on the other a stagnant African agriculture unable to provide even the bare minimum subsistence for its population and forced to release substantial amounts of migrant labour to the other sectors. The Tomlinson Commission of 1955, one of a long line of investigations into the state of the African 'homelands', considered that the latter's conditions had passed a point of no return and that a purely agricultural solution was no longer possible. It therefore recommended a drastic re-organization of African farming units which would render some 50 per cent of the population landless, and the establishment and manufacturing industries in the 'homelands' to employ the dispossessed. The South African government, however, while following the broad lines of the Commission's recommendations on land reform, preferred the establishment of 'border industries' within the country's white areas because this fitted more conveniently into its over-arching strategy of 'apartheid' or 'separate development of the races'.

Except in Kenya, these administrative re-organizations of African land tenure and land use did not, and were not intended to, challenge the predominance of European settler farming and planting in production for the market. By comparison with developments in West and Eastern Africa, and most of West-Central Africa, the post-war commodity boom tended to by-pass the African cultivators of Southern Africa, whose participation in the market economy was circumscribed by, and subordinate to, the demands of the other sectors.

MINING

Throughout the post-war years Southern Africa remained, as it always had been, the region where extraction of minerals made the most substantial contribution to earnings from external trade and the economies of the region, together with the Belgian Congo, were responsible for the greater part of Subsaharan Africa's post-war growth in mineral production. Eastern Africa supplied very few minerals to overseas markets, apart from diamonds from central Tanganyika and a little copper from western Uganda, and the primary producing foundations of its economies remained almost exclusively agricultural. In West Africa, the pattern of a few relatively isolated 'islands' of mining surrounded by African agricultural production was added to, but not substantially altered, by the opening-up of newly discovered deposits by foreign firms. Prominent among the newcomers were the American-owned Liberia Mining Company which from 1951 extracted iron ore from the Bomi Hills north of Monrovia, the Fria Company which was controlled by the same French consortium as the aluminium smelter at Edea in the Cameroons and which began to mine bauxite in Guinea in the mid-1950s, and the Shell-B.P. Petroleum Company which made its first small oil strike in the Niger Delta of eastern Nigeria in 1953. The penetration of West Africa by international mining-refining concerns proceeded at a more rapid pace after 1945.

Mining in West Africa, as well as in Eastern and most of West-Central Africa, tended to be highly enclavistic, inducing few changes

194

in other sectors of the local economy. Foreign-owned firms extracted crude ores for export to other locations for processing, refining and manufacturing and imported virtually every piece of equipment. They made little effort to foster local manufacturing of their inputs and repatriated their profits overseas. Through the payment of royalties and taxes, it is true, they contributed to government revenues—but against this, they normally made heavy demands on government for the provision of railways, roads, power and other public services. Only through their wage-bills, creating some local demand for goods and services, did the mines have any significant impact on the other sectors, but even this was limited by the use of capital-intensive methods of production which held back the growth of employment.

In a fairly typical West African economy like Nigeria, the share of mining in Gross Domestic Product during the late 1950s was only one per cent—as compared with 16 per cent in the Belgian Congo and 45 per cent in Northern Rhodesia. In the Congo the two giants, Forminière and Union Minière, continued to predominate in mining. The post-war rise in Forminière's output of diamonds, from 5,000 carats in 1947 to 16,000 in 1958, was a response to the growing world demand for industrial diamonds, for which the Congo was the principal source of supply in Africa. Union Minière's copper, however, remained the Congo's foremost export, and the company's highly profitable activities in Katanga further benefited from sales of cobalt, zinc and uranium associated with the copper deposits. Heavy investment in mechanized open-cast mining and the introduction of electrolytic refining rendered Union Minière's operations among the most efficient in the world, and in Katanga the company ran what was effectively a state within a state. Through its numerous subsidiaries it controlled coal-mining, electricity and the urban water supply, manufacturing enterprises which ranged from chemical and refrigeration plant to flour-milling and brewing, as well as banks, hotels and hospitals. Probably no other single private concern in Subsaharan Africa exerted such an all-pervading influence on the local economy as did Union Minière in Katanga.

The closest parallel may be found across the border in the Northern Rhodesian Copperbelt, where the two companies engaged in copper-mining, the Anglo-American Corporation and the Rhodesian Selection Trust, also invested in related industries and services—but they

195

left more to other firms and to the colonial government than did Union Minière. Northern Rhodesia's copper output, stimulated by strongly rising world prices, doubled between 1946 and 1954, and two new mines were brought into production during the latter 1950s. Copper-mining in Northern Rhodesia, as in Katanga, stood at an opposite pole from the mining enclavism of West Africa. The scale of production was greater, ores were smelted and refined at the point of extraction, mining was practically the only export-oriented activity, and a much higher proportion of the local population was engaged in extractive and related industries. Commerce, manufacturing and agriculture were all dependent upon its performance; the size of government revenues and the rhythm of economic activity mirrored the state of world demand for its single export.

The extremes of enclavism on the one hand and dependence on a single mineral export on the other were much less pronounced in the economies of Southern Rhodesia and South Africa, where inter-sectoral relations were both closer and more evenly balanced and where a greater part of the returns from mining accrued to locally resident European populations. In Southern Rhodesia, mining was carried out by a larger number of small firms than in Northern Rhodesia, involved a greater spread of products, and coexisted with a sizeable agricultural sector. Gold, long the mainstay of Southern Rhodesia's small-scale 'settler mining', received a temporary boost from the devaluation of the pound in 1949, but thereafter, with prices fixed and production costs rising, output remained static. But exports of such lesser minerals as asbestos, chromite, copper and nickel rose sharply, and the production of coal and iron ore for the domestic market also expanded. The most important post-war mining develop-ment in South Africa was the opening-up of the Orange Free State goldfields, which had been first discovered in the late 1930s and in which Oppenheimer's Anglo-American Corporation had a major stake. The higher-yielding ores from the Free State combined with the introduction of techniques to recover uranium from gold tailings to shelter South Africa's mining-financial houses from the fixed gold prices prevailing after 1949. They also contributed to a doubling of gold production between 1947 and 1956 and permitted gold to retain its position as South Africa's leading export. But although gold, and to a lesser extent diamonds, remained South Africa's most important mineral products, a diversification of mining activity broadened the base of export production. In a post-war international economy avaricious for industrial raw materials, South Africa's phenomenal wealth of natural resources placed it in a position to earn foreign exchange from mineral exporting which was unmatched by any other economy south of the Sahara, and substantial increases took place in the output of antimony, chromite, platinum, manganese and copper. At the same time, the on-going industrialization within South Africa generated higher demand for coal, iron ore and limestone.

INCOMES AND INDUSTRIALIZATION

Expansion of primary produce-exporting and enlargement of the infrastructure necessary to this function resulted in a marked improvement in real incomes in Subsaharan Africa after 1945. Unfortunately, the data on income trends are too fragmentary and their interpretation is surrounded by too many uncertainties, to permit any comprehensive or accurate measurement. Nor can it be assumed that the gains from the post-war commodity boom were equally shared, for political and institutional influences upon the distribution of income meant that some groups of people did better than others. In West Africa, for example, agricultural real incomes rose in both French and British colonies—but faster in the former than in the latter, where marketing boards held back producers' returns over the years of strongly rising commodity prices. Further divergences may be found in the pattern of real income movements for African peasant producers and urban wage-earners in West, West Central and Eastern Africa. In broad terms, both farm and non-farm incomes improved up to the early or middle 1950s but thereafter, with the decline in export commodity prices, the real incomes of peasant farmers tended to deteriorate—whereas those of wage-earners, employed in commerce, services, mining and manufacturing, continued their upward trend. The comparative 'success' of the wage-earners is to be explained partly by the growth of trade union organization among workers and partly by the changing political climate in most of Subsaharan Africa which rendered governments, often the largest single employer, sensitive to wage claims. But equally influential was the tendency of the larger private employers, usually foreign-owned concerns, to introduce more capital-intensive methods of production and to raise wages in order to encourage a settled work force and to end reliance on migratory labour.

The gap between urban and rural incomes widened in the course of the 1950s and this, together with the concentration of public services in the towns and the spread of formal education which motivated young men to take up employment outside agriculture, resulted in an accelerating drift of population from rural to urban areas. The labour shortages which were once such a pronounced feature of African economic history gave way to an overabundance of job-seekers attracted to the principal centres of wage-employment. When, in the later 1950s, the employment-creation effects of the export-led boom began to flag, their expectations became less capable of satisfaction.

In the pattern of income trends and differentials, South Africa presents a somewhat special case. Here the real income of the European population rose by 46 per cent between 1949 and 1954 while that of the African population apparently declined by 6·5 per cent. The latter figure includes estimates of income in the African rural areas, hit by falling per capita output as a consequence of population pressure on land, and it seems likely that the gap between African rural and urban incomes is to be explained more by a continuous decline in the former than by significant increases in the latter. Certainly, it has been demonstrated that the real earnings of African workers in the gold mines did not improve at all between 1946 and 1961. By comparison with the labour policies of governments elsewhere in Africa, the Afrikaner-supported Nationalist government which came to power in 1948 set its face against recognition of African trade unions and insisted that the gold mines continue to employ short-contract migratory labour. The mines, drawing a large part of their work force from outside the country, were not necessarily typical of South African employers, but the weight of official policy was firmly in the direction of advancing the real incomes of the European inhabitants at the expense of African labour drawn from impoverished 'homelands'.

The increase in real incomes, and the configuration of its distribution, impacted upon domestic demand for goods and services in Subsaharan economies. Examination of post-war trends in commerce and services would reveal a great variety of innovations—from a growth in the number of retail shops in peasant cash-cropping localities, through the rise of small businesses engaged in transporting produce and people to and from the towns and cities, to the construction of the department stores, hotels, bars and cinemas which catered for the higher income groups mainly resident in the urban areas. More significant perhaps was the growth of manufacturing industry—which proceeded more rapidly after 1945 than in early periods, but was relatively modest outside South Africa and Southern Rhodesia. Apart from the processing of raw materials for export—post-war developments in this field included groundnut-milling in Senegal and around Kano in northern Nigeria, the electrolytic refining of copper in the Congo and Northern Rhodesia, and aluminium-smelting in the Cameroons—the substitution of imported manufactures by locally made items was the most common form of industrial activity. In most African economies, however, import-substitution was confined to a narrow range of simple and cheap consumer goods for a low income mass-market—textiles, footwear, soap, cigarettes, furniture and household utensils—plus some inter-mediate goods like cement for the construction industry. Heavy industries and engineering industries capable of producing capital goods remained absent from the scene. Per capita incomes may have been rising, but in the greater part of Subsaharan Africa they were still low in absolute terms and the domestic market for manufactured goods was correspondingly limited.

Certain centres of manufacturing benefited from customs and transport arrangements which gave their products access to markets in other territories. Thus Dakar in Senegal was the principal location of manufacturing for the Federation of French West Africa, although its position began to be rivalled during the 1950s by Abidjan in the Ivory Coast. In Eastern Africa, similarly, the common market which linked Kenya, Uganda and Tanganyika operated mainly to the advantage of the emergent industries of Nairobi and Mombasa, so that Kenya's share of inter-territorial trade rose from 36 per cent in 1945 to 60 per cent in 1957. Both of these groupings had been estab-lished for many years and the only new post-war attempt to widen the market by creating a larger politico-economic unit was the Federation of Rhodesia and Nyasaland set up in 1953. This aspect of the Federation's establishment should not be over-exaggerated because few effective barriers had existed to trade between Southern Rhodesia and the greater part of Northern Rhodesia, including the Copperbelt. The major innovations, which also attracted most controversy, concerned government taxation and revenue allocation. Nevertheless, the creation of the Federation tended to strengthen and confirm the pre-eminence of Southern Rhodesia's manufacturing sector, the output of which was already three times greater by value than the combined manufacturing of Northern Rhodesia and Nyasaland.

By the late 1950s the share of manufacturing in Gross Domestic Product ranged from around two per cent in Nigeria and the Gold Coast to nine per cent in Kenya, 12 per cent in the Belgian Congo and 15 per cent in Southern Rhodesia. The higher figures of the latter two are to be accounted for principally by the existence of large mining sectors which generated demand for chemicals, cement and metal products, so that the manufacturing of intermediate goods and the emergence of engineering and allied industries proceeded further there than in most other economies. Southern Rhodesia, in particular, had the only iron and steel industry outside South Africa. Its state-owned Iron and Steel Commission brought the first blast furnaces into operation at Que Que in 1948 and with the addition of another blast furnace, two open hearth furnaces and two rolling mills developed a capacity of 90,000 tons of pig iron and 60,000 tons of steel by 1956. But the most highly industrialized economy was still South Africa, where by the late 1950s manufacturing accounted for 25 per cent of Gross Domestic Product and the value of its output was 53 per cent of all manufacturing value south of the Sahara.

South Africa's industrial foundations, laid down prior to 1945, were intensively and extensively enlarged in the post-war years—under state guidance and with heavy public investment. I.S.C.O.R.'s output of iron and steel, for example, practically quadrupled between 1945 and 1960, reducing imports of iron and steel from 80 to 58 per cent of total domestic consumption. Meanwhile, the Industrial Development Corporation financed such new state undertakings as S.A.S.O.L. (oil-from-coral and petrochemicals), S.A.I.C.C.O.R. (cellulose) and F.O.S.K.O.R. (phosphate fertilizers), and entered joint ventures with private capital in textiles and clothing. From these 'strategic' public and mixed enterprises linkages were developed with an ever-widening range of smaller industries, from plastics to automobile assembly. The government provided effective tariff protection for new lines of production and used a system of selective import controls which, by threatening overseas manufacturers with loss of their South African market, encouraged them to set up plants inside the country. A combination of foreign exchange earnings from gold and primary products, a relative abundance of local industrial raw materials, plentiful supplies of 'cheap' African labour, high levels of domestic capital formation as a consequence of the distribution of income in favour of the 'white' minority, and vigorous state promotion of industrial growth had created the only semi-industrialized economy south of the Sahara. Many observers, however, pointed to the low per capita incomes and therefore limited consumption of the 'non-whites' who comprised 80 per cent of South Africa's 16,000,000 inhabitants and questioned whether rapid industrial growth could continue without a substantial change in the pattern of income distribution and basic reforms in the country's political system.

Capital for the new industrial enterprises in Subsaharan Africa came from three principal sources—public, local private and overseas private. Except in South Africa and Southern Rhodesia, direct public investment in manufacturing was rare, most colonial governments preferring to allocate their revenues to infrastructure or services, like electricity, transport or urban construction and finance. Local private capital came from businesses, usually foreign or expatriate-owned, which were already engaged in commerce or mining-plantation activities but which began to diversify their interests into manufacturing. They ranged in size from mercantile giants like the United Africa Company, which set up seven wholly or partly owned manufacturing subsidiaries in Nigeria between 1948 and 1960, or mining giants like Union Minière, down to the Lebanese groundnut dealers who redeployed their profits into small-scale manufacturing in Senegal and Nigeria or the Asian trading community which by 1967 controlled 67 per cent of all locally owned industrial enterprises in Kenya. Comparative newcomers, however, were the metropolitan or international manufacturing firms which transferred some part of their production for African markets to African locations, sometimes in association with longer-established local firms. In French or Belgian colonies this post-war 'invasion' tended to be shielded from the public gaze by the adoption of trade names suggesting local origin or control, but in Anglophone Africa names which were already household words in Britain—like Portland Cement, Raleigh or Shell-B.P.—appeared on the scene. Manufacturing needs, therefore, was an important component of the capital inflows into Africa after 1945, and together with mining probably accounted for the bulk of new private investment from overseas.

201

The overall scale and distribution of private capital investment in Africa between 1945 and 1960 remains unclear. We lack such comprehensive studies as Frankel's calculations that the private 'listed' foreign capital invested in Subsaharan Africa between 1870 and 1930 amounted to £580,000,000, distributed in the following manner: 43 per cent in South Africa, ten per cent in other British colonies in Southern Africa, ten per cent in British West Africa, five per cent in British colonies in Eastern Africa, four per cent in French colonies, seven per cent in Portuguese territories and 17 per cent in Belgian colonies. After the Second World War, South Africa remained the most attractive location for private foreign investment, but neither its share of the total nor that of the colonial economies can be established with any precision. Figures on capital flows which are available for a few economies reveal a broadly similar pattern—strong inflows during the late 1940s and early 1950s and a levelling-off in the middle years of the decade. Then came a flight of capital as political developments, from the Gold Coast's achievement of independence as Ghana in 1956 to the Sharpeville incident in South Africa in 1960, temporarily discouraged overseas investors and encouraged some members of foreign business or farming communities to repatriate savings from colonies where metropolitan sovereignty was being withdrawn.

DECOLONIZATION

Towards the end of a period when trade between Western Europe and Africa, European immigration into Africa, European investment in Africa and European 'aid' to Africa was greater, and grew more rapidly than at any time in the history of interaction between the two continents, Britain, France and Belgium began to dismantle their colonial empires south of the Sahara. This seeming paradox requires some discussion for, just as the scramble for colonies in the last quarter of the third century had considerable economic significance for Africa, so too did the retreat from formal colonial authority in the third quarter of the twentieth century. Outside the settler minority-ruled South Africa and Southern Rhodesia, and the Portuguese possessions of Angola and Mozambique where the metropolitan regime used force of arms to maintain its sovereignty, authority to direct both the internal functioning of the African economies and their relationship with external economies formally passed from European to African hands. These pages, however, cannot pretend to provide a full account and adequate explanation of either the rising tide of African protest which coalesced into 'nationalism' or the various factors which impinged upon the decision of metropolitan governments to decolonize. Perhaps even more clearly than the original imposition of colonial rule, its removal was bound up with a multiformity of political, economic and intellectual trends which were often global in character—so that events on the battlefield of Dien Bien Phu or in the corridors of the United Nations General Assembly were as much a part of the overall picture as developments within Africa itself. Only a few broad generalizations, more immediately relevant to economic circumstances, can be made.

During the post-war years the advance of the interventionist powers and proclivities of the colonial bureaucratic state coincided with external economic conditions which produced an improvement in the incomes and welfare of many, if by no means all, Africans. The amelioration in material life, although more limited than in the industrial West, aroused expectations and aspirations which conflicted, or could be made to appear to conflict, with the methods and goals of the colonial regimes—whether in their restriction of private consumption to create public investment, their regulation of commerce in such a way as to favour established rather than emergent mercantile groups, their influence upon wage-bargaining and the creation of employment, their attempts to divert and alter land use, their continuing reliance upon expatriate civil servants in the enlarged state apparatus, and perhaps above all their underlying value systems which, permeated with differing degrees of racism, gave a pronounced bias towards European personnel and businesses in the shareout of earnings and income. Opposition to the colonial system, which in certain territories had its early roots in the inter-war years, was led by members of the small élite groups, sometimes described as an embryonic bourgeoisie, which had emerged in the restructuring of African societies—the professional men like teachers and lawyers, the wealthier African traders and businessmen, and at least some elements of the more commercially oriented farmers. These men, reformists rather than revolutionaries, aimed at a takeover of the colonial state, with its formidable powers of social control and economic management, so as to remove impediments to their own ambitions and to divert wealth from foreign to indigenous hands. To this end they formed a loose alliance with the urban wage-earners, although the degree of politicization of industrial disputes and the weight of the trade union role in the 'nationalist' movements are still hotly debated by historians.[2] The political élites also co-ordinated, and sometimes helped to instigate, 'populist' rural protest movements which ranged from chieftaincy disputes in West Africa to reaction against colonial pressures for change in agricultural techniques, land use or land tenure in British East Africa or the Belgian Congo. In British colonies like the Gold Coast, Nigeria or Uganda the pricing policies and accumulating reserves of the marketing boards were a particularly powerful focus of rural discontent. To workers and peasants the elites held out the prospect of a future management of the African 'mixed economies' which would be less oppressive and more sympathetic to their demands for public amenities. The general strategy of the African political leaderships, therefore, was not to dismantle the apparatus of the state, but rather to capture it, and redirect its functions of wealth creation and distribution.

Just as the configurations of the African 'alliances' and the timing of their successes differed from territory to territory, reflecting the variety of socio-economic conditions, so too might one point to diversity in the response of the metropolitan powers—from the more 'autonomous' traditions of British colonial theory and practice which seemed to render gradualist decolonization in Africa a logical extension of the retreat from colonial empire in Asia, through the French attempts at colonial 'assimilation' which foundered in Indo-China and Algeria and left the Fifth Republic to face up to the possibility of decolonization south of the Sahara, to the almost total lack of forward thinking in Belgian colonial strategy before being overtaken by events in the Congo in the late 1950s. But although all three used their military and police powers to control the timing and character of the handover—most notably in the containment of rural radicalism in Kenya—they eventually accepted the demise of the colonial system. It is difficult to discern any specifically economic trends which might account for the willingness of British, French and Belgian governments to abandon the advantages which formal control of African dependencies brought to metropolitan economies. The onset of decolonization certainly occurred at a time when industrial capitalism in Western Europe was reassessing the potential of African economies and beginning to invest in manufacturing production there, but whether or how far this development influenced the decolonization process remains an open question. The post-war role of the United States as the international economy's dominant financial and industrial centre, coupled with American hostility to the neo-mercantilist tendencies of European colonialism, may also be relevant. It seems likely, however, that the most important factor was the changing political climate within Western Europe itself, the growth of social-democratic parties and philosophies which were receptive to African demands for democratic rights and an end to foreign rule.

Acceptance of decolonization meant recognition that certain elements of the colonial economy and society which had enjoyed the patronage of the state in the past—expatriate civil servants, settler-planters or farmers, or the smaller European and Asian merchants and businessmen—would have to be considered 'redundant' or 'expendable' and be replaced at some point by African aspirants to their roles. The greater part of the capital outflows from colonial Africa in the late 1950s and early 1960s, it would appear, was the repatriated savings of such individuals. On the other hand, the larger, metropolitan-based or international firms engaged in commerce, plantations, mining and manufacturing were less immediately threatened by African goals of breaking into areas hitherto the preserve of lesser foreign capital. With their considerable financial resources and levels of technical and managerial expertise, and with their commanding positions in the local economy, they were better placed to reach an accommodation with incoming African governments. Most survived the transition from the late colonial to postcolonial periods of African economic history, albeit with modifications in their methods of operation and in their relationship with the state. The ambiguity of this situation, and the bargaining which went on, lend themselves to the charge that defence of 'big business' interests was the primary aim of metropolitan governments and that once assured of succession by relatively complaisant African governments they felt able to withdraw their formal sovereignty. Whether or not one accepts this 'conspiracy theory' of decolonization, with its assumptions about the motives of the colonial powers and the African political élites, the fact remains that the ex-colonies of Subsaharan Africa passed into the 1960s with economic power highly concentrated in the hands of the state and local representatives of international concerns.

The rapid export-led growth of the years between 1945 and 1960, resulting in a further erosion of African autonomy within the global system of production and exchange, was accompanied by, and in part helped to generate, demands for African autonomy in the political sphere. Towards the end of this period the major European powers abandoned the colonialism which had opened up Subsaharan Africa to foreign trade and investment and structured new 'proto-national' economies. In all but parts of Southern Africa, where a local 'colonial capitalism' was deeply embedded in the economy and exercised political authority, a new phase in African relations with the outside world appeared to be in the making.

The historic role of colonialism had been to create new politico-economic units in Subsaharan Africa and to lock them into a situation of interdependence with the international economy. It did so, however, by promoting African interdependence with certain Western European economies in particular, and this relationship was very one-sided. The European economies linked by the colonial nexus to Africa were, with the exception of Portugal, members of the central core of advanced industrial economies, the progress and performance of which rested upon the operations of the world economy as a whole. Their commerce with, and investment in, Africa represented but a tiny fraction of their total world activities and their national incomes, and the contribution of Africa to the overall economic development of Western Europe in the nineteenth and twentieth centuries had been slight, especially if semi-peripheral South Africa is excluded. This is not to argue that involvement with Africa was not profitable for individuals and firms in Europe, or that such private interests did not have a strong influence upon metropolitan policies towards African colonies. But in the context of Europe's political economy, the connexions with West, West-Central and Eastern Africa were considered to be side-shows, useful perhaps, but not of themselves essential to the material well-being of European societies. When the international economy was most unsettled and competition between the industrial economies for markets and/or raw materials most acute—in the 1880s and 1890s, between 1914 and 1923, in the depression of the early 1930s and between 1939 and 1948—voices proclaiming the 'necessity' of African colonies obtained their most receptive hearing, but the rapid growth of the international economy after the Second World War eroded support for such views and permitted the policy-makers of Britain, France and Belgium to face decolonization, and the possible loss of former colonial markets, with some degree of equanimity. Only the Portuguese regime, managing a metropolitan economy which had a semi-peripheral status in the world hierarchy, stood out against this trend.

The typical African colonial economy, on the other hand, had very strong links with a single European metropolitan economy, to which it sent the greater part of its exports and from which it drew most of its imports, investment, financial aid, new technology and skilled manpower. Interchange with other components of the international economy, although not completely absent, was relatively weak. The major phases of expansion and contraction in the global system as a whole, therefore, were transmitted to Africa through the medium of particular European economies, the needs and interests of which set the broad guidelines for public policy in the colonial economies. Decolonization opened up possibilities of, although it did not guarantee, a reduction in the close ties with the former metropolitan economies and the forging of new links with other economies, such as those of America, West Germany, Russia or China. Africa's interdependence with the international economy as a whole re-emerged into the open.

Political independence, however, came at a time when new trends were appearing in international commerce. From approximately 1955 onwards the world's industrial countries began to trade more with each other than with the primary producing economies, the growth-stimulating effects of the post-war commodity boom began to slacken in African economies and, with the development in the West of cheap synthetic substitutes for agricultural raw materials and low income elasticities of demand for foodstuffs and beverages, barter terms of trade moved against African exports. Behind the mood of optimism fostered by release from colonial rule lurked the harsher realities of a peripheral place within the international economy.

207

Eight

Retrospect

The assimilation of Subsaharan Africa into the global system of commerce and investment had lengthy historical roots, but first assumed its modern form in the course of the nineteenth century when the inhabitants of a few coastal and near-coastal localities began to move away from production and exchange of 'exotic' foraged commodities and/or slaves towards supplying agricultural raw materials and foodstuffs directly to the industrial markets of Western Europe. From being peripheries to other primary producing peripheries or to the maritime network which connected the international economy's industrial core to its overseas markets and sources of raw materials, these centres, notably along the West African coast and the fringes of Southern Africa, became direct peripheries of industrial Europe. Deficiencies in internal transport, however, confined this 'revolution' to a few favoured localities and the incorporation of the subcontinent as a whole into the new relationships of production followed the European scramble for colonies at the end of the nineteenth century.

The Partition of Africa was carried out partly to protect existing European commerce and investment in a period of intense intra-European economic and political rivalry, but mainly as a pre-emptive staking of claims for the future. Against a background of unstable industrialization in Western Europe and the desires of European commercial and mining capital on the African peripheries to gain access to and control over the interior, the advance of European colonial authority established a political-administrative superstructure which directed the erosion of African economic autonomy. The penetration of the interior by modern transport technology, tax-demanding colonial officials, and immigrant settler-farmers, merchants and traders and mining companies fashioned the economic base of most of Africa's contemporary nation states. Subsaharan Africa's politico-economic units became integral components of the global capitalist economy and shared its erratic progress through the disruption of two World Wars and the contractions of the inter-war depressions before reaching the more settled and expansionary period in world trade and investment after 1945.

The economies of post-1880 Africa were hybrid creations, artificially fostered by imposed political boundaries and infrastructural networks which encapsulated differing forms of intrusive European capitalism and indigenous, non-capitalist societies within the same 'national' or 'proto-national' entities. Reduced to a simple abstract model, however, each may be said to have comprised three principal sectors. The export sector generated the greater part of monetary income, was the locus of most technological and institutional innovation and obtained priority in official provision of overhead capital. Around it, there emerged a nascent intermediate or secondary sector which supplied some of the services required for export production, as well as local markets for foodstuffs and, to a very limited extent, manufactured goods. Finally, each economy had what may be called for convenience a 'subsistence' sector, comprising in the main agrarian communities ill-served by the transport and other public facilities which made participation in export or intermediate activities possible. This sector acted as a source of labour for the other two, and a refuge for labour pushed out of them by economic contraction, infirmity or old age. Its low productivity and earning capacity determined the labour costs of export and intermediate activities.

The years between the late 1890s and the First World War were a time when the structural foundations of most of the 'new' African economies were laid down. Continuities with earlier patterns of export-oriented activity were greatest in South Africa, where mines and immigrant estates and farms made up the export sector, and in West Africa, where African peasant farming dominated export production. Even so, the export sector in the latter region was both extended by the addition of new producing units and deepened by the adoption of new cash-crops, more especially cocoa in the Gold Coast and western Nigeria. Elsewhere, in Eastern and West-Central Africa and in the northerly territories of Southern Africa, the export sectors were substantially new creations, comprising some or all of four basic types of enterprise—mines, large company plantations, settler-estates and African peasant holdings. A period of plunder by concessionary companies in West-Central Africa delayed the introduction of new methods of primary production into that region until shortly before the First World War. Throughout Subsaharan Africa the intermediate sector was still tiny and 'subsistence', or marginally market-oriented, agriculture was still the mainstay of material life for a large proportion of the total population.

The inter-war years were generally unfavourable to the further expansion and diversification of the export and intermediate sectors. Here and there, and mainly in the 1920s, some new centres of export production emerged—the Northern Rhodesian Copperbelt, the Gezira and Niger irrigation schemes, new peasant cash-cropping localities like the Chagga coffee-growing in north-eastern Tanganyika, or diamond and iron-ore mining in Sierra Leone—and in some economies a broadening of the intermediate sector occurred, principally in the area of food production for local markets. But in many economies in the 1920s, and virtually all economies in the 1930s, slow rates of growth of international trade, low commodity prices and a major world depression meant limited opportunities for enlargement of incomes through external exchange and a loss of momentum in structural change. The principal policy issues of these years concerned the allocation of shares in, and the distribution of income from, relatively static external or domestic markets. The South African economy, however, enjoyed an early release from these restrictions, thanks to the peculiarity of its main export commodity, and entered a phase of state-induced industrialization which both substantially increased and altered the character of its intermediate sector.

The great majority of African economies had to wait for the commodity boom which followed the Second World War before experiencing any similar external stimuli to the growth and diversification of the export and intermediate sectors. On the whole, expansion of export production proceeded along well-established paths, with here and there the opening-up of new mines or ventures into new cropping patterns. In certain economies, however, notably the Ivory Coast, the Belgian Congo and Kenya, an official reassessment of the potential for peasant production, which first began in the 1930s, resulted in sizeable additions to agricultural exporting. Investment in public services and a broadening of the local market for goods and services also meant an increase in the scale and sophistication of the intermediate sectors. Nevertheless, everywhere, including South Africa, the 'subsistence' sector remained a large element of the national economy and, partly in consequence of a more rapid rate of population growth, now tended to release labour faster than the other two sectors could absorb it.

The persistence of the 'subsistence' sector may be explained in part by the accident of geography, which left many agrarian societies relatively remote from external and internal markets, in part by the bias in state policies of resource allocation in favour of the export and intermediate sectors, and in many cases, particularly in Southern and West-Central Africa, by a history of deliberate official neglect of areas which supplied migratory labour to the major centres of market production, a policy which lasted in differing degrees well into the post-war years. The economies of Subsaharan Africa, therefore, entered the 1960s not only with per capita Gross National Products substantially lower than in the industrialized West, but also with pronounced sectoral imbalances and strong inequalities of income between localities and social groups. Integration into and interaction with the international economy had produced, at best, only partial 'development'.

Notes

INTRODUCTION
1. The concept 'periphery of the periphery' was first suggested by S. Amin in 'Underdevelopment and Dependence in Black Africa', *Journal of Modern African Studies*, 10 (1972), p. 511.
2. A caveat about the use of international trade statistics is required. In 1880 most intra-African trade, especially important in West Africa, went unrecorded, so that transactions which entered European foreign trade statistics were omitted from African figures, which were largely those for external trade, i.e. trade with other continents. By 1960 methods of collecting trade information had improved but some under-recording of intra-African commerce remained, caused in part by illegal movement of goods to take advantage of differences in state marketing and pricing arrangements. The discrepancy between recorded and actual values was almost certainly greater in 1880 than in 1960. The effects of these deficiencies in trade figures is to understate the African share of world trade, while overstating that of other regions of the globe, and to overstate somewhat the growth of African commerce between 1880 and 1960.

CHAPTER ONE
1. R. Gray and D. Birmingham (eds.), *Pre-Colonial African Trade* (London, 1970) and C. Meillassoux (ed.), *Development of African Trade and Markets in West Africa* (London, 1971) provide useful surveys as well as case-studies.
2. Significant contributions include K. Polanyi, C. M. Arensberg and H. W. Pearson, *Trade and Markets in the Early Empires* (London, 1957); P. Bohannan and G. Dalton, *Markets in Africa* (Evanston, 1962), [especially the introduction]; G. Dupré and P. P. Rey, 'Réflexions sur la pertinence d'une théorie de l'histoire des échanges', *Cahiers Internationaux de Sociologie*, 46 (1969), and C. Meillassoux, 'From Reproduction to Production', *Economy and Society*, 1 (1972).
3. J. D. Fage, *A History of West Africa* (Cambridge, 1969), pp. 91–2.
4. Among contributions to the ongoing discussion are: J. Suret Canale, 'Contexte et Consequences Sociales de la Traite Africaine', *Presence Africaine*, 50 (1964); W. Rodney, 'African Slavery and other forms of

213

Social Oppression on the Upper Guinea Coast in the Context of the Atlantic Slave Trade', *Journal of African History*, 7 (1966); J. D. Fage, 'Slavery and the Slave Trade in the Context of West African History', *Journal of African History*, 10 (1969); C. C. Wrigley, 'Historicism in Africa: Slavery and State Formation', *African Affairs*, 70 (1971); G. N. Uziogwe, 'The Slave Trade and African Societies', *Transactions of the Historical Society of Ghana*, 14 (1973).

CHAPTER TWO

1. Differing interpretations and emphases are to be found in A. G. Hopkins, *An Economic History of West Africa* (London, 1973), esp. pp. 112–35; J. E. Flint, 'Economic Change in West Africa in the Nineteenth Century', in J. F. A. Ajayi and M. Crowder (eds.), *History of West Africa*, vol. 2 (London, 1974); C. W. Newbury, 'Trade and Authority in West Africa from 1850 to 1880', in L. H. Gann and P. Duignan (eds.), *Colonialism in Africa*, vol. 1 (1969); and R. A. Austen, 'The Abolition of the Overseas Slave Trade: A Distorted Theme in West African History', *Journal of the Historical Society of Nigeria*, 5 (1970).

2. W. K. Hancock, *Survey of British Commonwealth Affairs: Vol. 2, Problems of Economic Policy, 1918–39* (London, 1940).

3. Quoted in L. C. Duly, *British Land Policy at the Cape, 1795–1844* (Durham, N. C., 1968), pp. 47–8.

4. M. Gluckman, 'The Rise of a Zulu Empire', *Scientific American*, 202 (April, 1962); J. D. Omer-Cooper, *The Zulu Aftermath* (London, 1966), chs. 1–2; M. Wilson and L. Thompson (eds.), *The Oxford History of South Africa* (Oxford, 1969), pp. 336–64.

CHAPTER THREE

1. Much of the relevant literature is surveyed and/or presented as selected readings in the following works: R. F. Betts, *The Scramble for Africa* (Boston, 1966); R. O. Collins, *The Partition of Africa: Illusion or Necessity* (New York and London, 1969); M. E. Chamberlain, *The New Imperialism* (London, 1970); D. K. Fieldhouse, *The Theory of Capitalist Imperialism* (London, 1967); R. Owen and B. Sutcliffe, *Studies in the Theory of Imperialism* (London, 1972). J. Gallagher and R. Robinson, *Africa and the Victorians* (London, 1961) dominated the discussion of the early and middle 1960s, one response being R. Hyam, 'The Partition of Africa', *Historical Journal*, 7 (1964). A more recent contribution, upon which this chapter leans quite heavily, is A. G. Hopkins's analysis of the the Partition in West Africa in 'Economic Imperialism in West Africa: Lagos, 1880–1892', *Economic History Review*, 21 (1968) and *An Economic History of West Africa* (London, 1973), chapter 4. Also useful is E. Stokes, 'Late Nineteenth Century Colonial Expansion and the Attack on the Theory of Economic Imperialism', *Historical Journal*, 12 (1969).

2. Consul Sir John Kirk, 4 June 1886, quoted in J. S. Galbraith, *MacKinnon and East Africa* (Cambridge, 1972), pp. 102–3.

3. Lord Selborne, Under Secretary of State for the Colonies, 1896, quoted in J. Marais, *The Fall of Kruger's Republic* (Oxford, 1961), p. 327.

CHAPTER FOUR

1. W. A. Lewis, *Aspects of Tropical Trade, 1883–1965* (Uppsala, 1969), p. 49 and *Tropical Development, 1880–1913* (London, 1970), p. 50.
2. A. McPhee, *The Economic Revolution in British West Africa* (London, 1926, republished 1971), p. 304.
3. Among others: K. Arhin, 'The Ashanti Rubber Trade with the Gold Coast in the Eighteen Nineties', *Africa*, 42 (1972); R. Dumett, 'The Rubber Trade of the Gold Coast and Asante in the Nineteenth Century', *Journal of African History*, 12 (1971); P. Hill, *The Migrant Cocoa-Farmers of Southern Ghana* (Cambridge, 1963); R. H. Green and S. H. Hymer, 'Cocoa in the Gold Coast', *Journal of Economic History*, 26 (1966); S. S. Berry, 'Christianity and the Rise of Cocoa-Growing in Ibadan and Ondo', *Journal of the Historical Society of Nigeria*, 4 (1968); S. S. Berry, *Cocoa, Custom and Socio-Economic Change in Rural Western Nigeria* (Oxford, 1975); S. S. Berry, 'Cocoa and Economic Development in Western Nigeria' and J. S. Hogendorn, 'The Origins of the Groundnut Trade in Northern Nigeria', in C. K. Eicher and C. Liedholm (eds.), *Growth and Development of the Nigerian Economy* (Michigan, 1970).
4. S. H. Frankel, *Capital Investment in Africa* (London, 1938), pp. 149–53.
5. C. Bundy, 'The Emergence and Decline of a South African Peasantry', *African Affairs*, 71 (1972); G. Arrighi, 'Labour Supplies in Historical Perspective: A Study of the Proletarianization of the African Peasantry in Rhodesia', *Journal of Development Studies*, 6 (1970); I. R. Phimister, 'Peasant Production and Underdevelopment in Southern Rhodesia, 1890–1914', *African Affairs*, 73 (1974).

CHAPTER FIVE

1. See C. Ehrlich, 'Some Social and Economic Implications of Paternalism in Uganda', *Journal of African History*, 4 (1963).
2. See, inter alia, R. Van Zwanenberg, 'The Development of Peasant Commodity Production in Kenya, 1920–40', *Economic History Review*, 27 (1974), and J. F. Munro, *Colonial Rule and the Kamba: Social Change in the Kenya Highlands, 1889–1939* (Oxford, 1975), pp. 165–88.

CHAPTER SIX

1. G. C. Abbott, 'British Colonial Aid Policy during the Nineteen Thirties', *Canadian Journal of History*, 5 (1970) and 'A Re-Examination of the 1929 Colonial Development Act', *Economic History Review*, 24 (1971); I. M. Drummond, 'More on British Colonial Aid Policy in the Nineteen Thirties', *Canadian Journal of History*, 6 (1971); D. Meredith, 'The British Government and Colonial Economic Policy, 1919–39', *Economic History Review*, 28 (1975).

Notes

2. The Duke of Brabant, in the Belgian Senate, 1933, quoted in M. W. Van de Velde, *Économie Belge et Congo Belge* (Antwerp, 1936), p. 252.
3. W. A. Hance, *Population, Migration and Urbanization in Africa* (New York, 1970), p. 35.

CHAPTER SEVEN
1. J. C. Abbott, 'Agricultural Marketing Boards in the Developing Countries', *Journal of Farm Economics*, 49 (1967); P. T. Bauer, *West African Trade* (Cambridge, 1954); R. H. Green, 'Ghana Cocoa Marketing Policy, 1930–1960', *Nigerian Institute of Social and Economic Research, Conference Proceedings*, December 1960; C. Ehrlich, 'Marketing Boards in Retrospect—Myth and Reality', in *African Public Sector Economics* (Edinburgh, Centre of African Studies, 1970).
2. For example, the dispute between Warren and Berg: M. W. Warren, 'Urban Real Wages and the Nigerian Trade Union Movement, 1939–1960', *Economic Development and Cultural Change*, 15 (1966–7); E. J. Berg, 'Urban Real Wages and the Nigerian Trade Union Movement, 1939–1960: A Comment', and W. M. Warren's 'Rejoinder', *Economic Development and Cultural Change*, 17 (1968–9).

Appendices

APPENDIX I *Total Foreign Trade of Subsaharan Africa—Selected Years* (£ million)

	1897	1913	1919	1929	1932	1938	1945	1952	1960
WEST AFRICA	10·05	41·33	63·45	83·34	47·60	73·18	118·10	725·16	1,089·25
Nigeria	2·97	12·78	25·60	30·62	16·26	23·00	32·71	246·26	385·35
Gold Coast	1·76	8·51	17·89	21·93	13·29	23·06	25·78	152·99	234·28
Sierra Leone	0·85	2·70	4·08	2·87	2·07	3·74	7·69	20·94	56·07
Gambia	0·30	1·26	2·41	1·32	0·68	0·58	1·81	7·67	6·07
French West Africa	3·52	11·03	13·67[c]	20·07	11·48	17·93	39·60	(206·60)	(267·50)
Senegal and Mali	—	—	—	—	—	—	—	95·00	101·78
Guinea	—	—	—	—	—	—	—	19·64	37·50
Ivory Coast	—	—	—	—	—	—	—	70·35	96·78
Dahomey	—	—	—	—	—	—	—	11·78	17·50
Niger	—	—	—	—	—	—	—	5·71	9·64
Upper Volta	—	—	—	—	—	—	—	4·64	4·28
Cameroons[a]	0·48	2·73	n.a.	2·93	1·75	2·76	⎱ 6·79	60·60	64·64
Togo[a]	0·13	0·98	n.a.	1·50	1·05	0·81	⎰	9·00	14·64
Port Guinea	0·01	0·63	n.a.	0·85	0·59	0·44	n.a.	5·35	6·42
Liberia	n.a.	0·59	n.a.	1·25	0·43	0·86	3·72	19·75	54·28

	1897	1913	1919	1929	1932	1938	1945	1952	1960
WEST-CENTRAL AFRICA	*4·06*	*10·12*	*14·76*	*28·72*	*16·59*	*26·59*	*56·62*	*411·99*	*457·85*
Angola	2·22	2·76	2·75	5·51	3·55	5·13	11·62	66·82	90·00
Belgian Congo	1·48	5·04	10·24	19·35	9·00	18·17	37·19	238·82	284·64
Ruanda-Urundi	n.a.	n.a.	n.a.	0·40	0·21				
French Equ. Africa	0·35	2·30	1·77[c]	3·46	3·83	3·29	7·81	(61·35)	(83·21)
Gabon	—	—	—	—	—	—	—	12·85	26·07
Congo (Fr)	—	—	—	—	—	—	—	20·00	31·42
Ubangi	—	—	—	—	—	—	—	5·71	12·14
Chad	—	—	—	—	—	—	—	15·35	13·57
SOUTHERN AFRICA	*52·24*	*121·55*	*168·81*	*201·28*	*117·83*	*248·58*	*347·79*	*1,238·33*	*1,725·44*
South Africa	47·20	104·93	143·71	168·07	97·45	198·06	269·50	848·80	1,284·35
South-West Africa	0·30	5·68	7·58[c]	6·51	1·81	5·96	13·21	55·81	
Southern Rhodesia	n.a.	6·07	7·64	13·39	8·49	21·45	30·52	149·62	369·67
Northern Rhodeisa	n.a.	0·44	0·88	4·37	4·13	15·28	18·89	125·36	
Nyasaland	0·01	0·39	1·07	1·32	1·36	1·82	3·49	15·07	
Mozambique	4·62[b]	4·01	7·93	7·62	4·59	6·01	12·18	43·67	71·42

	1897	1913	1919	1929	1932	1938	1945	1952	1960
EASTERN AFRICA									
Kenya	4·57	14·90	27·35	42·32	22·33	43·32	80·88	413·71	509·69
Uganda	0·35	3·75	8·36	15·22	8·07	19·36	32·51	88·97	110·00
Tanganyika	0·81	4·44	3·83	7·74	3·89	7·49	15·33	85·46	68·92
Zanzibar	2·58	1·32	6·55	2·40	1·37	1·81	2·59	9·64	93·21
Sudan	0·15	3·28	8·03	13·43	6·65	12·53	21·78	104·45	11·07
Somaliland (Br)	0·66	0·47	0·58	0·71	0·38	0·75	n.a.	3·11	130·35
,, (It)	n.a.	n.a.	n.a.	n.a.	1·97	n.a.	1·02	7·57	} 19·01
,, (Fr)	n.a.	n.a.	n.a.	n.a.	n.a.	1·38	0·61	10·64	19·28
Ethiopia	n.a.	1·63	n.a.	2·82	n.a.	n.a.	7·04	31·89	57·85
TOTAL SUBSAHARAN	71·12	187·92	274·37	355·66	204·35	391·67	603·39	2,789·19	3,782·23

NOTES: ᵃ After 1919, area under French mandate only
ᵇ includes transit trade
ᶜ 1920

SOURCES: S. H. Frankel, *Capital Investment in Africa* (1938), pp. 196–7; *Statistical Abstracts for British Colonies/Overseas Dominions/Commonwealth*; United Nations, *Statistical Yearbooks*; Foreign Office, *Handbooks*, nos. 129–30 (1920); Dept. of Overseas Trade, *Reports on Economic Conditions in Angola, Mozambique and Ethiopia*

APPENDIX II *Percentage Change in Foreign Trade by Value Between Selected Years*

	1897/1913	1913/19	1913/29	1929/32	1929/38	1929/45	1945/52	1945/60
WEST AFRICA	*313*	*52*	*101*	*—42*	*—12*	*41*	*514*	*822*
Nigeria	330	100	139	—46	—24	6	652	1,078
Gold Coast	381	110	157	—39	5	17	493	808
Sierra Leone	214	51	6	—27	30	167	172	629
Gambia	316	91	4	—48	—56	37	323	235
French West Africa	213	23	81	—42	—10	97	421	575
Cameroons	469	—	—	—40	—4	} 53	} 925	} 1,008
Togo	617	—	—	—30	—46			
Port Guinea	5,655	—	34	—30	—48	—	—	—
Liberia	—	—	111	—56	—31	197	430	1,359
WEST-CENTRAL AFRICA	*149*	*45*	*183*	*—42*	*—7*	*97*	*627*	*708*
Angola	24	—0.3	99	—35	—6	110	475	674
Belgian Congo	239	103	283	—53	} —8	} 88	} 542	} 665
Ruanda-Urundi	—	—	—	—47				
French Equ. Africa	555	—23	49	10	—4	125	685	965
SOUTHERN AFRICA	*133*	*140*	*65*	*—41*	*23*	*72*	*256*	*396*
South Africa	122	36	38	—42	17	60	214	} 354
South-West Africa	1,758	33	11	—72	—8	102	322	

	1897/1913	1913/19	1913/29	1929/32	1929/38	1929/45	1945/52	1945/60
Southern Rhodesia	—	25	120	−36	60	127	390	⎫
Northern Rhodesia	—	100	893	−5	249	332	563	⎬ 598
Nyasaland	248	174	238	3	37	164	331	⎭
Mozambique	—	97	90	−39	−21	59	258	486
EASTERN AFRICA								
Kenya	*225*	*83*	*184*	*−47*	*2*	*91*	*411*	*530*
Uganda	⎱ 959	⎱ 122	⎱ 305	⎱ −46	⎱ 27	⎱ 113	⎱ 395	⎱ 450
Tanganyika	446	−13	74	−49	−3	98	457	508
Zanzibar	−49	396	81	−42	−24	7	272	327
Sudan	1,992	144	309	−50	−6	62	379	940
Somaliland (Br)	−29	23	115	−46	5	—	—	—
,, (It)	—	—	—	—	—	—	642	—
,, (Fr)	—	—	—	—	—	—	1,644	3,060
Ethiopia	—	—	73	—	—	149	352	721
TOTAL SUBSAHARAN	*164*	*47*	*89*	*−42*	*10*	*69*	*362*	*526*

SOURCES: Calculated from Appendix I

APPENDIX III *Foreign Trade as a Percentage of Total Subsaharan Trade—Selected Years*

	1897	1913	1929	1945	1960
WEST AFRICA	*14·1*	*21·9*	*23·4*	*19·5*	*28·8*
Nigeria	4·2	6·8	8·6	5·4	10·1
Gold Coast	2·5	6·5	6·1	4·2	6·1
Sierra Leone	1·2	1·4	0·8	0·6	1·4
Gambia	0·4	0·6	0·3	0·1	0·1
French West Africa	5·0	5·8	5·6	2·9	7·0
Cameroons[a]	0·7	1·4	0·8	} 1·1	1·7
Togo[a]	0·2	0·5	0·4		0·3
Port Guinea	0·0	0·3	0·2	—	0·1
Liberia	—	0·3	0·3	0·6	1·4
WEST-CENTRAL AFRICA	*5·7*	*5·3*	*8·0*	*9·3*	*12·1*
Angola	3·1	1·4	1·5	1·9	2·3
Belgian Congo	2·1	2·6	5·4	} 6·1	} 7·5
Ruanda-Urundi	—	—	0·1		
French Equ. Africa	0·5	1·2	0·9	1·2	2·2
SOUTHERN AFRICA	*73·5*	*64·6*	*56·5*	*57·6*	*45·6*
South Africa	66·4	55·8	47·2	44·6	} 33·9
South-West Africa	0·4	3·0	1·8	2·1	
Southern Rhodesia	—	3·2	3·7	5·0	} 9·7
Northern Rhodesia	—	0·2	1·2	3·1	
Nyasaland	—	0·2	0·3	0·5	
Mozambique	6·5[b]	2·1	2·1	2·0	1·8
EASTERN AFRICA	*6·4*	*7·9*	*11·8*	*13·4*	*13·5*
Kenya	} 0·5	} 1·9	} 4·2	} 5·3	2·6
Uganda					1·8
Tanganyika	1·1	2·3	2·1	2·5	2·4
Zanzibar	3·6	0·7	0·6	0·4	0·2
Sudan	0·2	1·7	3·7	3·6	3·4
Somaliland (Br)	0·9	0·2	0·1	—	} 0·5
,, (It)	—	—	—	0·1	
,, (Fr)	—	—	—	0·1	0·5
Ethiopia	—	0·8	0·7	1·1	1·5
SUBSAHARAN AFRICA	*100·0*	*100·0*	*100·0*	*100·0*	*100·0*

NOTES: [a] After 1919, area under French mandate only; [b] includes transit trade
SOURCES: Calculated from Appendix I

Select Bibliography

GENERAL

Anstey, R., *The Atlantic Slave Trade and British Abolition, 1760–1810*, London, 1975.

Coquery-Vidrovitch, C., and Moniot, H., *L'Afrique Noire de 1800 à Nos Jours*, Paris, 1974.

Curtin, P. D., *The Atlantic Slave Trade: A Census*, Madison, 1969.

Frankel, S. H., *Capital Investment in Africa*, London, 1938.

Gray, R., and Birmingham, D., (eds.), *Pre-Colonial African Trade*, London, 1970.

Goody, J., *Technology, Tradition and the State in Africa*, London, 1971.

Hancock, W. K., *Survey of British Commonwealth Affairs: Vol 2, Problems of Economic Policy, 1918–39*, London, 1940.

Herskovits, M. J., and Harwitz, M., (eds.), *Economic Transition in Africa*, London, 1964.

Kamark, A. M., *The Economics of African Development*, New York, 1967.

Neumark, S. D., *Foreign Trade and Economic Development in Africa*, Stanford, 1964.

Pim, A., *The Financial and Economic History of the African Tropical Territories*, Oxford, 1940.

Poquin, J. J., *Les Relations Économiques Extérieures des Pays d'Afrique Noires de l'Union Française, 1925–55*, Paris, 1957.

Robson, P., and Lury, D., (eds.), *The Economies of Africa*, London, 1969.

Sundstrom, L., *The Exchange Economy of Pre-Colonial Tropical Africa*, London, 1974.

Suret-Canale, J., *French Colonialism in Tropical Africa*, London 1971.

WEST AFRICA

Amin, S., *Le Développement du Capitalisme en Côte d'Ivoire*, Paris, 1967.

Bauer, P. T., *West African Trade*, London, 1963.

Berry, S. S., *Cocoa, Custom and Socio-Economic Change in Rural Western Nigeria*, Oxford, 1975.

Cox-George, N. A., *Finance and Development in West Africa: The Sierra Leone Experience*, London, 1961.

Davies, P. N., *The Trade Makers: Elder Dempster in West Africa, 1852–1972*, London, 1973.

223

Select Bibliography

Eicher, C. K., and Liedholm, C., (eds.), *Growth and Development of the Nigerian Economy*, Michigan, 1970.

Ekundare, R. O., *An Economic History of Nigeria, 1860–1960*, London, 1973.

Helleiner, G. K., *Peasant Agriculture, Government and Economic Growth in Nigeria*, Homewood, Ill., 1966.

Hill, P., *The Migrant Cocoa-Farmers of Southern Ghana*, Cambridge, 1963.

Hopkins, A. G., *An Economic History of West Africa*, London, 1973.

Kay, G. B., *The Political Economy of Colonialism in Ghana*, Cambridge, 1972.

Latham, A. J. H., *Old Calabar, 1600–1891: The Impact of the International Economy upon a Traditional Society*, Oxford, 1973.

Kilby, P., *Industrialization in an Open Economy: Nigeria, 1945–1966*, Cambridge, 1969.

McPhee, A., *The Economic Revolution in British West Africa*, London (reprint), 1971.

Meillassoux, C., (ed.), *Development of African Trade and Markets in West Africa*, London, 1971.

Pedler, F., *The Lion and the Unicorn in Africa: A History of the United Africa Company, 1787–1931*, London, 1974.

Szereszewski, R., *Structural Changes in the Economy of Ghana, 1891–1911*, London, 1965.

Thompson, V., and Adloff, R., *French West Africa*, London, 1958.

WEST-CENTRAL AFRICA

Amin, S., and Coquery-Vidrovitch, C., *Histoire Économique du Congo, 1880–1968*, Paris, 1969.

Anstey, R., *King Leopold's Legacy: The Congo Under Belgian Rule, 1908–1960*, London, 1966.

Katzenellenbogen, S. E., *Railways and the Copper Mines of Katanga*, Oxford, 1973.

Lacroix, J. L., *L'Industrialisation au Congo*, Paris, 1967.

Martin, P. M., *The External Trade of the Loango Coast*, Oxford, 1973.

Slade, R., *King Leopold's Congo*, London, 1962.

Thompson, V., and Adloff, R., *The Emerging States of French Equatorial Africa*, Stanford, 1960.

Union Minière du Haut-Katanga, 1906–1956, Brussels, 1957.

Van de Velde, M. W., *Économie Belge et Congo Belge*, Antwerp, 1936.

Wheeler, D. L., and Pelissier, R., *Angola*, London, 1971.

Ydewalle, C. D., *L'Union Minière du Haut-Katanga de l'Âge Coloniale à l'Independence*, Paris, 1960.

EASTERN AFRICA

Brett, E. A., *Colonialism and Underdevelopment in East Africa*, London, 1973.

Gaitskell, A., *Gezira: A Study of Development in the Sudan*, London, 1959.

Harlow, V., and Chilver, E. M., (eds.), *History of East Africa*, Vol. 2, Oxford, 1965.

Iliffe, J., *Tanganyika under German Rule, 1905–12*, Cambridge, 1969.

Leubuscher, C., *Tanganyika Territory: A Study of Economic Policy Under Mandate*, London, 1944.

Nicholls, C. S., *The Swahili Coast: Politics, Diplomacy and Trade on the East Africa Littoral, 1798–1856*, London, 1971.

Van Zwanenberg, R. M. A., with King, A., *An Economic History of Kenya and Uganda, 1800–1970*, London, 1975.

Wolff, R. D., *The Economics of Colonialism: Britain and Kenya, 1870–1930*, New Haven and London, 1974.

Wrigley, C. C., *Crops and Wealth in Uganda: A Short Agrarian History*, Kampala, 1959.

SOUTHERN AFRICA

Arrighi, G., *The Political Economy of Rhodesia*, The Hague, 1967.

Baldwin, R. E., *Economic Development and Export Growth: A Study of Northern Rhodesia, 1920–60*, Berkeley and Los Angeles, 1966.

Barber, W., *The Economy of British Central Africa*, London, 1961.

Coleman, F. L., *The Northern Rhodesia Copperbelt, 1889–1962*, Manchester, 1971.

De Kiewiet, C. W., *History of South Africa, Social and Economic*, London, 1960.

Doxey, G. V., *The Industrial Colour Bar in South Africa*, London, 1961.

Gray, R., *The Two Nations*, London, 1960.

Gregory, T. E. G., *Ernest Oppenheimer and the Economic Development of Southern Africa*, Cape Town, 1962.

Hall, R., *Zambia*, London, 1965.

Horowitz, R., *The Political Economy of South Africa*, London, 1967.

Houghton, D. H., *The South African Economy*, London, 1973.

Houghton, D. H., and Dagut, J., *Source Material on the South African Economy, 1860–1970*, 3 vols., Cape Town, 1973.

Isaacman, A. F., *Mozambique: The Africanization of a European Institution*, Madison, 1972.

Neumark, S. D., *Economic Influences on the South African Frontier, 1652–1836*, Stanford, 1957.

Wilson, F., *Labour in the South African Gold Mines*, Cambridge, 1972.

Wilson, M., and Thompson, L. (eds.), *The Oxford History of South Africa*, Vol. 2, Oxford, 1971.

Index

227